WHAT COMES OF TRAINING
WOMEN FOR WAR

COMMISSION ON IMPLICATIONS OF ARMED SERVICES EDUCATIONAL PROGRAMS

Appointed by the American Council on Education

EDMUND E. DAY, Cornell University, *Chairman*

HORACE M. BOND, Lincoln University

HOWARD A. CAMPION, Los Angeles Public Schools

J. WALTER DIETZ, Summit, New Jersey

ANNA L. ROSE HAWKES, Mills College

HENRY H. HILL, George Peabody College

HEROLD C. HUNT, Kansas City (Missouri) Public Schools

T. R. MCCONNELL, University of Minnesota

CARL H. MILAM, American Library Association

HARRY S. ROGERS, Brooklyn Polytechnic Institute

GEORGE F. ZOOK, American Council on Education, *ex officio*

ALONZO G. GRACE, *Director*

M. M. CHAMBERS, *Associate Director*

AIR-WACS ON AN EARLY MORNING HIKE

WHAT COMES OF TRAINING WOMEN FOR WAR

BY *Dorothy Schaffter*

FOR THE COMMISSION ON IMPLICATIONS
OF ARMED SERVICES EDUCATIONAL
PROGRAMS

★

AMERICAN COUNCIL ON EDUCATION
Washington 6, D. C.

PRINTED IN THE UNITED STATES OF AMERICA

FOREWORD

I N PLANNING its investigation of the educational lessons to be
derived from the training enterprises of the armed services
in World War II, the Commission on Implications of Armed
Services Educational Programs early determined to explore, as
one of the significant phases of that experience, the training of
women who wore the uniform as members of the Army, the
Navy, the Marine Corps, and the Coast Guard; and of the organization of women aircraft pilots who served with the Army
Air Forces.

For this part of its studies the Commission obtained the
services of Dr. Dorothy Schaffter, now research counsel, Legis-
lative Reference Service, Library of Congress, and well known
as former professor of political science at Vassar College, former
president of Connecticut College for Women, and author of
State Housing Agencies (Columbia University Press, 1942).

Not only descriptive sketches of the women's military services
in World War II, but also consideration of the traditions touch-
ing the education and training of American women and girls, of
social attitudes affecting in numerous ways the place of women
in the society, and of economic conditions and their bearings upon
employment prospects, necessarily enter into this report. There is
not at present unanimity of judgment and opinion on many of
these matters, but all will agree that they merit continuing observation and study.

The Secretary of War and the Secretary of the Navy approved the general purpose of the entire project of the Commission, and facilitated its progress by designating as official
liaison agencies respectively the Historical Division, War Department Special Staff, and the Standards and Curriculum Division, Training Activity, Bureau of Naval Personnel. These
agencies provided full access to documentary materials and
entree to the various headquarters and training installations of
the women's military services.

The same agencies also reviewed the studies in manuscript,

on occasion gave valuable suggestions, and finally approved the drafts as to factual accuracy and as to the safeguarding of information vital to the national security. It is understood, however, that opinions and assertions contained in this report are private ones of the author and are not to be construed as official or as reflecting the views of the War Department or the Navy Department or of the military or naval services at large.

All concerned with the future of education for women in the United States will find herein matter of interest and significance regarding how women were selected and trained to play multifarious roles in the armed services in time of war, how governmental agencies and voluntary associations cooperated in that enterprise, and some of the meanings which that experience holds for the future of the nation.

ALONZO G. GRACE
Director

June 1947

PREFACE

THE EXPERIENCE of approximately one-third of a million American women in the military services during World War II will have profound long-range effects upon the position of women as citizens. The operation of the various programs of training for women in the military services, devised to meet the exigencies of the war, brought to light interesting implications for the future education of women in civilian life. To explore those implications is the purpose of this report.

The report is presented in three parts: (1) an overview, (2) women in military aviation, and (3) women in medical, nursing, and related services. Fuller detail of its organization appears in the table of contents. On account of the complexity and variety of the subject, the treatment is selective rather than encyclopedic.

An abundance of informative data was available, though not always of the types most desired for this purpose. The principal types of materials and methods employed are here briefly noted:

1. Service histories in manuscript, original documents and records, and service studies based thereon. A few typical examples: (*a*) in the office of the historian of the Army Air Forces, the writer was permitted to use the entire series of histories of the WASP, together with several special studies of women pilots; (*b*) in the Training Division of the Office of the Surgeon General, United States Army, copies of all curriculums for training courses were available; (*c*) the histories of the training programs of the WAC, the WASP, the MCWR, and the SPAR were ready for use; and (d) original documents were used in connection with the training programs of the senior cadets of the Cadet Nurse Corps, in both the army and the naval hospitals.

2. Returns from a questionnaire sent to service women who had been teachers in civilian life, or in the service, or in both. (See chapter ii.)

3. Conferences with more that one hundred members of the Army, the Navy, the Coast Guard, and the Marine Corps train-

ing divisions; the WAC, WAVES, SPAR, and MCWR training divisions; the historical divisions of the major services and the women's groups named above; the historical division of the AAF; the historical division of the War Department Special Staff; the medical divisions of the Army and the Navy, and the Army and the Navy Nurse Corps; the officers of the Cadet Nurse Corps; and related military agencies.

4. Over a period of six months, continual comparison of information and evaluation of materials relating to the women's services, with materials being collected by other members of the staff of the Commission for use in their respective studies. This comparison was of great value in determining the extent to which the training programs for women had been altered and the extent to which they were like programs for men in the armed services.

5. One of the most valuable aids in preparing the study was the assistance rendered by a group of consultants. The consultants were used in two ways. One group acted as an advisory committee for the study as a whole, and three other groups assisted with specific aspects. The advisory committee attended an all-day session in Washington while the study was in its initial stages, and the subjects discussed were organized under an outline covering the following aspects of the training programs of the women's services: selection, classification, and assignment; instructional materials and methods; motivation and morale; the individual as a member of a military service; leadership; living conditions; health and physical fitness; and general implications. No attempt was made to arrive at any conclusions, but the general discussion by a group of women—military and civilian— who were competent to evaluate the military training programs in terms of civilian education was of great value to the writer. Since the session was "off the record" and entirely for purposes of assisting the writer in planning the study, no part of the discussion is included in the study.

Three meetings of women particularly interested in nurse training, aviation training, and industrial and business training, respectively, were held to give the writer the advantage of discussing these specific areas with persons who had experience in them. These were also "off the record" for advisory purposes only, and no reference is made to them in the study.

After the chapters dealing with the training of nurses and other medical personnel were completed they were read by Col. Florence A. Blanchfield, ANC, director, Nursing Consultants Division, Office of the Surgeon General, United States Army; Capt. Nellie Jane DeWitt (NC) USN, superintendent, Nurse Corps, Division of Personnel, Bureau of Medicine and Surgery, Navy Department; Lucile Petry and Minnie Pohe, chief and assistant chief, Division of Nursing, Public Health Service, Federal Security Agency; Mary E. Switzer, assistant to the administrator, Federal Security Agency; and Marjorie B. Davis, secretary, National Nursing Planning Committee, National Nursing Council for War Service, Inc.

The chapters dealing with women pilots and other aviation personnel were read by Phoebe F. Omlie, Division of Research, Civil Aeronautics Administration, Department of Commerce; Capt. Joy B. Hancock, USNR (W), director, Women's Reserve, Navy Department; Maj. Mattie E. Treadwell, WAC, Historical Division, War Department Special Staff; and Hazel Taylor, Bureau of Public Relations, United States Army.

All suggestions for changes, inclusions, and exclusions which were made by these experts were incorporated into the chapters.

After the entire study was completed, it was read by Bess Bloodworth, vice president, the Namm Store, Brooklyn; Virginia H. Blunt, formerly lieutenant commander, USCGR, now retraining and vocational education representative, Department of Labor; Ineva R. Meyer, formerly lieutenant commander, USCGR, now assistant dean, College of Letters and Science, University of Wisconsin; Margaret G. Myers, professor of economics, Vassar College; Jessie Pearl Rice, of Indianapolis, formerly lieutenant colonel, WAC, and commandant of the School for WAC Personnel Administration at Purdue University; Mary J. Shelly, formerly commander, USNR (W), now assistant to the president, Bennington College; and Cornelia D. Williams, formerly major, MCWR, now associate professor and counselor in the General College, University of Minnesota.

To each of these persons I am indebted for much information and numerous suggestions.

Other consultants who gave valuable services were Ruth M. Leach, vice president, International Business Machines Corporation; Louise McKellar, Training Division, Transcontinental and Western Air, Inc.; Lavinia L. Redd, major, WAC, Training Division, Women's Army Corps; Elizabeth C. Smith, major, WAC, chief, WAC Training Section, Office of the Director of Military Training, Army Service Forces; Chase Going Woodhouse, member, United States House of Representatives, and professor of economics, Connecticut College for Women. The generous encouragement and assistance from all the consultants added much to the pleasure of what was in itself a zestful and challenging task.

DOROTHY SCHAFFTER

Washington, D. C.
January 4, 1947

CONTENTS

Part Two: Women in Military Aviation

Part Three: Women in Medical, Nursing, and Related Services

CONTENTS

LIST OF ILLUSTRATIONS

LIST OF TABLES

Part One
THE OVERVIEW

I. THE WOMEN'S MILITARY SERVICES IN WORLD WAR II

CONSIDERATION of the implications for civilian education of the wartime training programs of the women's services includes of necessity the conditions under which those programs were developed and conducted, and the state of mind and purpose of the women who were students. The women's programs were conditioned by the larger training programs of which they were a part, by the attitudes of both men and women toward the place of women in the war effort, and by all the conditions existing in the women's services, including recruitment, classification and assignment to duty, and living conditions.

WHAT THE SERVICES WERE

The wartime women's military services were the Women's Army Corps (WAC), the Women's Reserve of the Naval Reserve (Women Accepted for Volunteer Emergency Service, abbreviated as WAVES), the Women's Reserve of the Coast Guard Reserve (SPAR), the Marine Corps Women's Reserve (MCWR), the Army Nurse Corps, and the Navy Nurse Corps.

The Women Airforces Service Pilots (WASP) and the Cadet Nurse Corps of the United States Public Health Service should not, strictly speaking, be included because these two services were not militarized. However, the WASP was like the women's military services in all other respects, and the work of the Cadet Nurse Corps was so closely related to that of the Army and Navy Nurse Corps that separation for purposes of description would have presented an inaccurate picture, and after consideration it seemed proper to include them.

The duration and status of these eight services varied. The WAC, established in May, 1942, as the Women's Auxiliary Army Corps (WAAC), became a regular component of the Army in September 1943. The WAVES, SPAR, and MCWR, established early in the war, from the beginning had the status of regular components of their respective services. The SPAR was terminated on June 30, 1946. At the time of writing it seems probable that the WAC, WAVES, and MCWR will be continued as permanent agencies, although the necessary legislation has not been enacted.

The Wasps, established early in the war and deactivated in December 1944, were civilians with civil service status. The cadet nurses were simply civilian students who had committed themselves to practice essential nursing for the duration of the war and who, in many cases, elected to perform that service in the Army or Navy Nurse Corps. The Cadet Nurse Corps was established in 1943, and the last students were admitted to training in October 1945. The corps will operate until all its members have completed training in 1948. The Army and Navy Nurse Corps had been in existence for many years before World War II and will continue in the future (see Public Law 36, 80th Congress, 1st Session).

In all cases, the members of the women's services were volunteers. The members of the WAC, WAVES, SPAR, and the MCWR enlisted for the duration of the war plus six months. The Wasps as civilian employees could resign at their pleasure, and cadet nurses were bound to engage in essential military or civilian nursing during the war, but they could drop out of training before graduation if they wished to do so. The term of enlistment for Army nurses was for the duration of the war plus six months. Most nurses who joined the Navy Nurse Corps joined as reserves, for active duty when needed in time of war or national emergency as declared by the President.

Wacs, Waves, Spars, and women in the Marine Corps had the same status as male reservists in their services. They served as enlisted people, noncommissioned officers, and commissioned officers, and provisions regarding their rank, pay, and other conditions of service were like those of the male personnel. Members of the two nurse corps held "equivalent rank" until the war was well advanced, after which they were given actual rank for the duration, and in general the conditions of their service were like those of men of the same rank. Wasps and cadet nurses had no military status. The women in all the services were uniformed, and the wearing of the uniform was required in all services except the WASP and Cadet Nurse Corps. The women in the military services and the nurse corps were treated as members of a military service in every sense, and it was required that they be extended all the rights and courtesies due their positions.

THE MAGNITUDE OF THE WOMEN'S SERVICES

Tables 1 and 2 contain summary data relative to the numbers of members of the women's military services.

TABLE 1

WOMEN ON ACTIVE DUTY IN THE U. S. ARMY AS OF JUNE 30 EACH YEAR, 1940–45

Women in Army	1940	1941	1942	1943	1944	1945
Officers....................				4,917	5,845	5,733
Enlisted women a..........				55,326	61,370	90,780
Nurses..................	939	5,433	12,475	30,316	40,018	54,291
Dietitians b..............				666	1,210	1,623
Physical therapists b.......				323	643	1,173
Doctors....................				c	c	72
Warrant officers...........					10	44
Total....................	939	5,433	12,475	91,548	109,096	153,716

 a Includes officer candidates.
 b Data not available until they had commissioned status, 1943.
 c Data not available.

TABLE 2

WOMEN ON ACTIVE DUTY IN THE U. S. NAVY AS OF JUNE 30 EACH YEAR, 1940–45*

Women in Navy	1940	1941	1942	1943	1944	1945
Navy:						
Officers.................				3,827	7,611	8,385
Enlisted women a........				21,717	57,981	73,813
Nurses.................	442	671	1,778	5,431	8,399	11,086
Marine Corps:						
Officers.................				244	797	831
Enlisted Women a.......				3,399	16,680	17,606
Coast Guard:						
Officers.................				235	704	867
Enlisted Women a.......				2,956	7,456	8,877
Total....................	442	671	1,778	37,809	99,628	121,465

 * Data from Table A-15, *Annual Report Fiscal Year 1945. The Secretary of the Navy to the President of the United States.*
 a Includes officer candidates.

In addition to the 153,716 women in the Army and the 121,465 women in the Navy on June 30, 1945, it must be added that by that date 16,454 cadet nurses had been graduated. Moreover, 916 women pilots were on duty with the WASP at the time of their inactivation in December 1944.

The number of something less than 300,000 probably approximates peak strength in the six military and two civilian services under consideration. By comparison this is a small group. An undetermined but undoubtedly much larger number of women was engaged in work closely related to the war, in business, in industry, and in the various volunteer services such as the Red Cross. Most of the women in the services were relatively young, and there were in the nation some thirteen million women between the ages of eighteen and twenty-eight, six million of them unmarried, to serve as a pool for all civilian and military war purposes. Since the idea of selective service for women had little chance of acceptance, there was considerable competition to recruit women in the younger age group. A fair number of women over twenty-eight years of age was enlisted in the military services, and many older women went into other types of war work.

On one or two occasions the opinion has been expressed that most women were not convinced of the need for their services; that, if there had been a real manpower shortage, a selective service for women would have been established, and not until such action was taken would they believe that their services were of vital importance in the war effort. In any event, important as was the contribution of the 300,000 women in the services described in this study, it must be remembered that this number was small by comparison with the number of women available, the numbers in business and industry and government service and volunteer service, and—even more strikingly—by comparison with the millions of men in the armed services.

REQUIREMENTS FOR ADMISSION

The requirements for admission to the women's services were definitely higher than the selective service requirements for men. In the great majority of cases, the women were high school graduates, and there were many women with college experience. No woman with young, dependent children was accepted. In the case of nurses, graduation from nurse training and registration in the profession were required. In general, the qualifications for the various services (WAC, WAVES, SPAR, MCWR) were alike; the qualifications of the Army and Navy Nurse Corps included professional status; the Wasps were required to show aptitude for pilot training as well as some previous flying training; and the cadet nurse candidates had to be high school graduates with aptitude for nurse training. If the high standards established were to be applied to all civilian women in suitable age groups, it is probable that many—perhaps the majority—would be disqualified.

MISSIONS OF THE VARIOUS SERVICES

The purposes of the various services differed. The over-all objective of assisting in the prosecution of the war in all cases determined the more specific functions. In general, women in the armed services were used either to increase the available manpower or to furnish some service, such as nursing, for which women were indispensable. The number and variety of duties which they could perform had been underestimated. Almost immediately their duties were enlarged, and this progress continued throughout the war until they were excluded from few types of duties which it was reasonable to believe they could perform competently.

In most cases if the women were not enlisted, trained, or utilized for particular types of services, the policy was based on reasons which related to the most efficient administration of the war. For example, more care had to be exercised about the housing of women than of men, and in many cases women were not used for certain duties because they would have to be assigned to duty in areas in which there was no suitable housing, or else labor and materials would have to be used to prepare special barracks. Sometimes it was not worthwhile to train women without proficiency in a particular skill because an adequate supply of competent men was available, or because men with a more suitable preparation for the training were being drafted into the service. Women served overseas, but they never engaged in combat duties. Few women served afloat except nurses, and no large number of women was assigned to pilot duty except the approximately nine hundred Wasps. The pilot duty of the WASP was the newest and most dramatic assignment which women performed in the services.

ORGANIZATION OF TRAINING

The organization of courses in the WAC, WAVES, MCWR, and SPAR was like that in the larger services of which they were parts. It would be quite erroneous to assume that these training programs were entirely separate from the general training programs of the military services. That is to say, the Army and the Navy developed vast training facilities and comprehensive training programs, and the programs of the WAC and the WAVES, the Army Nurse Corps and the Navy Nurse Corps, were simply parts of the grand total. The training of Wasps was planned and conducted by the AAF. In many cases the cirriculum, training aids, examinations, and instructors were furnished to the women's corps by the Army or Navy or Marine Corps or Coast Guard, and the instructors were often men, rather than members of the women's service. On the other hand, many women served as instructors of male personnel.

Although a few women were commissioned as officers without any training after entering the service, in most cases they entered as enlisted women and went to "boot" camp or basic training center; or, if they were accepted as officers, they went to officer-training school. Enlisted women could go to officer-candidate school if they met the requirements and if there were sufficient openings. After completion of the basic course, the officer or enlisted woman could be assigned to general duty; she could be assigned to duty which included in-service or on-the-job training in some specialty; or she could be assigned to further training in a specialists' school.

These three types of schools—basic or "boot" indoctrination, officer-training, and specialist—were like the equivalent schools in the men's services, except for the absence of training with weapons. In most cases men and women were given basic training in separate schools, and, with few exceptions, women officers were trained in their own schools. A different situation is found upon examining the training of women in specialists' schools, because many of them were sent to such schools which had been established for male personnel. Examples of this practice can be found in the training of women in aviation specialties.

Where separate schools for women were set up, they were not particularly different from the same kinds of schools in the men's services. When the first WAC and WAVES officers' schools were established, the educational content and method were almost exactly like Army and Navy officer schools. Since the backgrounds of prospective men and women officers differed considerably, and since the women were never trained for combat duty, changes in the courses for women officers were made in all the services. For example, the rigid physical conditioning necessary for men was found to be of little value for women, and military drill and physical training courses were adapted to the latter's needs in the types of duty to which they would be assigned. Because nearly all enlisted women were high school graduates, no illiteracy programs had to be prepared for servicewomen, as was found to be necessary in the men's services.

The women who were trained as pilots in the WASP had a course at Avenger Field in Sweetwater, Texas, similar to the course for young men at the AAF pilot training schools, except that the women were not trained for combat or overseas duty either in their basic course or in their later training. The military nurses were, of course, in a unique position, and no comparison can be made between their training and that of any similar group of servicemen.

II. WHAT SELECTED SERVICEWOMEN
THINK ABOUT THE EDUCATIONAL
IMPLICATIONS

IN MARCH 1946, the women officers in command of the WAC,
WAVES, SPAR, and Women Marines were asked to fur-
nish lists of teachers who had enlisted in their respective services,
and of their members who had served as teachers during their
periods of duty. A questionnaire was sent to 186 women chosen
from these lists. Fifty-two complete answers were received by
July 30, 1946. The resulting sample is very small, and there is
no reason to believe that it is authoritatively representative. It
is certain, however, that the considered opinions of some fifty
teachers from the four women's services do throw light on the
problem under consideration, and these opinions are worth
attention. It should be mentioned, in passing, that all information furnished, including the names of those replying, is confidential, and the women receiving the forms were informed of
this fact.

The first page of the questionnaire was designed to obtain the
following background information: education, rank attained in
service, occupation prior to service, the longest single course of
training received in service (except basic), the name and other
information about the courses taught in service, and present
occupation. The second page contained this paragraph:

On the basis of your own civilian and military experience, what features
of the military training courses in which you were a student or a teacher
seem most worthy to you of use in civilian education? (For example, the
Commission is giving particular attention to selection, classification and
assignment; instructional materials and methods; motivation, morale and
leadership; group living; recreation, health and physical fitness; integration
of vocational and liberal education; democratic aspects; the opening to
women of opportunity in new fields and its effect on plans for their education, and similar educational questions.)

BACKGROUNDS OF THE RESPONDENTS

A series of brief tabulations serves to show at a glance something of the military and civilian experience of the fifty-two women whose replies are to be examined. The highest ranks attained in service were as follows:

Major or lieutenant commander	5
Captain or lieutenant (SG)	27
First lieutenant or lieutenant (JG)	14
Second lieutenant or ensign	4
Enlisted grade (yeoman or seaman 1/c)	2

Educational attainment before entering the service was as here indicated:

Ph.D. degree	2
Master's degree	19
Some work in graduate school	17
College graduation	7
Some college work	6
High school graduation	1

Eight of the respondents had been in educational administrative positions before entering service. For convenience, these are grouped with "teaching" in the simple tabulation of teaching experience:

Teaching before, in, and after service	15
Teaching before and during service	20
Teaching before and after service	1
Teaching before service only	8
Teaching during service only	6
Teaching after service only	1
Not teaching at any time	1

Thirty-three were graduates of officer-candidate schools. Graduates of a wide variety of other service schools, both for commissioned officers and for enlisted women, were represented in smaller numbers. Those who had been assigned to teaching duties in the service had taught a great variety of courses for officers and enlisted personnel, and for officer candidates. WAC, WAVES, SPAR, and MCWR schools all were represented. The courses included basic training and indoctrination, military administration, communications, clerical training, mathematics, engineering, aircraft, ordnance, speech reading for rehabilitation of deafened veterans, physical training, and other subjects.

Having had a glimpse of the background of training and experience of the fifty-two women who replied to the questionnaire, we may now turn to a consideration of their replies to the question: "On the basis of your own civilian and military experience, what features of the military training courses in which you were a student or a teacher seem most worthy to you of use in civilian education?"

GENERAL COMMENTS

In a few cases the specific suggestions contained in these replies were preceded by general discussions which serve as an introduction to the subject. One officer with considerable and varied teaching experience in her service said:

I believe the lessons for civilian education, in the light of military experience, might well be divided into two categories: shortcomings in previous civilian training that showed up in military training, and practices in the military schools that might be tried in civilian education.

Another equally experienced officer wrote as follows:

Theoretically, civilian education applies all the principles advocated by the military training experts. Actually neither military nor civil education succeeds in a full application of the known basic educational principles, and we are off to a wrong start before we begin if we assume otherwise. The course of military education was set by civilian educators who donned the uniform. The unique character of military education and of its results came from the fact that the military groups were so organized and executed that there was little lost effort in most fields, although this was not necessarily true of the "refresher" and "maintenance" training. Military schools have three very effective factors that distinguish them from the civilian public schools. The first is that military discipline within the faculty is possible and frequently invoked; release and replacement of instructors who were not effective are much easier than in civil life. The second is that military schools have complete control of the students for twenty-four hours each day. And the third advantage is that the aims of military education have not only been specifically developed, they are defined in writing and well known to all who deal with training. Civil education can and should do little about the first two factors, but a great deal can be done toward achieving the third.

A third comprehensive evaluation and comparison of military and civilian education contains several important opinions: (1)

The features of military training courses most worthy of application to civilian education are physical screening before entry, current-events discussions, group living of a type which minimizes economic and social background, and extensive and active use of visual materials. (2) Compared with university training, military training is not faced with as aggravated a form of such problems as the influence of local social background, the lack of original motivation, and the lack of group spirit and problems. (3) On the negative side, military training is strictly vocational training, given in the briefest possible time. Therefore, it does not allow sufficient leisure or provide sufficient opportunity for independent projects, for spontaneous and undirected discussion among students, and for the development of reasoning ability rather than memory or mastery of a skill. (4) Unlike university education, military training has limited courses and openings for widely differing skills, does not allow the student much choice within programs, and offers instruction in skills which have an immediate and temporary use but neither future nor background of knowledge.

One officer in the WAVES stated her belief that few features of the basic course in her service were applicable to civilian education for the following reasons: (1) Students were real volunteers and, more than anything else, they wanted to be naval officers, so that "they would have learned Sanskrit standing on their heads if that had been required." Such a high degree of motivation rarely exists in ordinary education. (2) Students were highly selected for emotional maturity, for success in past educational endeavors, and for performance in civilian jobs. Only rarely would as competent a group of students be assembled. (3) The subject matter was simple, almost entirely factual, and required no high degree of ability to visualize or to comprehend. It was well organized and predigested by competent instructors, many of whom had had years of teaching experience. (4) The subject matter did not have to be retained for any great period of time before testing. Only a few courses were built on material presented earlier. This officer believed two aspects of training to be of value to civilian education; namely, having all students study the same courses at the same time, and use of visual aids.

AN EVALUATION OF MILITARY SERVICE AS A MEANS
OF EDUCATION

Opinion on this subject ranged between two extremes. One officer's observations led her to suggest that a compulsory military training program would be as beneficial to the young women of America as to the young men. In contrast were the opinions that military training has not helped women, that no formal courses could be recommended for civilian use, that the respondent found "nothing commendable" in her own course of training, and that actual experience after the training period had been of more value than any service school. One officer approved of the opportunities offered women of various professions and interests to pool their experiences for the common welfare, and thought education in service broadened personal as well as professional viewpoints. Another officer considered the benefit to the individual to be great, and said that military training brought out the finest qualities in each. In direct contradiction is the following excerpt:

It is true that the training period made for physical fitness, but military regimentation, although necessary and desirable for military service, is not the answer to achieve this result in civilian life. So, too, for group life! Our informal ways are better because they encourage individuality, as well as cooperation. They are more democratic.

Special advantages to two groups in particular were mentioned: (1) women with insufficient schooling had an opportunity in the services to realize their ambitions through schools, assignments, and group living; and (2) college graduates found opportunities to integrate vocational and liberal education on a larger scale than the usual civilian position would allow.

Finally, an officer with long teaching experience, and with experience both as a teacher and as commanding officer of a large training school in the Marine Corps Women's Reserve, wrote:

The courtesy and discipline exacted in a military training course are of infinite value and have carried over into civilian life. The courses in military life taught tolerance and made use of it constantly. All women became more patient, understanding, and sympathetic in their working and living together, and have all stated they would take nothing for their experience and all it has taught them in how to get along with people and be happy even under trying conditions.

Many respondents referred to particular aspects of military life as distinguished from the formal educational and training programs—for example, discipline, group life, drill, scheduling of time in programs, health and physical training and recreation programs, morale, motivation, leadership, and the democratic aspects of military training. Their comments on these phases are summarized in succeeding sections.

GROUP LIVING AND EDUCATION FOR CITIZENSHIP

Several women who replied to the questionnaire discussed the values of group living and, in all cases except one, this phase of military life seemed worthy of praise. Learning to live in close quarters, to adjust to different situations, and to get along with all kinds of people from all walks of life were specifically mentioned, as for example:

Most of the "misfits" that I have encountered in the service have been people who could not get along with people or did not realize that rules and regulations are made for the welfare of the group as a whole and not for one individual. . . .

The writer said that in civilian education instructors must stress the importance of group living to correct these faults and to guide the proper growth of the individual.

The opposing opinion was expressed by one officer:

The average citizen hasn't much need for learning to live in barracks with a hundred and forty-nine other goldfish, and such training has little carry-over value into civilian life though, doubtless, much human nature is observed. Family and neighborhood life are far more important to the average citizen, and intelligent guidance here will be much more valuable.

Some comments on education for citizenship appeared in the replies to the questionnaires. One officer remarked on the appalling ignorance of American history and government which existed among the students in her courses. Another officer said:

. . . one of the most far-reaching innovations in Army education which has implications for civilian education was the program to develop friendly attitudes toward our allies. Films with simple portrayal of fact, by their logical arrangement, handled a complicated emotional problem. A basis was thus formed for understanding the reasons for characteristics before opportunity had been given for them to be annoying. Some such effort toward understanding members of the United Nations is indicated now. These portrayals should be of high caliber, objective but sympathetic, and easily accessible to every section of the country.

If the American Council on Education could sponsor publications in the nature of "Army Talks" which would cover various problems of the day, both foreign and domestic, the cause of education would be greatly furthered. Citizens are supposed to be articulate in public affairs and to indicate to our legislators from time to time our attitudes toward problems of the day. But our supply source of facts is inadequate and at times warped. We should be able to turn to some sources for all pertinent facts objectively presented.

RECREATION, HEALTH, AND PHYSICAL FITNESS

Organized recreation was recognized as an essential part of the women's training programs, especially on bases where normal forms of recreation were not available. These programs were approved by women replying to the questionnaire. One woman said that the programs of various sports were not too different from a school program of team games, individual activities, and tournaments. Another officer said that the group games in planned recreational programs aimed at promoting teamwork, and that outdoor games and general exercise seemed more important to her than the development of highly skilled teams—a fact which some civilian schools could learn from the Army program of recreation. Approval was expressed of the military system of providing recreation and athletics for everyone rather than for a selected few.

The military emphasis on good physical and mental health was mentioned by many women in their replies, and several said that the "conditioning" rather than "muscle-building" objective should be called to the attention of civilian educators. Regular physical check-ups and adequate preventive medical attention were required, and in general women were compelled to recognize the necessity of good health and strength if their military jobs were to be accomplished satisfactorily. Both planned daily exercise and military drill were approved for consideration by civilian educators.

Military drill as a part of a physical education program would be popular with girls, in the opinion of an officer who had been a high school art supervisor before she entered service. Her reasons were that "it trains coordination, quick response, good posture and carriage, precision of movement, and leadership (providing that each individual assumes command at times)." Several other women made similar suggestions, and no one took occasion to object to military drill.

Several officers stressed the need for education in first aid, personal hygiene, venereal disease control, and sex education as parts of civilian educational programs.

Finally, a company commander who was in charge of the physical education program in a very large school for enlisted women, replied that, in her opinion, this particular course made the following valuable contributions: (1) Adequate supervised recreational facilities were afforded. The swimming pool was open and skilled instructors at hand. Plenty of equipment was available on weekends as well as on workdays. (2) Participation was compulsory. The civilian physical education teacher has no idea what the human body can stand and never gives pupils even adequate exercise. (3) A controlled situation made possible by the discipline of military life "made life more bearable in classes for all of us."

One reply is important because it emphasized the importance of physical training for adult women rather than training for students in school or college. The writer, a college teacher forty years old, said that at her age it was difficult to remember the importance of keeping fit, and that relearning this at officer-candidate school was one of her most important lessons. She had gradually dropped tennis and golf, and she used her car instead of walking. In training she learned bowling and walked every place, and upon her return to civilian life she actually liked physical exercise. She emphasized physical education for everyone, not just a chosen few, because people learn more easily if they are physically alert, and because they need relaxation and recreation.

Finally, a WAVES officer said: "The goal should be to so integrate physical and mental training that the students would recognize them as of equal value in producing well-adjusted adults."

SCHEDULING OF TIME IN PROGRAMS

No respondent dealt at length with the time element in the programs of service training, but there were many references to the subject. A few excerpts will indicate the general tenor of opinion.

. . . a well-rounded day to provide adequate time, opportunities, supervision, and training in use of leisure time.

. . . . .

Many women were unable to stand the pace of the accelerated training course. They were nervous and tired and therefore seldom did their best work. There should have been a military schedule of drill and physical education which still left them able to enjoy and study the courses presented.

. . . . .

The courses were done under tremendous mental and physical pressure. Selection was aided by this very fact in some instances, but in the main mature women learned more slowly and their capabilities were often overlooked in favor of some facile girl just out of college.

Approval was expressed of concentrated courses, with only essential materials included, to conserve time, and of repeated emphasis during such courses of certain important aspects—"a lesson to be learned by all teachers." One officer listed first in her recommendations "the capacity to teach in a comparatively short time difficult and technical courses and to insure that students will be able to make practical application of their knowledge upon the completion of the course."

MORALE, MOTIVATION, LEADERSHIP, AND DISCIPLINE

A summary of opinion on morale, motivation, leadership, and discipline is not possible because, although many replies to the questionnaire contained comment in this general and rather undefined area, the officers were reporting on different aspects and, even more important, their comments were seldom expressions of clear-cut approval or disapproval. Quotations in their own words will constitute the most accurate means of reporting.

One officer quite specifically recommended the increased classroom formality of the military services.

A second writer stated her belief, after almost ten years of public school teaching in a large city school, that school children simply exhaust themselves with disorder and noise, and that ·discipline would be beneficial to them. Upon her return to civilian life she had entered business and her reason for refusing to continue as a teacher was that she could no longer teach "in the modern manner." Without believing in "physical punishment or stern, stupid discipline," she did believe in reasonable peace and quiet, and she could not endure the prospect of further teaching under present conditions. Other officers approved the discipline maintained in the classroom, and the mental discipline demanded by the instructor. In fact, in the opinion of one woman, learning to think and mental discipline were of more value than actual subject matter in service school courses. Reference was made to "cajoling and fear of political reverberations by the teacher if the child is disciplined as he should have been at home," and "that the service wouldn't stand for that." However, the writer continued, those who are known and admired for what they are, do not have to rule with the whip.

A somewhat longer statement is worthy of quotation in full:

Many people were trained quickly and well for many jobs in the military machine in wartime. Surely some of its efficiency can be transplanted to civilian education. The training was highly competitive, done at high tension, its purpose clearly defined and understood by the participating student. Short cuts were the order of the day. The individual was forced to become a member of a group, live with them, bear with them, eat with them. It could be that civilian education with its namby-pamby purpose of "keeping the student happy" might conceivably be improved by a shot in the arm of military directness.

Approval of certain aspects of military discipline in training was expressed by a WAVES officer in the Educational Services Section who had been a college teacher before entering the service. She said:

One of the trends in civilian education which I view with great alarm is that of permitting the students a very considerable freedom in initiating action and a minimum of guidance and, I might add, compulsion. The results are obvious and serious; students trying to do everything and doing nothing well, failing to learn the necessity for thoroughness, failing to learn, because they have not been so taught, to discriminate between what is good and what is not (in literature, for example), failure to recognize authority. The military stand is, of course, obvious, and although it can be overdone, I believe that military discipline and emphasis on thoroughness could well be imitated by civilian schools.

One officer reported a procedure indicating that mere tight discipline was not the invariable rule. After basic required fundamentals were completed in courses with which she was familiar, students were asked their opinions of the course and, if necessary, the program was revised to meet their requirements. She stated that "the faculty's interest in the progress of their classes created confidence between student and teacher."

In discussing the democratic aspects of a wartime training program, the following paragraph offered a thoughtful evaluation:

There is some loss of efficiency in democratic education as opposed to authoritarian or military training which is counterbalanced by a gain in individual thought and achievement. Application in full of the military training methods would be to destroy initiative and individuality, though we must not forget the fact that the schoolroom is more often than not provided with the atmosphere of authoritarian discipline rather than with an autonomous air. Perhaps this will account for the fact that the doctrine of each new teaching method seems to wither and die after a period of trial. Traditional discipline is easier to maintain (and looks better to a casual observer) than the more desirable self-government. The wild sense of freedom in a child freed from the domination of teacher and school should be a danger sign to all whose responsibility is to prepare and maintain the program.

The questions of morale and motivation are closely related to those of discipline. There was no indication in any reply received that morale was other than satisfactory in the women's training programs, and many replies indicated that morale was consistently high. This situation appeared, in the opinion of many officers, to be due to motivation.

In discussing this subject a former college professor expressed her approval of the use by military services during wartime of motivation based upon advancement in rating, and she believed that it was effective. "As a strong liberal arts advocate as opposed to straight vocational education," she believed that the motivation for civilian education must be the conception of a job well done, a subject thoroughly mastered, a culture broadened, a horizon expanded. American young people are coming into their heritage in the *whole* world "where already too long the main motivation has been selfish interest, personal advancement—at any price. Many know now that victory and peace and human welfare have a price, and a high one. . . . At least I have the hope that this study made by the American Council on Education will have a strong statement to make on motivation, and let it not be the military angle. . . . Our job now is something bigger than that."

The two quotations below came, respectively, from the replies of a WAVES and a WAC officer. Each taught before entering the service, and taught in officer-candidate school in her own service. The officer in the WAVES in discussing motivation said:

Women officer candidates exhibited, on the whole, an earnest desire to learn as much and be as "perfect" as possible. There was a standard by which they could measure themselves—the ideal officer—leader, guide, and confidante. It occurs to me that civilian education offers no such standard by which one can measure herself. The standard of the Navy was the traditional "officer and gentleman." What is comparable in civilian life?

The most important feature of the military training was the *drive* behind it. The women are volunteers, not drafted. Their reasons for volunteering were many and varied, all having some relationship to the war, but they all had something in common and were working toward a common end. This, I believe, was behind whatever success the WAVES officers had in their later assignments.

The WAC officer considered motivation, morale, and leadership in one section of her reply:

Motivation, a necessary adjunct to all teaching, is limited in the public schools by a lack of sufficient reasons for including much of our subject matter. Eliminating this preliminary barrier by proper development of objectives, the next step consists simply in leading the student to see why the subject is pertinent to his own life. A well-conducted class will supply much of its own motivation by satisfying the needs of the developing citizen. A soldier in the infantry who knows his life hangs in the balance of training needs no special motivation for instruction in the use of his weapons. While it is hardly appropriate to assume such a strong motivation in a school child, he still feels an urge to be socially and economically successful and, if he sees his school classes as tools of achievement, motivation need be no large concern of the teacher.

Morale, on the other hand, depends on the use of wise leadership. A thorough training in leadership should be made a prerequisite to any teaching certificate, and the apprentice teachers seminars should continue leadership guidance. Since true and wise leadership is possible only in well-balanced individuals, a proper weeding out of the unfit should be accomplished in the colleges and universities through the use of properly trained counselors. It would be stupid to pretend that the military organizations were completely successful in providing proper leadership in all officer personnel, but its recognition of the need for such and its organized efforts to provide it are far ahead of our civil educational systems.

One officer, having said that morale was extremely high in her service, attributed this condition in part to the use of student platoon leaders. Outstanding girls were thus immediately located and sent to officer or specialist schools, and this prompt recognition had a desirable effect on all students. Another officer said that students were vitally interested in their courses, realizing the importance of the training period, and really worked hard. She also commented on leadership training. Since they were trying to make leaders of all students in officer-candidate school, they had "clashes of leadership rather than any lack of it." Mention was made briefly in several replies of the value of recognition of leadership qualities in the women's services. Finally, an officer of the WAVES said:

The leadership and authority of student officers is something that civilian schools might give heed to. It takes something to have to "hup" a platoon on the drill field or to stand a watch, and to know that you are responsible. Students develop leadership and a sense of responsibility under such circumstances, as well as resourcefulness.

SELECTION, CLASSIFICATION, AND ASSIGNMENT

About one-fifth of the servicewomen who replied to the questionnaire commented on some phase of the methods of selection and classification as a means of assignment to duty or to further training. Such comment was not entirely favorable and, in fact, no answer contained a recommendation for complete adoption of the military programs by civilian education, although there was general approval of the idea of a testing program as a basis for guidance.

One officer believed that "classification by mentality makes those of average or lower mentality the losers. They lose the incentive, the burning interest of the bright boy or girl who is in the same room with them, close enough to them so they know what it is like to have some one stand head and shoulders over them in their work. It will be that way later. Why give them false security?" A second officer, who was not a teacher while in service, believed that, considering the size of the effort, her particular service did as well as could be expected. All tests given, in her estimation, left out the personality of the individual "which in the long run is almost more important than her ability or past experience." As a line officer, she was dealing with people, not cards, and her job was in part adjusting mistakes arising from the system used.

Contrasting with the opinion just expressed was the following statement: "The best of the available personnel were selected in the numbers needed. Emphasis was placed upon a well-rounded personality, maturity, and adaptability rather than upon any specific skills. The individuals were carefully observed and studied in a variety of situations." After careful classification, assignments were made. Owing to military necessity it was not always possible to assign personnel to jobs best suited for them, but in normal circumstances it would be possible to coordinate classification and assignment more satisfactorily.

One reply contained strong approval of carrying over to civilian education the processes of selection according to skills, aptitudes, and intelligence quotients used for military training. If this were done the methods would have to be perfected and made acceptable to the public and the student. The experience of "washing out" left such a residue of bitterness among many women that it might have a permanent bad effect. But if only those individuals best suited for a given occupation could be identified and trained, greater efficiency of the individual would be achieved, and both time and money would be saved. Careful selection would cut down costly error—costly to the individual and to the public pocketbook.

A similar point of view is contained in the following quotation:

Civilian schools do not as effectively screen and select their students. . . . There is some selection done, of course, but too frequently counselors are imbued with the idea that college is the answer for everybody. Military schools attempt to place students in fields for which they have demonstrated an aptitude. Other important factors are also realistically considered—for example, an officer candidate must demonstrate officer aptitude as well as academic aptitude. Assuming that the criteria for selecting are fairly sound, the product is likely to be a happier, better-adjusted person than he would be if he lacked one or the other aptitude.

One particularly thoughtful answer came from a former science teacher whose military experience was in a supervisory and command position directly connected with training:

Public schools do not exercise much choice of students for the lower levels. Some selection is used on the secondary and university levels, though stringent exercising of a selective right is not democratic. Tailoring the schools to fit the school public is much more in order. Classification of high school students into college-preparatory and trade groups in the high schools and channeling the high school graduate into an immediate vocation or further schooling in a trade school or college, when used properly, can be a much better use of the selective function.

Most schools already give intelligence and aptitude tests. Some of them still use the "IQ" tests for homogeneous groupings of the pupils, thereby inducing a sense of inferiority or superiority in the pupils according to the group in which they find themselves (and, incidentally, creating a negative reaction in the teacher who must teach the slow group). Other tests are recorded and filed away. They come to light when a child becomes a problem. Someone is seeking justification in low scores for the fact that his teachers and principals cannot "handle" him!

Properly trained faculty advisors can use such tests to an advantage. High school and college training can and should be slanted more toward the interests, aptitudes, and abilities of the students, though the subject of beginning professional training before entrance into such schools as law and medicine is highly controversial at present, and the dangers of early and concentrated specialization for those who plan to attend school at or beyond the college level cannot be overlooked.

A WAC officer stated she believed that "the greatest factor in the success of the WAC training programs was the excellent selection and expert classification of trainees. Women were given opportunities for intensive specialized training in fields which, economically, in civilian life would have been unavailable."

"Selective education" based on a classification and selection program, was approved in another reply, if it were used to make learning available for the best brains, regardless of family income. Civilian education must "apply the pressure to boards of trustees, parents, some members of the faculty, even college presidents and deans" to make them understand and adopt such a program.   In the services many executives refused to use the excellent systems of classification and selection.

METHODS OF INSTRUCTION

Although many teachers in women's service training schools singled out visual aids for specific approval, even more of them approved a combination of various teaching methods usually including visual aids.   Several such proposals are presented below:

1. Varied methods of instruction to meet group needs, stressing applicatory phases and performance testing.

2. A combination of lectures and films.   One of the best statements was to the effect that:

. . . the value of movies is supplementary to teaching facts. They are excellent for motivation and for acquainting the learner with the subject. Of course, he learns while viewing the film, but there is so much that is new that he can't absorb it all at one time. Thorough knowledge comes only through integrational study and discussion which should follow. The emotional value of films can be a powerful weapon in the hands of the educator for developing the desirable characteristics of citizenship. I can remember very well how impressed I was with the need for security, accuracy, and efficiency, and the pride in country which I felt on seeing some of the films.

3. The intensified training method making use of visual aids, teacher demonstrations, and field trips.

4. The close coordination between films and classroom work; the lecture method; and, most important, student participation. "Since we were training officers, we wanted to see how they would perform before a group, so they frequently gave the lectures and led the discussions."

5. Although with few exceptions the subject matter used in military training courses would not be suitable for use in civilian education, "the method of presentation, the liberal use of conferences, the constant emphasis on morale and leadership, the valuable experience which evolved from group living, the active program of health and physical fitness have contributed many splendid ideas which may be included in civilian school programs."

6. A combination of (a) use of small-scale models, preferably working models; (b) extensive use of visual-aid materials; (c) use of personal experience or application of theory to current situations; (d) actual field trips or demonstrations of points involved; (e) lectures or short talks, followed by discussions, given by an authority on the points under consideration. "If the above points are used in conjunction with the standard lecture method, either the lecture or the practical course is far better retained by the student."

7. In teaching communications, conditions were almost ideal. Actual devices were used, there were no discipline problems, there were natural interest, high degree of adaptability, and eagerness to learn on the part of students. "The instructor's chief worry was clarity of explanation so that much could be learned in a short time. Explanations were brief, with concentration on *doing*."

In addition to the combinations of teaching methods described above, many women mentioned other excellent teaching methods used in the services, as summarized below:

1. The use of practical problems in connection with the course —for example, the use of muster rolls and payrolls in the administration courses.

2. In the intensive courses the generally high motivation was a natural result of being in the service, and many classes achieved excellent results.

It was of most interest to me as a military novice to see how quickly the class could be drawn into participation and discussion in courses which were ordinarily treated as straight hour lectures. Wherever there were actual discussion and exchange of personal experience, the resulting scores on tests of factual knowledge were higher for the class as a whole. This is, no doubt, one of the well-proven facts of educational theory, but it is one of the unexpected developments and adaptations of military classes.

3. Objective tests. The purpose of basic training was to acquaint women with military customs and terminology as rapidly as possible. Recognition tests were satisfactory for such results, but "in civilian education we stress the recognition angle too much already . . . in the objective quizzes which are used ex-

clusively in some schools with the result that the learner really does not know anything thoroughly."

4. Having all students study the same subjects at the same time. Discussion among the students in their spare time was possible because everyone knew what the other was talking about. Material not made clear by one instructor to her students could be explained by others who had fared better with a different instructor.

5. The close association of subject matter and future application.

6. Learning by doing. Courses in which this method was used successfully were office procedures, communications, motor transport, bakers and cooks. Practical, workable situations were created for the student, and actual experience provided interest and stimulated the effort of the trainee. "Army administrative training far surpasses that offered in most civilian business schools, as was proven by the rapid increase of speed and accuracy in both beginning and advanced typists in clerical training."

7. Field trips to air bases and Navy yards in connection with courses in ships and aircraft. Several included field trips in lists of teaching practices which they approved for civilian use.

8. Standardization of methods in the Army as a whole was an aid in making the rapid, intensive training a success. For example, the system of Army abbreviations, once mastered, was applicable to all jobs.

9. Army reference materials—concise, accurate, standardized, and readily available—were invaluable to training and on-the-job needs.

10. Finally, a SPAR officer discussed at some length a teaching device not mentioned by others who replied to the questionnaire, but which seemed most constructive; namely, the group and forum discussions of the daily topic.

The school was divided into groups of 16 or 17 students for this purpose. The staff leaders of the groups were rotated daily. The composition of the groups was rotated at midterm. This tended toward varying the presentation of the topics by the leaders and the assumption of leadership in the discussions by individual students, thus insuring maximum participation and greater inclusive stimulation toward constructive thinking.

Objective questions directing thought build-up toward the topic for discussion were presented on mimeographed forms to the students who filled in answers and omitted names. These were collected and answers tallied by the student chosen to represent the group in that day's forum discussion. Then the topic was attacked and controversy encouraged until the group could arrive at some satisfactory conclusions and suggestions. At a later hour, this "summing up" of the group's discussion was presented by each group's representative at the forum held by the entire student body. Thus each individual was benefited by the thoughts, opinions, and ideas brought out by each group. Each representative was subject to challenge by any member of the forum.

In conclusion it may be suitable to quote from one of the replies:

Here one must pause to note that some adult re-education will be necessary. In general, parent and teacher alike distrust any school which departs radically from the methods by which they were taught.

VISUAL TEACHING AIDS

More favorable comment has been made about the various training aids used in the military schools than about any other one aspect of the training programs. The replies to questionnaires confirmed this opinion. In at least two-thirds of the replies favorable mention was made of visual and other teaching aids, and there were only a few adverse criticisms, chiefly directed toward insuring their correct use.

One of the conclusions to be derived from a careful consideration of replies is that no *one* teaching method alone is the ideal in the minds of service-school teachers. In most cases, the recommended use of visual aids, for example, would be made in connection with a description of a good training program which was based on lectures, field trips, and so forth, and usually the necessity of a first-class teacher was included.

The various visual aids which were recommended were films, slides, filmstrips, mock-ups, cutaways, flash cards, recognition devices, charts, diagrams, handouts, maps, posters, pictures, small-scale working models, and in one case, even books! Attention was called to a training-aids library containing projectors, films, and other materials to supply all classes with what they needed. Moreover, "the close cooperation between various branches of the service made any training aids developed by one service available to all services through headquarters training-aids departments. When teaching physical education in boot camp, we had all the sports equipment we needed plus an extra supply to cover loss and damage."

These women called attention to the cost of such elaborate aids used in quantities and raised the question of availability of funds to operate similar programs in civilian schools.

Specific values inherent in the use of visual aids are, according to different officers: (1) "Most of the students got more background and information from the training films than from any amount of lectures. More use of visual aids would be of distinct value in civilian education, especially in holding the interest of young people and presenting ideas to them graphically and in a way best calculated for them to understand and retain." (2) "The showing of movies, slides, and diagrams helps immensely to clear up many questions and statements which would be hard to put across verbally." (3) "Training films have a more lasting effect than hours of lecture."

A SPAR officer replied at considerable length on the subject of the importance of visual aids. In her own training experience and observation of the training of men, she found films invaluable and thought that they could have been used even more if films had been available. Instructors found films particularly useful when there were accompanying study guides. Charts were useful, and pamphlet study guides were recommended. Models furnished practical experience in working with motors, parts of guns, planes, boats in training "rules of the road," navigational aids, and piers. In "night lookout" training, a Navy device—an electrically controlled panel to show ships and planes by night and day, under storm and battle conditions—aided in eliminating men with poor night vision. Such a device might be useful in civilian aviation or industry or anywhere where night vision is important. For blinker instruction men were divided into small groups—usually not more than three men—having the same proficiency. A competent signalman instructed every group. As a man improved his speed, he moved on to the next instructor. This proved to be a highly successful method of instruction.

Finally, instructors used models for visual-oral examinations in such courses as boat handling, seamanship, piloting, chart reading, gun handling, use of fire extinguishers, and so on. "The results were astounding, for skippers and mates and their instructors discovered weaknesses of which they were entirely unaware." This type of examination was conducive to greater efficiency and keener interest, and could be adapted in many ways to civilian education.

One former training officer criticized the aids as being "too complex materials and machines. The interest is on them instead of the subject being illustrated." Several writers warned against excessive use of aids, particularly films, by teachers who depended upon them to do the total teaching job. For example, one teacher said: "Training films can be excellent training aids, but their use is not always well timed or pertinent. Films are used to fill up the regularly scheduled weekly movie period. Sometimes they are neither in keeping with the subject being studied in class nor scaled to the abilities of the group. They are almost always shown to an audience of several classes at once, with no preliminary introduction or follow-up discussion."

One woman said: "Visual education has received a much-needed boost from service training. I have already noticed it upon return to teaching."

SIZE OF CLASSES AND CLASS ENVIRONMENT

The use of small groups for instruction was mentioned by several persons who replied to the questionnaire. One woman called attention to classes of ten or twelve students in technical courses. Another said:

The most salient of the military teaching methods is the use of small training groups, well supplied with pertinent training aids and provided with an environment as near like the real situation as possible (mock-ups). I believe that without exception every course offered in the public schools and colleges would profit by imitating the military in this respect. Laboratory courses are a step in this direction. But, in most of these, the laboratory occupies a secondary place and is so full of material that the student frequently works under too much pressure. All too often he is more concerned with the results of a problem than with the methods used or the

PLATE I.

—*Official Photograph, U. S. Navy*

WAVES RECEIVING INSTRUCTION AND PRACTICE IN NAVAL AIR COMMUNICATIONS

principles illustrated. The "area studies" are, in a measure, also a step in this direction, and it is too early to predict their ultimate outcome.

One officer in pointing out very briefly the three military practices which she would recommend to civilian educators included "the increased classroom formality of the military."

Finally, an officer replied that she believed that "the advantages of equipment, training aids, and teaching facilities (classrooms, fields, sufficient instructors, comparatively small classes) were far superior to conditions in public schools and were the greatest contribution to theories on education which were the outcome of the war."

TEACHING OBJECTIVES

The difference between military and civilian training objectives was recognized by all who discussed the subjects in replies to the questionnaire. The following is typical:

Military schools have definite goals in view. They must produce men and women with a specialty. In this respect, trade and professional schools are similar; not so the public school, whose Mother Hubbard diploma fits all and reveals nothing. Military schools aim at producing good soldiers or sailors, the civilian school at producing a good citizen. This comparison would have no significance except that the requisites for good soldiers and sailors are well known, propounded and enforced by all military organizations, whereas the public school leaders lose themselves in controversy over what constitutes a good citizen and how one may be developed out of the raw material afforded by the wide-eyed six-year-old who begins a tedious six- to twelve-year program with them.

Another officer wrote that she believed:

. . . persons with military experience returning to the classroom will endeavor to stress to the students that the objective of any course is not the grade or time exposed to the course but how well they can use the knowledge obtained on the actual job or assignment. In brief, civilian education should stress the practical side of education more. This can be done by improving instructional materials and methods. Military training courses stress actual problems that the members of the class will be confronted with after leaving the classroom.

The elimination of nonessentials was frequently mentioned in connection with clarifying the objectives of military courses.

The most comprehensive expression of this point of view is as follows:

The need for speed during the war eliminated nonessential instructional material in Army and Navy training. The "curriculum" was constantly being scrutinized in the light of new developments and something was done about it. Mobilization Training Programs were published, revised, and republished. Knowledge of what they wanted to accomplish made the task of planning training programs easier. Public education remains like a rambling house with extra rooms added here and there, but with no coordinated floor plan. If something can be done in the direction of definite aims of public education, the revamping of the curriculum will be able to take on a really constructive aspect. Such aims must be developed in several steps, and it is important that the first step be the classification of the objectives of the entire educational program. Other steps must follow in order from the aims of each individual school system, through the breakdown of responsibility to each school or department, to the course objectives that actually are the working objectives. Not until this is done will the selection of instructional material be efficiently done.

A further criticism of civilian education may be quoted:

To my mind, public education in America has reached an all-time low. This is because of uncertainty as to what the aims are, resulting in ineffectual teaching and a diffusion of effort. Military schools know what they are supposed to accomplish and all energies are bent in that direction. The results have been startling. Most graduates of civilian schools must, however, go through a training period in which they frequently must unlearn attitudes as well as learn skills and techniques which they should have learned in school.

Finally, a rather emphatic statement:

In the services men and women learned and learned fast. Information given was frank, honest, and, above all, to the point. Civilian education spends too much of its time beating around the bush with vague words and meaningless terms which are much too wordy—in the schoolroom, as well as in professional associations and in teachers colleges.

INTEGRATION OF VOCATIONAL AND LIBERAL EDUCATION

Although the questionnaire under discussion made the suggestion that the integration of vocational and liberal education might be affected by training programs of the war period, only two persons who returned the questionnaire commented on this. One officer believed that there was no implication here, because

in service training programs the military aim was entirely vocational and liberal education was purely secondary. She stated
that, on the contrary, public education has a dual aim, though
vocational education has been largely slighted in favor of the
so-called cultural aspects.

A second officer, having expressed approval of more extensive
use of in-service training in civilian education, proceeded to discuss the value of specialty schools. The latter type of training
gives confidence, in her opinion, because it is special and comprehensive, and it gives a sense of being well equipped for the
job ahead. Such training, to be offered in advanced under-
graduate classes, and in graduate and professional training, "is
a thing far different from the basic and general education required for any intelligent citizen in a democracy, where English,
history, science, music, art, drama are almost required—even for
stenographers, iron welders, motor mechanics, gas station men,
grocery clerks, bank clerks (as well as presidents), insurance
men, certainly doctors, lawyers, merchants—even brokers! If
they are to be anything but *just* that. . . . I think you know
what I mean. I believe in the liberal arts tradition (and I think
it is more than that) in America."

THE TEACHERS

Opinion as to the quality of teaching in the women's military
services is not unanimous and, consequently, recommendations
vary. It is well known that the services conducted large-scale
teacher-training programs both because of the shortage of trained
teachers and because those who were experienced needed indoctrination into military teaching methods and information on subjects which they were to teach. That all teachers were properly
prepared, is unfortunately not true. One woman who had not
been a teacher in civilian life made this comment:

I felt the lack of proper preparation prior to teaching in a service school.
From being commissioned one week I was to teach a class a week later.
Although there was a need for instructors there should be advance preparation so that the prospective teacher can become familiar with the teaching
material. This may have been only a wartime measure, however. I also
had had no civilian teaching training or education courses and was com-

pletely surprised to get my assignment. Someone with prior experience in the educational field should be assigned as a teacher.

Another woman without previous teaching experience who was assigned as instructor in a service school wrote: "The experience of teaching a group of adult women has given me self-confidence which I needed, plus the ability to express myself clearly and concisely."

A third officer commented:

My own personal feeling is that in general the teaching done during indoctrination was of very low caliber—complete memorizing with not many aids. The few good instructors had had previous experience, which was evidenced in the organization and presentation of their material and the aids, visual and otherwise, that were used.

Contrasting with these adverse criticisms, the following excerpts are offered:

Where former teachers were the teachers in these courses, the teaching was excellent. Very few visual aids were available and there was little time for study or practice, and as a result one had to depend on memory to pass the courses. As a whole, with the adjustment to be made in a new life to women, the teaching and courses were good and results gratifying.

· · · · ·

In spite of the danger in regimenting teachers, civil education can learn from the Army's supervisory and teacher-guidance programs. The training period for a school teacher ought to be enlarged to include a one- or two-year postgraduate apprenticeship. The apprentices would be given lighter teaching loads, be closely supervised, and be required to attend regular seminars and conferences with the supervisors. Problems and mistakes could be discussed and a collective solution arrived at through intelligent guidance.

Others who answered the questionnaire commented favorably on the in-service training of instructors in their particular services. In one case it was reported that officer-candidate school considered each officer a potential instructor and that the training was based on this consideration.

The qualities of a good teacher are discussed in the following quotations:

In all the courses, both civilian and military, the greatest prerequisite of a teacher has appeared to be vitality, originality, and vividness of presentation. In too many cases the teacher has appeared to be disinterested or else unsure of the material to be presented. Genuine interest seems to be infectious and is passed on to the student only when felt by the instructor. In short-term courses of instruction, rapidly presented material does not persist in the student's mind unless presented vividly with force and imagination. Accurate, concise, and logical development of points must be the basis of course treatment, interspersed with color and application for truly effective education. Although these points are old and time-worn, they are still the ones which appeared most vivid to me. Too often the instructor is a parrot and not a teacher. No matter where, or under what conditions, the teacher must be a leader by virtue of his presentation and delivery, his humor and understanding, confident yet not overbearing.

.   .   .   .   .

A plan worked out at WAC headquarters and used only experimentally for a more accurate selection of leadership material for officer-candidate school might furnish invaluable assistance to teacher-training institutions by providing an instrument that would give a concise objective picture of the strength and weaknesses of prospective teachers. With this fundamental understanding of the student at the beginning of his training, a much stronger teacher could be developed.

The following paragraph taken from one reply to the questionnaire serves well as a conclusion to this section:

Teaching in a military setting is little different from teaching in a large civilian organization. Where administrators had vision, and where individual instructors had courage and experience with good techniques, excellent results were obtained. Where administrators felt that the way to cover one hundred pages of text was to assign ten pages a day and at the end of ten days give a test, the results were the usual ones. Similarly, no matter how well the administrators might plan the integration of visual aids or class participation, unless the individual instructors were familiar with these devices and willing to perfect their use, the introduction of new ideas and methods of teaching had little effect.

COSTS OF EDUCATIONAL PROGRAM

One officer who replied at some length concerning teaching materials and methods was somewhat critical of the use of training films by civilian teachers. She continued as follows:

Not all of these mistakes can be pinned on the teachers. If substantial improvements are to be made in instructional methods, the schools must fall heir to a vast increase in public funds. The money will be necessary to increase the number of teachers, enlarge the building space to provide for a larger number of classes, insure adequate teaching equipment, and pay the teachers salaries high enough to attract men and women of the highest abilities into the profession.

Another reply contained the statement that "increased respect for the teaching profession and better pay for the job in civilian schools in the United States would, in my opinion, increase our classroom efficiency. We are probably, in American education, getting about what we are paying for, and we aren't paying enough."

A third officer described an elaborate program of training at the Army Command and General Staff School. This was based on visual aids and, in her opinion, the cost of similar equipment might be prohibitive for civilian schools. However, results obtained seemed to justify the methods used.

Finally, one reply contained approval of the increased use of audio-visual aids in civilian schools. "These cost money, of course, but the public ought to get around to recognizing that education is as important in its own way as waging war is, and that it is far more constructive. A little of the money spent in a day of total war might, if spent on schools, do much to prevent a recurrence of war."

OPPORTUNITY FOR WOMEN IN NEW FIELDS

Although the opening to women of opportunity in new fields and its effect on plans for their education seemed to some educators to constitute one of the most significant implications of the wartime training programs of the women's services, only eight of the fifty-two women replying to the questionnaire mentioned this point as important in their estimation. Seven of the eight stated without qualification that new fields for women's activity had been opened.

To quote the minority opinion first, one officer wrote:

I see little implication here. Women were used during the war in work hitherto considered to belong to the masculine world. But civil life in peacetime continues inexorably on, and woman's place in the business end of it will continue to be secondary. The major reason for this is obvious in the biological functions of the sexes; others are hidden and obscure but none the less real. As long as little girls are taught "ladyhood" from the cradle, as long as they must look on the activities and privileges of their brothers with wistful longing, as long as the word "tomboy" remains an epithet, we shall have a large, neurotically unstable feminine population, while our sturdier, less inhibited brothers and husbands will continue, generally, to be more stable and more dependable in the eyes of employers.

The schools are at present powerless to change this situation, for it involves feelings too deep-seated in the social consciousness to be changed in a matter of several generations—if at all. As long as the family remains the basic unit of society, motherhood is a career in its own right, and should be given primary consideration in the education of women. We can eliminate much of this feminine hungering after man's rights and reduce the neuroses of women accordingly.

I am not prepared to discuss the merits and demerits of masculine and feminine personalities, which seem to me to lie at the root of this particular problem. However, it is my feeling that, in America, the pendulum has swung from the slavery of women across its nadir, and now feminists are striving to carry it too far on the opposite upward swing.

The majority opinion, equally emphatic in the opposite point of view, is represented by the following statement:

Women in the services proved to the world at large that they are able to succeed in vastly more fields of endeavor than has been thought in the past. Mechanical as well as clerical fields were opened to them and they proved that they were as adept at one as at the other. I think this should tend to make our educators try to open more fields of training for them in our schools and colleges and try to find out by classification tests which fields students are best qualified for, and are most interested in, before they get too far along in their education.

Other women educators in the four services thought that there would be new openings for women in the technical aspects of communications (radar, high-frequency direction finding, etc.) and in the mechanical and technical aspects of aviation; and a WAC officer wrote that the most satisfactory courses, from the standpoint of her service, were those that were open both to men and women. Through such courses the Army became aware of the possibilities for utilization of women in jobs which they formerly thought only men could handle. Experience of women in these fields will have a certain carry-over into civilian life, both in change of jobs and in further civilian education.

III. GENERAL IMPLICATIONS OF THE TRAINING PROGRAMS

THE FACT that women were admitted to the armed services because their participation in the prosecution of the war was needed, that their usefulness rapidly increased as the war progressed, as evidenced by the number of military occupations opened to them, and that the training and utilization of women were much like the training and utilization of men—in short, that the occupation of waging war was opened to women on conditions which tended toward equality—this fact has implications of great importance for the education of women in the civilian world.

EQUALITY IN MILITARY SERVICE

Irrelevant sex distinctions tended to disappear, and women's field of usefulness tended to broaden.

If one examines the women's military services the fact just stated is demonstrated to be true. The WAC, WAVES, MCWR, and SPAR sought relatively large numbers of recruits possessing certain skills which the military services needed immediately. The indoctrination and the semiskilled and semiprofessional courses were designed to make the skills of the women recruits available in military form within the shortest possible time. In most cases, these skills were in fields in which women had received civilian training and in which many women were employed—in short, they were "women's jobs." The training and utilization of these servicewomen resembled that of servicemen very closely, and the significance for civilian education lies in the fact that women were permitted, practically for the first time, to practice these skills in a *milieu* from which they had been excluded, and that they were employed on a basis of equality with men soldiers in the same types of positions.

The generalization just stated is only a generalization, and every serviceman or woman knows many exceptions.

Servicewomen advanced in military occupations new and old—as in aviation and nursing.

The women who were trained for employment in military aviation were entering a field which was new not only for women. Military aviation was the most recent, the most dramatic, and the best publicized of the different branches of the services, and this fact was of importance to women. Because, for example, the Army Air Forces had so much less of tradition behind them than the other Army branches, the utilization of women presented a less marked change in their pattern of organization for warfare. So many experiments in the testing, classification, training, and assignment of personnel were conducted in the Army Air Forces that the addition of a group of women was not particularly striking.

On the other hand, the entire air force was of the greatest interest to the civilian public, and the fact that women were permitted to be pilots and mechanics and control tower operators was widely known. In fact, there was an overdramatization and overpublicizing of the work of women in this branch of the service which appears to have led most people to believe that many more women were used in more important duties than was actually the case.

The use of women in military aviation was truly experimental. The work of a pilot, and in fact of any member of an aircrew, is highly skilled and requires certain rather special abilities. No one could offer even a reasonable guess as to how many women could be taught which of these skills, or by what methods. The Army Air Forces were ordered to conduct the training and utilization of women as pilots as an experiment, and as a result these questions can now be answered with some degree of authority.

As for the nonflying jobs for women in aviation, some of them can scarcely be called "aviation." Many women were assigned in clerical and medical positions in the air forces of all the services, and a considerably smaller number was trained to perform mechanical and administrative duties properly classifiable as aviation jobs. Most of the nonflying duties were semiskilled or semiprofessional, and in many cases the training for them was done on the job.

The importance of the training and utilization of a few thousand women in aviation branches with personnel numbered in the millions is out of proportion to their numerical strength. As an experiment it was of sufficient scope and duration to answer the questions basic to determining affirmatively that this new occupation had possibilities for women not only in war but in peace.

In contrast with aviation, nursing is one of the traditional fields for the employment of women. They have not only been nurses in civilian life for a long time, but their use in the Army and Navy in times of war and peace is well established. It was not necessary to prove that women were needed, or that they could be trained and used, as it was in the case of aviation.

In spite of the established status of women as military nurses, certain developments of real importance to educators occurred in their training during World War II. In Part Three of this report separate consideration is given to nurses, who are highly skilled professionals, and to other medical assistants trained for semiskilled and semiprofessional jobs. In the training of the former group, the establishment of the Cadet Nurse Corps under the auspices of the federal government is of outstanding importance not only in the field of education for nursing, but for education in general.

The use of federal funds to subsidize civilian training of various sorts is under continual discussion, and concrete experience under a successful program should be carefully studied and evaluated. In the training of nurses and of other medical personnel for military duty there were many changes in the methods of teaching. Civilian educators will study with interest the complex relationships developed within the training programs. The federal and state governments, the Army and Navy medical branches, civilian and military hospitals, and professional associations of nurses worked together to prepare and to operate these programs; and other professional groups, including educators, will find value in their experiences during the war.

IMPLICATIONS FOR WOMEN IN CIVILIAN LIFE

The implications to be derived from the study of training programs for women to serve as military personnel in aviation and in nursing, respectively, are stated at some length in chapters vi and xi.   At this point certain general implications derived from the experiences of the eight women's services collectively are to be observed.

1. *Social attitudes and employment prospects will continue to affect educational opportunities for women.*

The place of women in our culture has not yet been fixed, but the major determinant is no longer the demonstration of their ability.   What men and women *want* women to do will continue to have heavy weight, and women are still disqualified in many areas as a result.

A second set of conditions will be found to have a close working relationship with the public attitudes toward the employment of women in many occupations.   If there is a general shortage of labor, or if there are shortages in certain occupations, women will find admission to employment and to training for such employment not only open to them but active recruiting will be instituted to obtain them.   If the shortages are sufficiently acute, we will have a reproduction of the situation of 1941-45.   Business, industry, government, educational institutions, and the women's services were competing actively during those years for the available woman labor supply, and inducements and counter-inducements became increasingly attractive.

Two illustrations, taken from the situation as of July 1946 will illustrate this point.   There was a serious shortage of teachers in the country, and a large surplus of young men with every sort of training in aviation.   Any young woman who questioned the advisability of educating herself to be a teacher could be certain that the shortage of teachers was so extensive that opportunities in the profession would exist for her at the end of a rather long educational program.   On the other hand, if she wished to go into aviation she could be equally certain that, outside of a few types of positions such as airline hostess and clerical work, there was only the most remote possibility that she would be able to get a position. Some women do not wish to teach, no matter what opportunities there may be, and some women insist upon trying to force an entry into such an occupation as aviation, knowing the probable hazards. Nevertheless, the work opportunities which are open to women at the time do have a strong influence upon the pattern of education for women.

2. *The education of women must take some account of contemporary cultural conditions.*

In spite of the fact that women can be taught to do what men can be taught to do, with allowances for physical differences in cases where they are relevant, there will undoubtedly have to be differences provided for teaching men and women in many cases because of the influence of contemporary cultural conditions. However, the experiences of women during the war, not only in the women's military services but in all sorts of occupations, have lessened the cultural difference between men and women. It will never again seem revolutionary for women to fly fast pursuit planes, and traditional barriers in many occupations are similarly weakened or completely broken down.

The military training program had one main objective—to fill quotas established by the service forces and release men for combat. Trying to give men and women equal educational opportunities was not even a secondary objective. This was, of course, quite right, and there is no criticism to be implied. Since the objectives of civilian education in a democracy include the offering to all young men and women of equal opportunities to develop their capacities, the implication of their equal ability to profit by educational opportunity, even though it is derived from military programs in which this objective was *not* recognized, is important to civilian educators.

3. *The trend toward coeducation was continued by the war experience.*

Basic military training courses for women differed from those for men because the men were being trained to use weapons in combat and the women were not. In very large part it would have been difficult to conduct coeducational basic training with such divergent objectives.

On the other hand, the training of specialists in all branches of the armed forces was conducted on a coeducational basis. Frequently, women trainees were sent to schools which had been set up for men. Sometimes the schools were planned to be operated for both sexes. Occasionally, women could not be sent to a men's school because there were no housing accommodations for women, and in such cases a separate school exactly like the one for men was established for women.

The implication for civilian education appears to be that there may be reasons arising from the different status of men and women in our contemporary culture which will make it expedient in some cases to have separate schools for men and for women; but, on the other hand, there is a strong implication that men and women can and should be educated together, particularly if the education is for an activity in which both men and women will engage. Since men and women continually do fewer things alone, the field of coeducation progressively expands. Little argument can be offered for separate colleges of liberal arts on the basis of the experience afforded by the wartime training programs of the women's services.

The existence of well-established men's and women's institutions of higher learning which offer a high grade of educational opportunity will undoubtedly mean that the sexes will continue to be separated in a large number of cases, and the writer is neither attacking nor defending this situation. The sole point which is made as the result of the present study is that there is no implication to be derived from the training programs of the women's military services in support of separate colleges, and that there is strong support for coeducation except in the diminishing number of situations in which the cultural position of men and women varies so widely that different subjects must be taught, in a different manner, or from a different standpoint.

4. *The war experience produced permanent gains in the status, freedom, and capacities of American women.*

The opportunity, both in the armed services and in all aspects of civilian life, which was offered to women during World War II, undoubtedly produced results which will have important effects for years to come. The reduction of male enrollment in colleges made possible the education of many more than the usual number of civilian young women. Women in the military services, business, industry, government, education, and volunteer services played important and interesting roles in the conduct of the war.

Generous recognition was given to these services and to the individual women who participated. Women wore the uniform —whether it was the uniform of a nurse or an administrative officer or a mechanic—and they attained the prestige of membership and status in men's groups. They tasted the glory of hearing men who had opposed women's admission to these groups actually support their membership. Women who had held subordinate posts rose to excellent administrative positions. This history cannot be erased by the return to conditions of peace.

5. Various aspects of the women's services can yield information of great social value.

There were no precedents precisely applicable to the training, administration, or utilization of large numbers of women in a military organization. The considerable modification of Army and Navy practices in this respect that occurred by the end of the war only emphasizes more strongly the dearth of information as to what effect military discipline and group living could be expected to have upon adult women, what capacity they had for leadership and military command, how differently from or similarly to men they were motivated, and so on. Systematic exploration of the materials derived from the record of some 300,000 servicewomen should furnish valuable data.

Group living. Prior to the establishment of the women's services, few women lived in groups, except girls under twenty-one in boarding schools and colleges. The experience of close contact with large numbers of women was entirely new to many servicewomen. Provisions for group living which had been reasonably satisfactory in the men's services were carried over into the women's services when they were first set up, but not all of them were found to be usable. Neither could women's living arrangements be patterned upon those which are suitable for college and preparatory schoolgirls. The causes of these differences are obscure, and they are worth at least preliminary consideration by competent social psychologists to determine whether more thorough study should be made.

The effects of discipline. The situation of having thousands of adult women living and working under conditions of military discipline was so far from normal that it attracted great public attention, and the servicewomen themselves were deeply interested in it. The reaction of women to a military situation, the effectiveness of military types of punishment, and similar problems were carefully considered both by men and by women in the services, and their observations and conclusions, supported by ample data, should be made available for civilian use.

Leadership and command. Investigation should be made by competent psychologists into the available information relating to women's capacity as military commanders and leaders. Tests were developed to discover potential leaders, courses were provided, and evaluative procedures were devised. Probably no other extensive body of information on this particular subject exists, and if it could be used to answer questions of long standing as to women's capacities to lead or to command, the results would have great value.

Colleges commonly make the statement that they are training women to be leaders, and they point with pride to their alumnae who attain positions of leadership. Apparently no one has seriously tried to discover whether girls with leadership qualities tend to go to college, whether the college teaches them leadership or merely provides a situation in which natural qualities have an opportunity to develop, whether college graduates have better opportunities to become leaders because of their social and economic positions, or whether college women's leadership records are actually better than those of noncollege women. Similarly, all the statements commonly made comparing the leadership qualities of women and men are without scientific foundation.

The officers of the women's services who conducted the training programs were very often former civilian teachers, and they were interested in comparing leadership training in the services with student government in high schools and colleges. Many servicewomen in noncommissioned positions were responsible for the command of the enlisted women and these were positions of *real* responsibility. This situation was contrasted with student government, to the disadvantage of the latter. The principal criticism was directed against the unreality of student government, particularly on the grounds that the student leaders were not leading in any direction, and that in any case there were no adverse results if the leaders were poor. In general, the women officers favored student government entrusted with important duties for the performance of which they would be held responsible, without any attempt to protect student leaders from the results of their poor leadership.

Adaptability. Great stress was laid on the characteristic of adaptability as an important factor in successful performance of duty assignments in the services. This characteristic was defined in social, rather than educational or occupational, terms. Women with highly specialized training seemed to be less adaptable and less successful outside the range of their specialty. These are tentative impressions, but their importance would justify careful investigation.

Motivation. It is probably true that women are moved by rather different reasons than men. Probably the most important cause is the different roles of men and women in the American family. No one knows how many high school and college girls and young women in business or professions are interested in careers outside the home, but a considerable number of them consider such careers as secondary to marriage and homemaking, and they consciously or unconsciously believe that they will be supported by a husband. Similarly, most young men believe that they must be successful business or professional men because, among other reasons, they will be sole support of a wife and family. This persistence of an "amateur" or "temporary" attitude on the part of so many young women is a fact of great importance to educators and to employers.

Indoctrination. The methods of indoctrination, the purposes, and the results are closely related to the preceding problems.

We have not been accustomed to the idea of total indoctrination, nor have we cared to use the word in schools and colleges. Freshman "orientation" weeks and football rallies are, nevertheless, common examples of deliberate attempts to induce desired attitudes, and there are many others. The women's services necessarily conducted indoctrination courses, and they used all the devices of clothing, language, and surrounding conditions to convert the civilian women to membership in a military unit.

To the surprise of many members of the services, the women took to regimentation very easily and in a great number of cases they actually liked it. The reasons for this adaptability have been discussed at great length with the writer. Women like security, it is argued, and in a military service all one has to do is to learn the formula and carry it out. On the other hand, many women said frankly that their civilian lives were secure, to be certain, but very dull, and they joined the services in a spirit of seeking adventure rather than more security. To many women it was satisfying to be a part of a great venture, and to have their small effort gain recognition as a contribution to the whole. Some women who disliked regimentation were willing to forego freedom temporarily in the fight to guarantee permanent freedom. The state of mind of servicewomen was thus in part a result of the causes which led them to enlist and in part a result of indoctrination processes, and to a large extent their motivation was the result of what happened to them after the initial period of intensive indoctrination was concluded.

Indoctrination is a dangerous business. It is no more possible to forget or to forego the use of indoctrination than it is to pretend that atomic energy was never discovered. Unfortunately, the means were discovered before we were able to define the ends for which they are to be used. The combination of the use of indoctrination to support aggression carried out with atomic weapons is the greatest danger that mankind has ever faced. On the other hand, indoctrination and atomic energy can be used for constructive purposes.

It is obvious that we must have every possible bit of information about indoctrination, and data are available to study certain special aspects in relation to adult women who were deliberately indoctrinated into a new situation as rapidly and as completely as possible. Certain preliminary and tentative conclusions indicate the types of study which could be made.

One officer stated that, in her opinion, indoctrination and morale programs were better on paper than in practice; that "Washington was always having a good idea, but the field rarely caught on." As a teacher, she was inclined to believe that a similar situation existed in education. Research in education and publication of results give the appearance of progress. But how far down the line are there any resulting changes? She believed that the most successful morale-builder and indoctrination instrument was the series of motion pictures titled "Why We Fight."

Health, physical fitness, and recreation. There is a wealth of raw material, much of it in statistical form, in this area. Most available published material on the subject is based upon data relating to civilian women under twenty-one years of age, in schools or colleges. The services dealt with an older age group, and with many women who were several years out of educational institutions. Studies based on such materials should be prepared by researchers with special experience in health and physical fitness and recreation programs, and the military experience should be evaluated to determine implications of value for civilian women.

Part Two
WOMEN IN MILITARY AVIATION

IV. WOMEN AIRFORCES SERVICE PILOTS (WASP)

THE PLAN to use women pilots with the Army Air Forces was proposed in the summer of 1941 but was not accepted at that time because there were more than enough male pilots to handle available planes and because the plans for organization and administration of the program were not complete. In September 1942 the program was activated in two parts which for the time being were independent of each other.

THE WAFS AND THE WASP

The Women's Auxiliary Flying Squadron (WAFS)—an experimental squadron of experienced women pilots to do ferry work in the Air Transport Command with no other preliminary training than a few weeks of transition and concurrent ground schooling—was established September 10, 1942, at Newcastle, Delaware, under the command of Mrs. Nancy Harkness Love. Later, three more units were activated in Michigan, Texas, and California.

Miss Jacqueline Cochran was director of the Women's Flying Training Detachment, activated September 15, 1942, in the Flying Training Command, and she served with the general staff of the FTC in Fort Worth. The detachment was located first in a contract school at the Howard Hughes Airport in Houston, Texas; and after May 1943 at Avenger Field, Sweetwater, Texas. The first class of twenty-five trainees entered school at Houston, Texas, on April 24, 1943, and in November of that year was assigned to duty with the Air Transport Command.

On August 5, 1943, women pilot trainees and WAFS were merged into one organization—Women Airforces Service Pilots (WASP). Miss Jacqueline Cochran became special assistant to the Assistant Chief of Air Staff, Operations, Commitments, and Requirements, with the title of Director of Women Pilots. Mrs. Nancy Harkness Love, at the same time, became WASP executive with the staff of the Ferrying Division of the Air Transport Command. Complete regulations defining all aspects of the WASP program were promulgated at this time.

When the WASP was inactivated on December 20, 1944, there were 916 women pilots on operational duty as follows:

	Number
Headquarters, AAF	1
Training Command	620
Air Transport Command	141
First Air Force	16
Second Air Force	80
Fourth Air Force	37
Weather Wing	11
Proving Ground Command	6
Air Technical Service Command	3
Troop Carrier Command	1

They had flown approximately sixty million miles on operational duties, with an average for each woman pilot of 33 hours a month.

Women pilots were civil service employees, not members of the armed forces. Recruitment, except for the original group of Wafs, was handled directly by the office of the director of Women's Flying Training. Thirty women pilots were taken directly into the WAFS; all others passed through the training program. At no time was any effort necessary to secure prospective trainees, as there always were several hundred applicants on the waiting list. In her final report, the director said: "The selection was entirely a matter of choosing clean-cut, stable-appearing young girls, of proper age, educational background, and height, who could show the required number of flying hours properly noted and certified in a log book."

The stated purposes of the woman pilot program were:

To determine whether, in any grave national emergency, women could serve as pilots. Such determination involved a performance study of capabilities and limitations; of health, welfare, and discipline.

To organize a nucleus which could be expanded to almost any degree should the requirements of war so dictate.

To release male pilots for higher grades of duty and for combat by using women for the routine, noncombat jobs.

To decrease the Air Force's total demands for the physically and mentally perfect young men—the cream of the over-all manpower pool, from which the military services and industry must draw men.

In 1942 very little was known about women as pilots. There were about three thousand women qualified for licenses, but less than a hundred could meet ferry-duty standards without further training. A few women had done outstanding air work. England and Russia were using women pilots. Basically, however, the American program was started without benefit of precedent. There were no clear-cut physical standards available and, although there were nearly six million single women between the ages of eighteen and twenty-eight, only ideas and opinions were available as to their capacity to fly military aircraft regularly. It was necessary to determine whether a whole group of women without special selection except for physical requirements—not merely a few chosen pilots—could take over efficiently, effectively, and regularly, flying duties that would otherwise have to be performed by men. In these circumstances, changes in requirements, in training curriculum, and in other features of the program as it developed, were natural.

THE WASP TRAINING PROGRAMS

A description of the training program for Women Airforces Service Pilots must include as its major feature the work of the training school which was located for about six months at Houston, Texas, and from May 1943 to the end of the program in December 1944 at Avenger Field, Sweetwater, Texas.

There were 25,000 applicants for admission to the WASP training program. Of the 1,830 women who were admitted, 1,074 completed the course successfully and were assigned to operational duty. The remaining 656 were eliminated for the following reasons:

	Number	Percentage of Total Number Admitted
For flying deficiency	552	30.1
Resigned	152	8.3
For medical reasons	27	1.4
For disciplinary reasons	14	.8
Killed	11	.6

CURRICULUM

There were continual changes in the course content of each phase of training. The first program of the WASP training

WASP TRAINING PROGRAM
December 9, 1943

| | HOURS OF TRAINING | | |
FLYING TRAINING	Dual	Solo	Total
Primary: Fundamentals of flying (9 weeks)	28	42	70
Intermediate (9 weeks)			
Transition (AT–6)	14	21	35
Instrument (BT–15)			
Basic	14	7 [a]	21
Advanced	10	4 [a]	14
Link trainer	—	—	25
Advanced: Navigation (9 weeks)			
Navigation (PT–17), day	1	14	15
Navigation (AT–6)			
Day	10	29	39
Night	2	4	6
Night local	2	2	4
Instrument	4	—	4
Formation	2	—	2
Link trainer	—	—	5
MILITARY TRAINING			
Customs and courtesies of military service			2
Honor indoctrination			2
Organization of Army Air Forces			2
Safeguarding military information			2
War Department publications			2
Military correspondence			2
Close-order drill and ceremonies			54
ACADEMIC TRAINING			
Mathematics			20
Physics			14
Maps, charts, and aerial photography			18
Navigation			58
Aircraft and principles of flight			18
Engines and propellors			42
Weather			50
Code practice			30
Instruments			18
Forms and procedures			12
Pilots' information file			12
Communications			7
AERONAUTICAL EQUIPMENT MAINTENANCE TRAINING (MINIMUM)			10
PHYSICAL TRAINING			81
MEDICAL TRAINING			10

[a] Team rides

school took four months and consisted of 135 hours of flying training and 180 hours of ground school. The academic courses were revised very soon after initiation of the program, with a new breakdown totaling 315 hours. The entire course was actually very flexible and was adjusted to the previous experience of the individual trainee, because the flying experience of the first groups of trainees varied so widely. In April 1943 the curriculum was increased to 24 weeks, and in October of that year the program was again lengthened to 27 weeks and consisted of 210 hours of flying instruction in three equal phases of nine weeks each and 476 hours of ground-school instruction.

There were several innovations in the 27-week program. All instrument flying was concentrated in the intermediate phase. Twin-engine training was eliminated on the theory that a better pilot was produced if the advanced phase was concentrated on AT-6 training. New materials were added—ground-school courses in instrument flying, communications, pilot's information file, forms and procedures. Cross-country navigation training was increased and concentrated in the advanced phase, with two extended flights—one in an AT-6 and one in a PT-17.

The major changes in the training program for women pilots developed out of dissatisfaction with the results of the original program, criticism of the proficiency of early graduates after assignment to duty, and the declining experience level of accepted applicants. By the end of the first year, there was in effect a carefully worked out systematic plan for flying and ground-school training.

In March 1944 when it appeared likely that Congress would enact legislation militarizing the WASP, the curriculum was lengthened to 30 weeks and the military training program was expanded to 137 hours. Medical training was increased to 23 hours. The curriculum then consisted of 210 hours of flying training and 393 hours of ground-school instruction.

There were eight WASP classes in 1943 and ten in 1944. The number of trainees in each class and the number and percentage of graduates are shown in Table 3.

TABLE 3

NUMBER OF TRAINEES IN EACH OF THE 18 WASP TRAINING CLASSES, AND
PERCENTAGE GRADUATED

Class	Number Entering[a]	Number Graduated	Percentage Graduated
43–W–1	28	23	85.2
2	60	43	79.6
3	37	38	97.4
4	142	112	81.2
5	127	85	66.9
6	122	84	67.8
7	101	59	59.3
8	96	18	54.5
44–W–1	99	49	49.5
2	111	49	44.1
3	100	60	60.0
4	95	50	52.5
5	132	76	57.6
6	126	72	53.7
7	85	59	60.2
8	108	49	41.5
9	117	55	56.7
10	107	68	53.7

[a] Figures in this column represent new students and do not include small number of holdovers from preceding class.

In the third class, 97.4 percent were graduated and, in general, the rate was high in all 1943 classes because many trainees came in with considerable flying experience. In 1944 the most successful class had a graduation rate of 60.2 percent, and the lowest rate was 41.5 percent. The 1944 figures are probably more significant than those of 1943. In the *History of the WASP Program* written at the Central Flying Training Command, the elimination rate at Avenger Field was discussed. The average elimination rate in 1943 was 26 percent and it was 47 percent in 1944. The command stated that "the rates compared favorably with cadet training in the command, where elimination rates varied from slightly less than 25 percent to over 55 percent in the same years." Of 158 trainees who were held over for the next class, 50 percent were graduated, 26 percent were eliminated, and the remainder resigned or were discharged for various reasons.

The relation between age and success in training, based on the records of all 1,830 trainees, is summarized as follows:

Age Group	Percentage Graduated
18–20	70
21–24	65
25–29	54
30–35	34

The rate of graduation for the eighteen- to twenty-year-age group was double the rate for the thirty- to thirty-five-year-age group. The breakdown of eliminations for flying deficiency, resignations, and medical discharges offered additional evidence that young trainees were most successful, as shown in Table 4.

TABLE 4

RELATIONSHIP BETWEEN AGE AND PERFORMANCE IN TRAINING OF 1,066 WOMEN IN THE LAST TEN WASP CLASSES

Age Group	Number	Eliminated for Flying Deficiency	Resigned	Medical Discharge	Graduated
18–20	93	20 (22%)	3 (3%)	2 (2%)	68 (73%)
21–25	649	183 (28%)	63 (10%)	11 (2%)	392 (60%)
26–30	243	102 (42%)	31 (12%)	11 (5%)	99 (41%)
31–35	81	44 (54%)	11 (14%)	6 (7%)	20 (25%)

SPECIAL TRAINING PROGRAMS

After a considerable number of Wasps had been assigned to the Flying Training Command for operational duties, certain special training programs were initiated to increase their usefulness. These programs were carried out during the latter part of 1943 and in 1944.

	Number Entering	Number Graduated
Transition, C-60	16	6
Transition, B-17	17	13
Transition, B-25	20	19
Transition, B-26	57	39
Co-pilot, B-26	24	Discontinued
Advanced instrument	246	232
AAF School of Applied Tactics	460	460

C-60 transition

The women pilots admitted to this type of training were being prepared for glider-towing assignment, and the proficiency standards were high. Results were not entirely satisfactory because women appeared to lack strength and stamina for this exacting, fatiguing work. The trainees who were graduated were rated "minimum satisfactory for glider towing under ideal conditions." The course was abandoned upon recommendation of the Flying Evaluation Board. There was some indication that leg length and stature in general were important factors.

B-17, B-25, and B-26 transition

The results of these courses were reasonably satisfactory. Of the 94 women who entered the courses, 71 completed them successfully and checked out on these three types of aircraft.

B-26 co-pilot

This was a training program of short duration, undertaken at flexible gunnery schools in the Eastern and Western Flying Training Commands. The commands determined the length of the course and the amount of flying time. Trainees were to be prepared for work as co-pilots in tow-target missions. When they had reached high enough proficiency, they were to be checked off as first pilots.

It was difficult to get qualified trainees for the course because quotas had to be met at the same time for the instrument-training course and for the advanced training course at Orlando. Moreover, a B-26 pilot had to be at least 64 inches tall, and had to have twin-engine experience and possess an instrument card. The course lasted about one month, after which most of the women trained as co-pilots were returned to their original stations. Apparently no further use was made of their special training.

Advanced instrument-training course

In September 1944 notice was sent to the several commands and air forces of the AAF announcing the establishment of an advanced instrument-training course for WASP personnel. All who had not successfully completed the instrument-instruction course at Bryan Army Air Base, Bryan, Texas, were to receive this advanced training at Sweetwater, Texas. The entrance dates of five classes and the quotas to be sent from each command and air force were announced.

The student-instructor ratio for the course was fixed at 3:1, and the student-airplane ratio at 2.3:1. The hours of instrument flying were divided fairly equally between a basic-instrument phase, a radio-range phase, and Link-trainer instruction. Ground training consisted of 14 hours in a basic phase, 17 hours in a radio phase, and 23 hours in a weather phase.

The objective of the course was to qualify Wasps as instrument pilots, and those so qualified were to receive an instrument card (AAF Form 8, white). The course lasted five weeks and consisted of 51.20 hours of instrument flying, 54 hours of ground school, and 15 hours of physical training. The course was given from August 7 to November 24, 1944, and was then discontinued because of the imminent inactivation of the WASP. Of 246 women pilots who entered the course, 232 completed it successfully.

WASP Training Course at AAFSAT

Early in 1944 the AAF planned to request Congress to transfer the WASP from civilian to military status, and at first it appeared that this action would be taken. The WASP Training Course at AAFSAT (Army Air Forces School of Applied Tactics) at Orlando, Florida, was instituted as a means of military orientation for women pilots and was operated from April 19, 1944, to September 29, 1944. In May of that year, expanded military training was also offered to all trainees at Avenger Field, and graduates of this school who completed the expanded course were not to be required to attend the AAFSAT course. Earlier graduates were to take the course at Orlando after not less than ninety days of operational duty, and they were chosen on a quota basis from the various commands where they were stationed.

The term "officer training" caused some opposition to the course, and the AAF was accused of "jumping the gun" in sending women to the school before the bill was acted upon by Congress. Actually, nearly all pilots in the AAF were officers, and the women's training was in reality advanced pilot training for service whether as civilian or military personnel.

Within a few weeks after the institution of the programs of expanded military training, it was apparent that not only would the WASP not be militarized, but that it would be inactivated by the end of 1944. Several classes of Wasps nevertheless took the course at Orlando, and the history of the school contains the statement that, although not used for its original purpose, "it is by no means meant that the value of the AAFSAT training was lost, for at AAFSAT the leaven of sound tactical doctrine concerning military employment of air power was spread among a group of women who, without a doubt, will become the leading female pilots of the future in this country." Four hundred and sixty Wasps entered the course, in ten classes ranging from 39 to 50 trainees. All entrants completed the course successfully. Their morale and application were rated "Superior."

The staff and special training department of the School of Applied Tactics was assigned to direct the new WASP course, and Capt. Horace R. Smith of that department was appointed chief, WASP Training Course Division. The curriculum was worked out with Miss Cochran and it remained in effect throughout the program with only a few administrative changes. Many curricular revisions were planned but not adopted. There were, however, constant revisions of subject matter and of the treatment of subject matter within the curricular framework.

The curriculum was organized in two phases. In the first phase of fourteen instructional days were included subjects of a basic military nature; in the second phase of six instructional days the technical and tactical aspects of AAF operations were studied. The consolidated schedule of a typical course appears on page 61.

The examinations were all of the objective type and their preparation and results were carefully studied. An analysis of the testing program for the first two classes showed that in some of the short subjects in the first phase it was difficult to prepare examinations that were hard enough. Nevertheless, the examinations were used because it was believed that stu-

CONSOLIDATED SCHEDULE (IN HOURS) OF THE WASP COURSE AT
THE AAF SCHOOL OF APPLIED TACTICS, ORLANDO, FLORIDA

Subject	Lectures (Phase 1)	Exams	Demonstration	Lectures (Phase 2)	Total
Address of welcome	1	...	...	...	1
Army orientation	3	...	...	...	3
Personal transportation	1	...	...	...	1
Base and staff functions	12	2	...	...	14
Aircraft recognition	13	1	...	...	14
Communications	7	1	2	2	12
Weather	5	1	...	...	6
Supply	5	1	...	...	6
Administration	6	1	...	...	7
Safeguarding military information	2	...	...	...	2
Organization War Department and AAF	8	1	...	...	9
Military law	13	2	...	...	15
Military courtesy and discipline	3	...	...	...	3
Physical training	2	...	...	2	4
Aeromedical	7	1	...	...	8
Chemical warfare	4	1	2	...	7
Tactical air force	...	...	...	1	1
Strategic air force and air service command	...	...	...	1	1
AAF weapons and CWS	...	...	4	...	4
Reconnaissance aviation and air defense command	...	...	...	1	1
Antiaircraft artillery	...	...	...	1	1
Airdrome security	...	...	...	1	1
Troop carrier aviation	...	...	...	1	1
Strategic air force	...	...	...	1	1
Automatic pilots, gunnery and air-sea rescue	...	...	3	...	3
Fighter aviation	...	...	...	3	3
Fighter control	...	...	3	1	4
Tactical bombardment	...	...	...	1	1
Cross-country navigation	...	...	...	2	2
Training films	...	...	...	8	8
General exam and critique	...	1	...	...	1
Graduation	...	...	...	1	1
Reserved for director	7	...	...	7	14
Total	99	12	14	35	160

dents could more readily prepare for tests in individual subjects than for a comprehensive general examination, and because the length of a single comprehensive examination would have made it extremely fatiguing in Florida summer heat. In the history of the WASP program in AAFSAT it is noted: "On examinations which were also taken by officer and enlisted cadres at AAFSAT, it was estimated that the Wasps averaged eight to thirteen points higher than the men."

Their work in general received most favorable comment and commendation from the school authorities, and there were no adverse criticisms recorded. "Accompanying the thorough preparation for teaching was a spirit of critical evaluation of the teaching processes and procedures in use. This evaluation resulted in constant improvements in the teaching of the course." One method used to improve the quality of the course was to solicit student ratings of each lecture and demonstration, both as to content and presentation. Lectures were rated Superior, Excellent, Very Satisfactory, Satisfactory, and Unsatisfactory. Ratings were tabulated and the results circulated to teachers as representing the students' conception of the value of each lecture. However, so elaborate an evaluation method was used only for the first class. Later classes merely evaluated each course as a whole.

COSTS OF WASP TRAINING PROGRAM

It is always difficult to estimate unit costs for a small part of a much larger training program. Approximately eleven hundred women were graduated from the WASP school at Avenger Field, and this group was only a small fraction of the larger number of male pilots who were given similar basic flight training. Certain items of overhead in the program for male trainees were not increased by the addition of the WASP program, while other overhead items were increased.

The Director of Women Pilots in her final report made the following statement:

The cost of training a Wasp is the same as the cost of training a male cadet to do the same work. Elimination rates are equal. One instructor can handle an equal number of students, male or female. Like equipment is used, and similar courses given. The precise cost for Wasp or male cadet involves so many indirect items that differences could always be arrived at by any two persons. Indirect costs through general overhead are almost all of an increment nature in the case of any flying student, because there would be no lessening of general or command staffs if there were no WASP program. The direct cost of WASP training should be treated as almost the entire cost. This has been approximated as $12,150.70 per Wasp, including tuition, salary, plane depreciation, maintenance and supplies, personnel, equipment, travel, all uniforms and functional clothing, medical examination, communications, amortization of equipment, maintenance of administrative vehicles, and adjustment for eliminees. Sizable amounts, even for wartime, have been quoted publicly on the cost of the WASP program. Perhaps greatest enlightenment would come from consideration of the fact that most of the enlarged WASP program's costs would have accrued during the budget year of 1945. The Army Air Forces requested, and Congress granted, in the Army Appropriations Bill for fiscal 1945, a sum of slightly over $6,000,000 to cover all contemplated WASP costs!

The Committee on Civil Service of the House of Representatives, in its report of June 5, 1944, on the proposals for expansion and change in civil service status of the Wasps, made a statement which differs in some respects from that quoted above, although the same estimated unit cost of $12,150.70 is used:

At the outset of this inquiry information was sought as to the cost of the Sweetwater course. On February 26, War Department presented this cost as $6,540.90. This same figure had earlier been presented to the Truman Committee. However, request for more complete analysis of the cost resulted in the submission, on April 21, of further detailed figures, showing the cost to be $12,150 per graduate. This larger figure includes additional items not previously mentioned:

	Cost per graduate
Original figure (tuition, student salary, plane depreciation)	$6,265.35
Additional costs:	
Maintenance cost, material, labor, gas, and oil	3,023.50
Personnel, military and civilian	540.10
Equipment	89.56
Travel	18.00
Uniform	326.06
Medical examination and hospitalization	66.59
Communications	8.80
Amortization, crash truck, Link trainer, vehicles	95.66
Maintenance, administrative vehicles	13.64
Adjustment for eliminees	1,703.44
Total additional costs	$5,885.35
Total cost per graduate	$12,150.70

It is important to consider that the $12,150 figure last submitted includes only the cost at Sweetwater, and that graduates of Sweetwater are qualified to operate only the lighter type ships, generally used in training, courier, and liaison work.

Training for operating this faster and heavier equipment is much more expensive than for the lighter types. It is necessary that these fledgling pilots have many hours of dual and solo instruction, which is costly in fuel, equipment, instructor time, and other direct and indirect expenses.

It is the studied opinion of the staff that complete training of a WASP pilot qualified to handle the faster and heavier ships costs a minimum of $20,000 per pilot. This estimate is supported by the considered opinion of highly competent civilian and military authorities.

CHARACTERISTICS OF WASP PERSONNEL

The first women pilots (30 members of the WAFS) were chosen in September 1942. They met the following requirements: American citizenship, high school education, twenty-one to thirty-five years of age, possession of a commercial pilot's license, 500 hours of certified flying time as a pilot, a CAA rating on 200-horsepower planes, and a minimum height of 60 inches. They were assigned to take a short orientation course before they went on duty in ferrying operations.

QUALIFICATIONS FOR ADMISSION TO WASP TRAINING

The first set of requirements for WASP trainees, with modifications which were made for later groups, was as follows: American citizenship, high school education or its equivalent, twenty-one to thirty-five years of age, 200 hours flying time, minimum height of 60 inches, medical examination by an Army flight surgeon, and a personal interview with an authorized recruiting officer.

Early experience indicated that younger women were more successful in training than women in the higher age groups. The minimum age for admission was eventually reduced to eighteen and one-half years, and most of the women who were admitted were under twenty-seven years of age. This action was prompted by the fact that the rate of elimination for flying deficiency and the rate of medical discharges and resignations increased markedly in the upper-age groups. Data from the training of male cadets tended to confirm the decision.

Very few women had enough flying experience to meet the original high requirements. The flying time was reduced to 100 hours, then to 75 hours, and eventually to only 35 hours. Of the 343 women in the first four classes of 1944, only 39 had more than 105 hours of flying experience before entering training.

Height, weight, other measurements

No precedents had been established and no physical standards were available on which to base suitable heights and weights for trainees. At first, Table AR 40-105, "Weights and Heights of Officer Candidates" was used and it was adapted to women by deducting four pounds, by age groups. An analysis of 1,383 WASP trainees, as seen in Table 5, led to revisions.

TABLE 5

AVERAGE HEIGHT AND WEIGHT OF 1,383 WASP TRAINEES, BY AGE GROUPS

Age Group	Average Height in Inches	Average Weight in Pounds
18–20	65	124
21–25	66	128
26–30	65	128
31–35	65	130
Average for group	65¼	127½

(NOTE: Range from 60 inches, 101 pounds in the 18-20 age group, to 72 inches, 186 pounds in the 31-35 age group.)

This standard table was based on the average weight of all trainees of a certain height in the various age groups, which was found to be three or four pounds less than the earlier weight table. The minimum weight permitted was the same in the two tables, but the maximum weight was lowered by fourteen to sixteen pounds in the second table. This decision to require a relatively lower maximum weight for women pilots was based upon differences in the physical make-up of females and males. A woman who approaches maximum weight is usually obese, with poor musculature.

After some experience it was found desirable to admit only those women who were at least 64 inches tall. Very short persons have to use so many cushions that they are too close to the stick to permit free movement in many types of planes.

Among 1,383 trainees, 12 signed waivers for weight over the maximum (seven were graduated and five eliminated for flying deficiency), 59 signed waivers for weight under the minimum (39 were graduated, and 20 eliminated, in the majority of cases for flying deficiency), and 15 were admitted who were less than 62 inches tall (10 were graduated and five eliminated for flying deficiency).

To select and classify women pilots properly it is necessary to know something of the muscular requirements in handling various types of aircraft, particularly Classes IV and V. It is especially necessary to give attention not only to "standing height" but also to "sitting height"; and adequate leg length is important. The differences in measurements between a woman pilot and a man pilot, as shown in Table 6, demonstrate that the variations are not uniform. For example, the difference in standing height is 4.3 inches, but the difference in sitting height is only 2.3 inches.

TABLE 6

COMPARATIVE ANTHROPOMETRIC MEASUREMENTS OF 450 WASPS AND 2,961 AVIATION CADETS

Measurement	WASP	Aviation Cadets
Anterior arm reach	31.8 inches	35.2 inches
Sitting height	34.1 "	36.4 "
Buttock-to-knee length	22.6 "	23.6 "
Patella height	20.1 "	22.0 "
Stature	64.9 "	69.2 "
Weight	128.6 pounds	153.1 pounds

Educational and occupational backgrounds

Although a trainee could be admitted with high school graduation or its equivalent, approximately two-thirds of the trainees in six classes had had additional education. The proportion was even higher in the WASP group on duty.

The occupational background of the Wasps on duty in October 1944 with the Western Flying Training Command is far from typical of the average background of an unselected group of women of the same ages. Twenty-four of these Wasps had been engaged in an occupation in the field of aviation, 14 in various mechanical occupations, 52 in office work, 27 in education as teachers or students, 15 in various professions, 2 in the WAAC, and only 4 listed themselves as "housewife." Many of the occupations in which considerable numbers of women are engaged did not have a single representative.

Performance on aviation tests

In anticipation of the possibility that a selection and classification procedure similar to that used for aviation cadets might be desired for selection of women pilots, the Psychological Section of the Office of the Air Surgeon, AAF Headquarters, prepared a report entitled, "Performance of Wasps in Training upon Aviation Cadet Qualifying and Classification Tests." The Shipley Personal Inventory and numerous specific classification tests were also given. These tests were adapted for women pilots by the omission of materials relating to combat duties.

The validity of comparing the performance of women pilots on these tests with the performance of male pilots is subject to question, as the Psychological Section was careful to point out. In the first place, relatively few women trainees were examined. The tests in some instances were administered to as many as six classes in training at Avenger Field.

Wasps who were selected for training made slightly better scores than unselected male applicants, but their scores were definitely lower than those of qualified male aviation students and fully qualified cadets. Their best scores were on the tests for rudder control, reading comprehension, and general information. Their poorest scores were on tests having a large mechanical component. The Psychological Section concluded that the pattern of abilities in the WASP group was quite distinctive.

Physical and medical considerations

Capt. Nels O. Monserud was medical officer at Avenger Field for sixteen months. With the assistance of the Professional Division in the Office of the Air Surgeon, he prepared a study entitled *Medical Consideration of Wasps* which reviewed the experiences of AAF surgeons, commanding officers, flying safety officers, and other interested personnel at fields where Wasps were stationed both as trainees and as operating personnel.

The evaluation of medical adaptability to flying is difficult because we have no accurate criteria of human physical and psychological normality. This is particularly true in the case of women aviators. Speculative opinion has been expressed that women pilots are physically and psychologically unsuited to fly Army types of aircraft. Captain Monserud's study, which was based upon both training and operational phases of WASP work, may be useful in the future, both in military and in civil aeronautics, because it offers some concrete evidence rather than unsupported personal opinion.

The policies of WASP training were drawn in the main from the Army Air Cadet program, and the variations were caused by the nonmilitary status of the Wasps rather than by their sex. Evaluation of their work in operational phases was less objective and was based upon letters and interviews. Captain Monserud said: "Throughout this report appear several impressions that may be classified as reliable, maturely considered presumptions, because even lacking statistical support, the preponderance of authoritative opinion renders other conclusions untenable."

In spite of the warning which appears frequently throughout the AAF reports on the WASP program that "there should be no attempt to compare Wasps to male pilots," such comparisons are probably justifiable. The only information about women pilots is based upon the relatively small number who joined the WASP and is of doubtful statistical validity. If comparison with data based upon very large numbers of male aviators can be used to substantiate tentative indications shown by WASP data, it is valuable to make the comparisons. It is necessary, however, to view all comparisons between men and women pilots with the greatest care, and to be certain that all variables have been given due weight.

Experience with this women's program indicated that the most favorable age physically is from eighteen to twenty-eight years, although younger women (eighteen to twenty) may lack responsibility.

Women can meet the physical requirements of the War Department examination for pilots. The Army Air Forces examination was found to be adaptable to women with certain necessary changes which listed the causes for rejection peculiar to women.

Physiological problems.—When the program was initiated, headquarters staff was concerned with the physiological problems peculiar to women in their relation to flying activities, but nothing on the subject appeared in the early directives. In March 1943 a letter was sent to all group commanders setting forth a policy in line with the current CAA rules governing women pilots; namely, that no woman pilot was to be assigned to any flying duties during pregnancy, and that during the menstrual period a woman could not fly from one day before the beginning of the period to two days after the last day of the period. The effect of the second regulation would be to ground every woman pilot for six to eight days every month. The Air Transport Command Surgeon agreed on pregnancy as a flying disqualification, but disagreed on the second regulation. In his opinion, flight during the menstrual period should be treated as an individual problem to be regulated by the local WAFS leader and by the Station Flight Surgeon when his assistance was required. This opinion was thereupon endorsed by the Air Surgeon with orders that the matter was one to be handled locally, and that delay in cross-country ferrying trips due to the menstrual period was not to be censurable.

Actually it would have been almost impossible to enforce the original directive, and in practice several women pilots even continued to fly for months after the beginning of pregnancy. In the official history of the WASP in the Air Transport Command it is stated that earlier fears about loss of flying time for physiological reasons were "much exaggerated" and women pilots simply were not grounded for six to eight days each month. Even when grounded, they were nearly always able to attend the continuous ground school operated by each ferrying command, to take care of the post work required of all pilots, to get their gear in order, and in general to attend to the details which all pilots have to postpone while on ferrying trips.

Captain Monserud's study contains important data on the subject of menstruation and flying based upon 430 cases, all doubtful cases having been rejected. This group of WASP trainees included women from eighteen to thirty-five years of age, of whom 12 percent were married but had not borne children, and 6 percent were married and had borne children. Very

comprehensive data were collected concerning the objective fore-
warning of menstruation and the perceptible effects before,
during, and after the period. Concentration, coordination,
reaction time, and tenseness tests were given, with the result
that 75 percent of these trainees were found to be normal, 19
percent were below normal, and 6 percent were not known to
vary. Depth perception and visual acuity were normal in 88
percent of cases, altered in 6 percent, and in another 6 percent
there was no known variation.

Records showed the percentage of women grounded for
menstruation "to be less than heretofore popularly supposed.
Thus, one might expect approximately 30 of these 430 women
to be on duty not involving flying the first day of their period
as indicated by statistics during training. Yet the experience
of surgeons and operations officers failed to find the figure to
be that high. At Love Field, for all causes, Wasps lost less
than one-tenth day per girl per month. Other stations report
time lost was negligible and did not interfere with the job."
At Avenger Field six women instructors lost less flying time
than did male instructors.

Of the 430 women included in the study, the 18 who resigned
listed no menstrual disturbances. There was no relation demonstrated between menses and elimination. In the 11 fatal accidents, and in the 112 major, nonfatal accidents, there were no
demonstrable contributing menstrual factors. Of 263 minor
accidents, 28 percent occurred within five days after the first day
of menses.

To sum up, the studies at Avenger Field and the experience
of surgeons connected with graduate Wasps revealed that menstruation in properly selected candidates is not a problem, and
it has little if any effect on the training or operational phases
of the program. There is no relation demonstrated between
accidents and menses. About 20 percent of trainees observed
reported moderate to severe menstrual disturbances, and of these
about 30 percent were grounded during training. The average time in two classes of trainees which was lost to flying was
about seven-tenths day per girl per month, and in operational
flying, the time lost at most fields was negligible.

The records indicated that severe dysmenorrhea should be disqualifying if not amenable to treatment or if tending to recurrence, because of the frequency of neurotic or psychosomatic tie-up in such cases. Amenorrhea, if not due to pregnancy or menopause, might be imposed by tension which in at least one case was removed by the solution of conflicts. In the predominant age group observed, menopausal conditions were of rare occurrence, but because of vasomotor and emotional instability such cases required careful evaluation. Under some conditions, a subtotal hysterectomy was not disqualifying, but total and panhysterectomy did disqualify.

Important decisions were made to apply to pregnancy and its relationship to flying. Unintentional abortion was found to be the most likely obstetric complication during early stages, and the next in importance was excessive vomiting. Upon discovery of pregnancy, temporary disqualification should begin, extending through delivery and long enough after to help to preserve mother-infant relationship. Application of this principle would tend to discourage the re-entry of a woman whose loyalty was divided and who might later wish to resign because plans for the care of her child were not satisfactory. The proper period was established as from three to six months after the date of anticipated normal delivery, thus reducing the possibility of induced abortion to shorten the time of disqualification.

Fatigue, stamina, endurance.—Captain Monserud writes:

Operational fatigue is an illness manifested by emotional and fatigue symptoms, generally revealing itself in a state of anxiety—it is the result of the current stress incidental to flying—it is not the result manifested in the anxiety ridden personality which is really poor structural response. It is the reaction of normal people and does not mean psychoneurosis. Some of the Wasps showed a low threshold of endurance, but most of them seemed to possess the necessary structure to adequately tolerate normal apprehensions and fears. That a pilot would "rather fly than eat" does not necessarily eliminate her from involvement if she is mentally so constituted as to not adequately handle conflicts peculiar to her. It is not the degree of the conflict about flying, but more the adequacy with which it is handled. Operational fatigue among women pilots is not based upon physical factors. While these may play an accessory role, they are not primary, in fact an arduous physical training program is an important factor in combat of fatigue states due to flying. Menstrual tension, as such, is in some cases alleviated by the "sedation of flying," (a term used by the Surgeon, CFTC, in personal communication with the author) many women stating they feel better if they fly.

The sources of conflict contributing to operational fatigue were many—financial worries, marriage and engagements, fear of pregnancy, home problems, resignations—but most were directly related to problems on the flight line. Instructors changed, policies on elimination changed, and weak trainees were prone to charge favoritism and to add to each other's concern by gossip among themselves. Separation from home and customary conveniences, and unaccustomed regimentation were also factors. Captain Monserud repeated, "Again the adequacy of solution is the most important thing." Trainees with dormant neurotic tendencies, overlooked at entrance, showed tendencies to nostalgia and were unable to accept regimentation. Some of these anxiety-ridden trainees resigned, and others flew so poorly that they were eliminated. "Checkitis"— a condition in which the girl was doing well but for some reason slumped and failed on her check rides—was common, but was usually reported to the medical officer who helped the trainee to analyze the situation, to rationalize and evaluate her status, and to finish training.

Armstrong [1] states that 10 percent of all pilots eventually develop subjective symptoms of mild functional neurosis. The rate at Avenger Field over a 21-month period was 0.7 percent. Captain Monserud believed that this low incidence might be speculated upon as follows: Possibly all cases were not reported to the medical officer. Perhaps the medical officer was not thorough enough or used the wrong approach. That might have been true to a certain extent, because the medical group did not always know exactly what was expected of them in an entirely new situation. Some doctors might have been over-diligent and have lost the confidence of trainees and failed to secure proper cooperation. There were instances of "over-diagnosis." The male medical point of view is well expressed

[1] Harry C. Armstrong, *Principles and Practice of Aviation Medicine* (Baltimore: Williams and Wilkins, 2d ed., 1943).

by Captain Monserud in the statement: "When one considers the over-all feminine capacity to broad emotional trend and the tendency to cry as easily in anger as for any other reason, much care must be exercised lest the state is misinterpreted." Finally, the low reported incidence might be due to the more highly selected group, plus the fact that these women were highly motivated in their desire to fly and anxious to show that they were as good as men pilots.

The rate of incidence of functional neurosis was lower with early trainees who had more flying time, and increased later as younger candidates with less flying experience were admitted.

Aerotitis and upper respiratory conditions.—At Avenger Field there was evidence of an increase in nasopharyngitis and upper respiratory diseases after the admission of each new group of trainees. They were instructed about colds and did not hesitate to seek advice and carry out treatment. "These women, on the whole, seemed most meticulous in matters of health, hygiene, and cleanliness," says Dr. Monserud.

No cases of aerosinusitis or other diseases related to changes in atmospheric pressure occurred. There were no known complications, such as tympanic ruptures and secondary otitis, nor was any one forced to resign because of tendencies toward recurrence. Otitis, non-aero, was more prevalent during the summer swimming season. There were no cases that lost more than a few days at a time from flying due to otitis externa, mycotic, although some cases were frequent repeaters. From time to time it was suggested that there was a connection between tension and ability to clear the ears, but there were no supporting data. In the cases in which trainees came to "have their ears checked" during instrument training, it was found that difficulties were caused not by aural or auditory fatigue but by the radio equipment or by failure of the trainee to know what to listen for in radio work.

Altitude chamber reaction.—The results of altitude chamber tests of 386 Wasps were compared with those for 719 aviation cadets chosen at random and were found to be approximately the same. Table 7 shows the percentage frequency of indicated reactions occurring during simulated flight to an altitude of 28,000 feet, in a low-pressure chamber:

TABLE 7

ALTITUDE CHAMBER REACTIONS OF 386 WASPS AND 719 AVIATION CADETS

Reaction	Wasps [a]	Cadets
Tolerance to anoxia at 18,000 feet	3.6	0.8
Incidence of aerotitis media	24.4	18.8
Incidence of aerosinusitis	1.6	1.2
Incidence of toothache at altitude	0.5	1.0
Gas distress at altitude sufficient to cause premature descent	0.0	0.0
Collapse or shock	0.0	0.0

[a] There was no correlation between menses and adverse reactions.

Terminal physical examinations.—Captain Monserud included in his study a tabulation of 745 terminal physical examinations, although he could not, from available records, compute the percentage of all applicants eliminated for physical reasons. Standards for Wasps did not vary in the main from those imposed on other AAF flying personnel.

It was possible to compare over one-half of the terminal examinations with entrance examinations. There were few changes in physical standards. "They apparently maintained a good physique throughout their stay in the program," concluded Captain Monserud.

ACCIDENTS AND FATALITIES

As might have been expected, great interest was taken, both by AAF authorities and by the public in general, in the safety factor of the women pilots program. Since there was considerable misinformation on the subject prevalent while the program was in operation and since it is such an extremely important part of flying, careful consideration was given to it by the persons in charge of the program.

The Statistical Control Division, Office of Management Control, AAF, tabulated all Forms 14, "Report of Aircraft Accident," furnished by the Office of Flying Safety. This included all Wasps on duty as pilots, co-pilots, and students, but excluded observers and passengers. The material taken from the accident reports is listed under date, name of pilot, station where the accident occurred, injuries, type of mission, and type of plane.

The tabulation made by the Statistical Control Division covering all accidents in the period from November 1942 through December 1944, classifies the injuries as follows: fatal 36, missing 1, major injury 7, minor injury 29, no injury 337.

From November 1942 through December 1943, the largest cause factors in accidents were faulty technique, carelessness, and poor judgment. In 1944 the largest factors were misuse of controls, misuse of brakes, lack of proficiency in the particular type of aircraft involved, failure to observe, and other pilot errors. In the Air Transport Command 62 percent of all WASP accidents were due to poor technique, carelessness and disobedience, and poor judgment. Although this percentage may seem high, all the factors are of types which can be influenced by training and experience. The remedy would be to insure fully qualified instructors for training, and to refuse to allow women to "check out" in as many aircraft as possible to permit shortening of the transition period.

Captain Monserud's analysis of WASP accidents covered 394 which occurred between November 1942 and October 1944, a period two months shorter than that covered by the Statistical Control Division.

With the customary warning as to the validity of comparing the records of men and women pilots, Captain Monserud presented the following statistics based upon experience in the Air Transport Command: from October 1942 to April 1943, the comparative pilot error accident rate per 1,000 hours of flying in the ATC was .22 for Wasps, and .62 for male pilots; from April 1943 to June 1944, the rate was .60 for Wasps, and .32 for male pilots. These figures indicate that as Wasps with less flying time were assigned to operational duty, the pilot error rate increased; whereas, as the male pilots accumulated more flying time, their error rate decreased.

Of the 394 accidents which were studied, 185 occurred at Avenger Field during training. In 29 percent of the total of accidents, the plane was either wrecked or required major overhaul. In 82 percent there was no personal injury, and in 9 percent there was a fatality. The number was undoubtedly affected by conditions at the field, which was under construction during most of the time the WASP training program was located there.

Commenting on the psychological reactions of Wasps to plane accidents, Captain Monserud indicated it was the consensus that they were not easily distracted and seemed to have the situation well in hand. Since he was stationed at Avenger Field for sixteen months he had ample opportunity for observation. During training, women pilots were most upset, after accidents, by the loss of flying time due to clearance procedure following accidents. Statistical evidence was not available on "this matter of self-preservation and distractibility or flightiness" and it must remain a matter of opinion. Captain Monserud cited examples of the "composure and level-headedness of the girls" and called them "outstanding." This evaluation was concurred in by "most of the surgeons, operations officers, and flying safety officers."

DUTY ASSIGNMENTS

In September 1942 the Women's Auxiliary Ferrying Squadron (the WAFS) consisted of a small group of women pilots who had extensive flying experience. They were attached to the Army Transport Command, and their mission was to deliver various types of military aircraft. Almost immediately there came indications that women pilots would be asked to perform other duties. In November 1942 General H. H. Arnold stated that the objective of the Air Forces program was to provide at the earliest possible date a sufficient number of women pilots to replace men "in every noncombatant flying duty in which it is feasible to employ women." The plan included both the improvement of the trained pilots and the training of women with little or no previous flying experience.

The Flying Training Command was asked to furnish a list of suitable positions. Although it was very early in the program and there was incomplete information on the subject, the command suggested that, in addition to ferrying, women pilots could act as instructors in women's flying schools, primary pilot schools, elementary glider schools, and liaison pilot schools;

PLATE II

—*U. S. Army AAF Photo*

A WASP ON DUTY AT ROMULUS ARMY AIR FIELD, ROMULUS, MICHIGAN

as tow pilots in basic glider schools; as gunnery tow-target pilots; as instrument flying instructors; and as Link-trainer operators.

The August 1944 report of the Director of Women Pilots to the Commanding General of the Army Air Forces contains a description of the status of Wasps then on duty. At that time, 773 women pilots had been trained and 699 were on operational duty, as follows:

Training Command:
Instruction, engineering flying, target towing, etc. 300
Air Transport Command:
Ferrying 299
AAF Weather Wing:
Liaison flying 12
Continental Air Forces:
Target towing and related flying duties ... 81
Materiel Command:
Testing flight clothing, engineering flying .. 2
Proving Ground Command:
Target towing 5

Effort was made to assign women pilots on the basis of their preferences and capabilities but, as in all military services, the necessity of meeting quotas and, in general, of fitting into a rapidly expanding program took precedence. Rating sheets were submitted on all trainees covering the entire period at Avenger Field, by flight line, ground school, physical training department, Link department, student officers, and staff advisers. These were prepared from day-by-day records. Immediately before graduation each class member filled out a preference sheet indicating the type of plane she preferred to fly, the location preferred as a base, and the members of her class with whom she preferred to be based. She could also indicate which one of these factors was of the greatest importance to her. In nearly all cases, the type of plane to be flown received preference. A chart for each graduate was prepared from the rating sheets, plus the number of disciplinary demerits, and the over-all rating of the individual was determined. Assignments then came in from the Central Flying Training Command and graduates with the best over-all ratings were given preferences, provided that their record on the flight line indicated that they could fly the type of plane requested.

Upon graduation a Wasp was given a Class I flying rating, the same first rating as that of a male pilot. Wasps on operational duty followed the regular pattern of on-the-job training and school attendance, and they advanced to higher ratings as flying officers.

In June 1944 the 635 Wasps on operational duty were classified as follows:

No.	Class	Type of Aircraft
122	I	PT, BT, AT–6, BC–1, C–43, C–61, C–64, C–71, C–72, C–81.
158	II	AT–7, AT–8, AT–9, AT–17 (C–78), AT–10, AT–11, AT–15.
216	III	A–29, OA–9, OA–10, B–23, B–18, C–33, C–39, C–47, C–53, C–56, C–59, C–60, C–57.
59	IV	B–25, B–26, C–46, A–20, A–30, P–38.
14	V	B–17, B–24, A–24, A–25, B–29, C–69, C–54, C–87.
66	Fighter Class	P–39, P–40, P–47, P–51, P–63.

FERRYING

The ferrying service began in October and November 1942 with the delivery of a few planes over short distances. In December, with a full complement of twenty-five women pilots, thirty-four primary trainers and liaison aircraft were delivered in 507 hours of flying time.

As the program continued, longer distances were flown. By July 1943, with 88 Wafs on duty, 305 planes were delivered and the average flying hours each month rose to 52 for each pilot—a record for their service. The number on duty increased to 303 in April 1944, but many pilots were later transferred to the Training Command. During the last few months of operation in 1944 an average of only 140 women remained in the Transport Command ferrying service.

After April 1944 the ferrying activities of Wasps and male pilots differed considerably, and pursuit-plane flying became the main WASP activity. Immediately the accident rate rose. This same difference in accident rate was shown in the total record for the Ferrying Division. From June 1942 to the end of 1944, 20 percent of their operations were pursuit-plane ferrying, and 37 percent of all accidents occurred in such work. In the continental Air Forces in 1944 the accident rate for heavy bombers was 0.29 per 1,000 miles flown; for single-engine pursuits the rate was 1.34, and for the P-39 alone the rate was 2.88.

In evaluating the work of WASP ferrying pilots, the Air Transport Command said, "The most interesting conclusion to which these considerations lead is that throughout their career the women ferry pilots, for a variety of reasons, concentrated on types of ferrying essentially more hazardous than done by their male colleagues. So far as is known, there was no tendency among them to complain about this; if anything, at least in the pursuit period, it was a matter of pride."

In twenty-seven months the women ferry pilots completed 12,650 movements, flying approximately 9,224,000 miles, "a record of useful achievement and of solid contribution to the prosecution of the war. In their latter months they specialized in the delivery of a type of aircraft which did not fit into the transition program, thereby facilitating the advancement of male pilots to foreign duty, combat and noncombat. That this type was essentially dangerous to fly, that many of them crashed and some were killed, did not make them hesitate."

Reference was made in the quotation above to the "transition program" of the Ferrying Division. Pilots came into the division in Class I, capable of flying the easiest planes, and they were gradually upgraded to Class V, which signified that they could fly four-engine transports. It was necessary to maintain a continuous flow of men through this process and it was difficult to fit women pilots in because, if they were frozen in any one class, men could not pass through it. The Pursuit Class was independent of the system set up to include Classes I to V, described earlier, and it was not necessary for male pilots to pass through it. For that reason women were of the greatest service to the Ferrying Division if they could fly the pursuits and, as noted above, there were more women pilots in this class than in any other at the termination of the WASP program in December 1944.

Ferrying work was done practically entirely by daylight but most other operational duties were done by day and night. Wasps were fully utilized on operational duties within eight months from the time they started training.

WASP personnel were used successfully in tracking and searchlight missions, simulated strafing, smoke laying, and other chemical missions, basic and instrument instruction, administrative and utility flying. A few exceptionally proficient women pilots were assigned to the testing of rocket-propelled planes, to work with radar-controlled targets, and to the piloting of jet-propelled planes.

TARGET TOWING

In July 1943, women pilots were first assigned to target-towing jobs in support of antiaircraft and aerial gunnery training. The project was under the constant supervision of a board which established the necessary schedules for transition and tests, set up a daily reporting system and received daily progress reports, made recommendations, and investigated cases requiring disciplinary action. The policy to be established on the use of Wasps was to be based on the findings of the test, and "it was imperative that this test be conducted in such a manner that the conclusions derived therefrom will permit no debate."

There were some difficulties reported in utilization of Wasps in target towing: some women pilots lacked proper training for the mission; in some cases the women pilots were spared risk and responsibility, making it difficult to evaluate their work comparatively; it was difficult to use partially trained women pilots in existing programs; and resentment of some male pilots and inactivity of women pilots were occasional causes of low morale.

The service history continues: "In general, it seems that

women pilots proved capable of tow-target work.   The chief
of the Tow Target Section, Fourth Air Force Headquarters,
stated that in many respects they were better adapted to the
activity than most pilots returned from combat.   Former combat pilots and Air Corps pilots at large, he stated, looked upon
tow-target work as a dull chore, whereas nearly all of the Wasps
considered it a 'high adventure.'   A conference at Fort Worth
in September 1944 concluded that Wasps were suitable for
assignment as tow-target pilots."

GLIDER TOWING

Wasps were not successful as glider-towing pilots chiefly because the operation of C-60s turned out to be physically too
strenuous for women.   The commanding officer of one of the
four air forces reported that Wasps were subject to certain
limitations unconnected with their flying ability, which affected
their availability.   For example, he said: "On heavy airplanes
involving a crew of enlisted men and a co-pilot, the pilot must
exercise command.   It is important, in emergency situations,
that this command be instantly recognized and accepted without
reservation by the crew.   Only in rare instances can women pilots
win this reaction.   This crew prejudice, though admittedly irra-
tional, must be acknowledged and reckoned with."

INSTRUCTING

There were a few types of operational duties in which Wasps
were not sufficiently successful to justify their continued use.
At the suggestion of General Arnold in 1944, an experiment
was begun in two flying commands in the assignment of women
as instructors in basic flying schools for male trainees.   In one
command there was a large surplus of male instructors, and in
the other it was agreed by the commanding officers, supervisors,
and Wasps that women should not be used for this work because
in most circles women pilots are considered to be inferior to
men.   Consequently a woman would have to do a much better
job than a man.   Also, it was considered bad psychologically
for an aviation cadet if a Wasp and not a male Air Corps graduate were his instructor.

EVALUATION

Pages were written in the various command histories in the attempt to evaluate the experiment of training and using women as noncombatant flyers in the Army Air Forces. The history of the WASP, based upon all the other histories, contains the following statement:

The actual contribution to the war effort made by WASP operations is difficult to assess. The favorable unfolding of events in the theaters of operations changed the needs on the home front, and by the time women pilots were ready to make their chief contribution it seemed that there was no longer a pressing need for their services. Their utilization apparently gained its chief significance as an experiment, though the results in this instance may not be considered conclusive. It was demonstrated that women are capable of performing a variety of flying and aviation administrative duties. Whether they are equally as capable as male pilots in these respects and other types of piloting and ground activities will perhaps continue a point of controversy.

. . . . .

In the course of more than two years with the Army Air Forces, women pilots made a contribution to the war effort and demonstrated that they were capable of performing several flying duties which would release male pilots for combat duty. They were frequently confronted by hostility on the part of male pilots and commanding officers, but doubts about the capabilities and fears of limiting physical or temperamental characteristics in women pilots seem to have been removed or substantially lessened, in many cases, as their total of hours and miles flown mounted. In ferrying, target towing, administrative flying, and in several capacities in connection with the pilot training program, they showed their usefulness. In General Arnold's judgment, "their very successful record of accomplishment has proved that in any future total effort the nation can count on thousands of its young women to fly any of its aircraft."

The program was instituted to release men for theater assignments, and women could not make a greater contribution than they did because the male pilot program resulted in a surplus. As an experiment to determine the capabilities of women pilots, the fact that it was a wartime program limited the opportunities for adequate testing. There were conflicts with major training and operational missions both in ferrying and tow-target work. The program did indicate that women pilots can replace men in certain types of flying and administrative duties and it revealed some of the strong points and weaknesses of women flyers. Further experimentation would probably have given additional valuable information and provided an opportunity to explore new fields of aeronautical usefulness to women.

V. WOMEN IN THE OTHER SERVICES ON DUTY IN AVIATION

THE PRECEDING chapter deals with the civilian women in the Army Air Forces who actually flew planes during World War II. In addition to this small but important group, women in the four women's military services performed duties in connection with aviation. In a few cases they were trained for and assigned to flight duty, but usually they were in the aviation ground services.

CHARACTERISTICS COMMON TO THE FOUR SERVICES

With numerous unimportant variations, the histories of aviation personnel in the four women's military services are similar. There was no expectation that women with the necessary skills could be recruited in sufficient numbers to meet the needs of the aviation branches of the Army, Navy, Coast Guard, and Marine Corps. The WAC for a time recruited women specifically for the Army Air Forces (Air-Wacs), but recruits understood that they would be used in their civilian skills and were never promised any aviation or specialist training of any sort. The object was to get women already trained.

The following data, adapted from a study prepared by WAC Major Lavinia L. Redd for the Historical Division, War Department Special Staff, "History of Military Training, WAAC/WAC Training, Army Service Forces," indicate how very small was the number of women who had any background of aviation experience. Of 29,140 WAC enlisted women who were classified at Fort Des Moines between July 20, 1942, and February 29, 1944, only 70 were found who had civilian occupational specialties in the field of aviation.

Airplane pilot	5
Aeronautical engineer (student)	1
Airplane electrician	22
Airport control operator	4
Airplane engine mechanic	11
Airplane and engine mechanic	7

Airplane engine service mechanic   8
Airplane fabric and dope worker   5
Parachute repairman   1
Parachute packer   6

There were three types of duties in aviation—flying, ground
services which relate specifically to aviation, and ground services which need to be performed at an air base or station but
which are properly classified under some other occupation.
Yeomen and clerks and cooks and personnel specialists were
used by the aviation services in large numbers, but the duties
of these women were not "aviation," nor were those duties
fundamentally different from those performed by the same
categories of workers in nonaviation services. The present
chapter deals with the second category mentioned above—
women who were trained for ground services specifically related
to aviation.

The women's services handled the training of personnel for
aviation in a similar manner. In all cases, the newly enlisted
women were sent first to "boot" camp or basic training center.
A number of women were assigned to training schools to take
aviation courses, depending upon the needs of the Army, the
Navy, the Coast Guard, and the Marine Corps, upon the availability of graduates of basic military training courses who had
suitable qualifications for training in aviation specialties, and
upon the availability of suitable facilities for their training.
The three factors just named produced different results in the
four services as a whole, and different results at different times.
For example, the Coast Guard sent only 52 Spars to aviation
training courses for the stated reasons that the complements of
Coast Guard air stations were very small, there was difficulty
in housing women at their air stations, and it was difficult to
use women in outdoor mechanical work. On the other hand,
relatively large numbers of women were trained in aviation
specialties in the Marine Corps.

The training of women in aviation specialists' courses in all
of the services was in most cases just like the training of men
in the same specialties. Usually the two sexes were not separated
in the courses. The duty assignments were the same, except

in the case of men who went overseas. In some cases a relatively large number of women received training—for example, more than 2,700 Waves were trained as aviation machinist mates and more than 1,700 Waves were trained as Link-trainer operators. In many other cases, fewer than 20 women were sent to a particular school. In total, the number of women as contrasted with the number of men was so small that comparisons of their relative abilities are not valid.

WAVES

A description of the basis for selecting enlisted Waves for training in aviation specialties, of the training courses in such specialties, and other related information was contained in the *Interviewers' Classification Guide, Supplement for Enlisted Women* (NavPers 16705), prepared by the Training Division, Bureau of Naval Personnel, in March 1944. This guide was designed to aid interviewers in the classification of recruits by supplying information about the various duties for which they might be classified, and the qualifications required. These duties included ratings for which schools were conducted, ratings granted upon completion of training at Naval Training School (WR), and seaman assignments. A separate page for each rate or school was included, and of the twenty-two so described, eight were in the field of aviation specialties.[1]

The twenty-two rates or schools described in the *Guide* were classified in four general groups, and the aviation schools and rates were in three of the four groups, as follows:

Clerical and communications. None. Ratings in this group required considerable clerical aptitude.

Technical. Aerographer's mate, aviation instrument mechanic, aviation machinist's mate, camera repairman, specialist (Y) control tower operator. Ratings in this group required theoretical background and a knowledge of mathematics and physics.

Personnel. Specialist (G) aviation free gunnery school, specialist (T) Link-trainer instructor. These ratings all involved work with people, individually or in groups. The functions performed by teachers, personnel workers, group workers, and interviewers were included.

Miscellaneous. Parachute rigger.

[1] Four additional rates or schools were later open to women: aviation metalsmiths, pigeonmen, SP(V) storekeepers, SP(V) transport airmen.

In the introductory portions of the *Guide* it was stated that certain rates not included were open to WAVES personnel, but no school training was provided for them. Some special billets and general detail assignments provided the opportunity for striking on the job for a rating, and among this group was aviation radio technician (ART). A specialist (X) rating could be given to essential specialists who did not fit in any existing rating, and one of the designations in this field was air station operation desk time shack (TS). Seamen not assigned to a school or selected for a special billet were classified for general detail to be assigned according to the needs of the Navy. One such assignment was duty as checker at an air base. On-the-job training was provided for general detail personnel.

Returning to the eight types of assignments for which school training was provided, the data indicate that 123 officers and 7,308 enlisted women completed these courses, constituting the bulk of the 571 officers and 7,564 enlisted women who received specialist training in aviation courses. Table 8 shows the numbers of WAVES officers and enlisted women who completed aviation-specialist courses prior to January 1, 1946.

TABLE 8

NUMBER OF WAVES COMPLETING AVIATION-SPECIALIST COURSES IN THE NAVY PRIOR TO JANUARY 1, 1946

Course Completed	Officers	Course Completed	Enlisted Women
Aerology	113	Aerographer's mate	650
Air combat information	11	Aviation machinist's mate	2,731
Aircraft recognition	9	Aviation machinist's mate (instrument)	649
Air navigation	146		
Aviation indoctrination	135	Aviation metalsmith	236
Communications procedures	20	Link celestial navigation trainer	235
Gunnery officers	10	Parachute rigger	419
Link celestial navigation trainer	46	Pigeonman	20
Photo interpretation	11	Specialist (G) gunnery	505
Radio-radar administration	121	Specialist(P)(ACR) camera repair	51
		Specialist (T) Link trainer	1,701
		Specialist (Y) control tower	602
Total	571[a]	Total	7,564[b]

[a] Actual total of courses completed is 622. Two different courses were completed by 51 individuals.
[b] Actual total of courses completed is 7,799. Two different courses were completed by 235 individuals.

Three courses for enlisted women were not included in the *Guide* for the use of interviewers.   These were the courses for Link celestial navigation trainer, in which there were 235 graduates; pigeonmen, 20 graduates; and aviation metalsmiths, 236 graduates.   Quotas had been filled, and the needs of the service had been met in these classifications.

Very soon after Waves began to be assigned to duty, they were sent to naval aviation activities in the field and to the Bureau of Aeronautics.   At the end of the first year of WAVES activity, 200 of their officers, petty officers, and seamen were at work in the photographic, flight, training, and maintenance divisions of the Bureau.   They served as film cutters, Link-trainer instructors, messengers, statisticians, clerks, and business machine operators. One officer, a fabric tester in civilian life, tested fabric in planes and other equipment.   Another officer who held a civilian pilot's license was following her civilian experience in the field of aviation medical research.   Women chemists and civil and aeronautical engineers held billets in the Bureau.

On July 30, 1943, the following number of Waves were on duty at forty different air fields, under the jurisdiction of the Bureau of Aeronautics:

Naval Air Primary Training Command 1,550
Naval Air Technical Training Command   225
Naval Air Operational Training Command   600
Naval Air Intermediate Training Command 1,000

Total 3,375

These women manned traffic control towers at air fields, packed parachutes, taught gunnery and instrument flying, and served as aerologists, members of ground crews, and navigation aides.

Nine hundred women aviation machinist's mates reported for duty in October 1943 at two dozen air fields, and 90 women aviation metalsmiths were assigned at the same time.   These women worked with Navy men trained in the same specialties. The machinists cared for, operated, adjusted, and overhauled internal combustion engines of the various types used on aircraft, overhauled and adjusted carburetors, ignition apparatus, and starting gears, aligned and assembled aircraft and individual parts, adjusted and repaired rigging and fabric, and spliced wiring and manufactured terminals.

One of the best jobs which the machinist's mates took over was the job of plane captain. Four women went on duty as plane captains at the Naval Air Station, Jacksonville, Florida, in October 1943. The following description of their work was written by an observer:

Bright and early they report to the hangar for duty. After these "mechs" have checked plane schedules they go to the plane that has been assigned to them. Each goes to her plane to (1) prepare it for flight, (2) fill out the yellow sheet which is a daily or preflight check on the plane and its operations, and (3) warm it up. After this is done, if the plane is scheduled to go up, the "mech" in charge checks out two 'chutes and in some cases two life jackets. When the time for the "hop" arrives she tunes the motor and puts the radio equipment in working order. When the pilot is ready to take off she helps him don his 'chute and fastens the safety belt. He checks the operation of the plane and if he accepts it for flight, he signs the preflight check sheet. Then comes the time for "thumbs up" and the take-off. Until the pilot returns, the plane captains do everything from gassing transports to spotting planes. When the pilot returns he signs the yellow sheet once again, this time listing all complaints—if any. On the job again, the "mechs" take over and, after checking the gas and oil, secure the plane for the night.

The metalsmiths did repair work on high-caliber instruments, radiators, pipe connections, and other metal parts of planes.

By December 1943 approximately one-fourth of enlisted Waves on duty had been assigned to naval aviation. Officers were being trained in aerological engineering, navigation, and gunnery, and in two new fields—aircraft recognition instructor and photographic interpretation. Among the enlisted women the expansion of the training program was even more marked. A year before, the first aviation technical schools were scheduled for opening within a few weeks. In addition to such schools, there were, in December 1943, schools for aviation instrument mechanics and gunnery instructors, and enlisted women could earn petty-officer rating as aviation radio technicians by study while at a duty station.

The work as air gunnery instructor was taught at the Naval Air Training Center, Pensacola, Florida. In December 1943 the first class of Waves was in training, to qualify for petty-officer ratings as specialist (G). A number of enlisted women were already serving as synthetic gunnery instructors and these women, first rated as specialists (T), had demonstrated that women could handle arms effectively on the range and that, therefore, they could be used in the much broader field of general gunnery instruction. To qualify for admission to the Pensacola school, women met the same rigorous technical requirements that men had to meet. It was found that women with hunting experience or any other knowledge of guns and ordnance, knowledge of machine equipment, and teaching experience were especially desirable for specialist (G) training. The course was eight weeks long, half of the time being spent in learning range firing. Two weeks were devoted to each of the two major synthetic training devices, one for free gunnery and one for fixed gunnery.

To qualify for the third-class specialist (G) rating, enlisted personnel had to meet the following qualifications: ability to instruct in aviation free gunnery on any firing range (excluding turret machine gun), on synthetic gunnery training devices, and in a classroom; ability to fire properly a shotgun, a service pistol, a machine gun, and a turret machine gun; ability to assemble and dismantle arms, identify common types of ammunition and belt a machine gun; ability to operate and repair synthetic training devices. The trainee also had to know ordnance regulations, be able to recognize friendly and enemy ships and aircraft, have a general knowledge of leading and sighting in gunnery, range estimation, and standard nomenclature. While it was not anticipated that women would be used in large numbers as instructors on firing ranges, they would be fully qualified for this duty, and as an experiment, several enlisted women had served successfully as range instructors at Pensacola. Their admitted ability overcame any reluctance the men might have had about learning to shoot from women instructors. The principal duty planned for the women specialists (G) was assignment to air stations to help to train aircrews in fixed and free gunnery. Their pupils were fighter pilots and the crewmen on fighter, bomber, and torpedo planes. Approximately five hundred women were graduated from this course.

In July 1944 approximately one-third of all enlisted Waves on duty had been assigned to air stations as mechanics, metalsmiths, control-tower operators, instructors in gunnery, instrument flying, and celestial navigation, aerographer's mates, and radio technicians. The successful assignment of women to duty as aviation free gunnery instructors had led to the establishment of a new course. The first class of enlisted women had just entered training at the Naval Air Training Center at Pensacola, Florida, to become gunnery instructors. Upon completion of their training they were to be assigned to teach enlisted men to shoot the enemy from the sky.

In July 1944, WAVES officers were on duty as air navigation instructors and air combat intelligence officers. Training for the latter duty had begun in March with the entrance of women into classes at Quonset Point, Rhode Island, where a two-month course was offered at the Air Combat Information Training School. In general, the duties of an officer graduate included briefing and interrogating pilots, preparing and analyzing action reports, and providing information necessary to effective air operations, and after their graduation they were to be assigned to one of the seven Air Combat Information Centers in the United States. Eleven WAVES officers completed the course successfully.

Early in 1945 Naval Air Transport Service began to use enlisted Waves as flight orderlies on continental trips, with the rating of specialist (V), the transport airman's rating. The women's training program was under the supervision of a WAVES officer who was a former airline hostess. It included practical instruction in flight control, space control, the cargo shed, and the air transport office, including actual work in supervising the loading and unloading of cargo and passengers, and familiarization flights in transport planes. By July 1945 approximately a hundred WAVES flight orderlies were serving as flight crew members on almost every NATS route in the United States and to Hawaii and Bermuda, and on the ground at most NATS stations.

On the third birthday of the WAVES, in July 1945, approximately 30 percent of enlisted women were assigned to naval aviation. Although the great majority were on duty in continental United States, a few officers and enlisted women had gone to air stations in Hawaii, as volunteers. More than a thousand Link-trainer instructors were giving lessons in instrument flying to approximately four thousand men a day, and women were on duty operating Link celestial navigation trainers at seventeen naval activities. At least four control towers were manned entirely by Waves. At one station, Waves controlled the traffic in the block of air in which night fighters trained. WAVES officers in air activities included those serving as aerologists, air transport officers, and air navigation and Link celestial navigation instructors. Eighty officers had recently been designated naval air navigators, the first women officers in any United States military organizations entitled to perform duties as part of a military aircrew. They wore the wings of the naval air navigator on their uniforms, were assigned to duty as transocean navigators in areas to which Waves could be assigned, and served in crews flying to such points as Hawaii and the Aleutians.

As the needs of the field were met, the variety of types of training gradually decreased in the last months of 1944 and in 1945. At the time of the third anniversary, aerographer's mates and control-tower operators were the only aviation specialists' courses in which women were enrolled. After the defeat of Japan, procurement was discontinued, no new quotas were assigned to recruit school, and women currently in schools completed their training and were assigned to duty in the field.

An interesting comment on the work of Waves in naval aviation was made on May 3, 1946, by Commander Joy B. Hancock, USNR, in an address before the Industrial College of the Armed Forces, in Washington, D. C. During the first three years of the WAVES program, Commander Hancock was assigned as the Women's Reserve representative in the Bureau of Aeronautics, Deputy Chief of Naval Operations for Air, and in such a position she was able to suggest fields of work for women and to aid in setting up the training. On this part of her work, she commented:

That was comparatively easy. I had the wholehearted backing of the aviators. The difficult part was awaiting the results and comments regarding the performance of the women after graduation from the specialized schools and assignment to their new tasks. The women did a magnificent job. Our first trial balloons, so to speak, met with such enthusiasm on the part of the men that the cry started which continued throughout the war—"Send us more Waves; they can do the job. . . ."

Almost immediately the aviation requests had to be handled. In carrying out the training in aviation the women were sent to the schools already established for men, took their instruction with the men, and competed for class standing. This method of training was adopted because it was more economical and because training with the men more readily and quickly assured their acceptance on the jobs they were to do. The experiment was highly successful.

Commander Hancock described the training programs for women which were established in the aviation trades at various schools for men, and she said:

Assignment of women to many phases in the field of technological development, both research and operational, proved to be highly successful. To give but one illustration, I point to the night-fighter program. Early in the Pacific war it became evident that trained night-fighter pilots were urgently needed in carrier operations. We had none. At Naval Air Station, Vero Beach, Florida, the training was set up. Operations involved the extensive use of radar in connection with night navigation and landing approaches on decks. The project was manned almost entirely by Waves, including the night traffic control. Information concerning continuing development of some of the phases of this program has recently been released to newspapers—specifically, the ground-controlled approach techniques which will undoubtedly be one of the greatest safety factors in future commercial air transportation.

The work of aerographers was too confidential to receive publicity during the war, but in Commander Hancock's opinion the importance of their contribution was recognized within the service. Speaking of all types of service including aviation, she said in conclusion that, in some cases, the performance of women "has surpassed that of the men. We found that when physical limitations were taken into consideration and proper classification carried out and applied, we could count on a woman per man replacement."

MARINE CORPS WOMEN'S RESERVE

The Women's Reserve of the Marine Corps trained and assigned to various duties in the aviation division of the corps a much higher proportion of its personnel than did the other three women's services. Slightly more than 23,000 women joined the Reserve, and approximately 1,000 of them were commissioned. About one-third of all these women received instruction in various specialist training courses, both aviation and nonaviation (Table 9).

TABLE 9

NUMBERS OF MARINE CORPS WOMEN RESERVISTS COMPLETING ALL SPECIALIST COURSES
(AVIATION AND NONAVIATION) DURING WORLD WAR II

Type of School	Officers	Enlisted Women	Total
Navy schools..................................	78	2,943	3,021
Marine Corps schools...........................	255	4,252	4,507
Civilian contract schools.......................	27	189	216
Other schools.................................	26	....	26
Total..................................	386	7,384	7,770
Additional trainees not completing the courses......	12	433	445
Percentage of attrition........................	*3*	*6*	*5*

Table 10 deals solely with the courses directly related to aviation. More than 2,000 women completed courses in this category.

TABLE 10

AVIATION-SPECIALIST TRAINING OF MARINE CORPS WOMEN RESERVISTS DURING
WORLD WAR II

Type of School	Course	Length in Weeks	Number of Graduates	Attrition
Navy:				
Officers.........	Link celestial navigation	22	6	2
Enlisted Women..	Aerial gunnery instructor.....	6	2	0
	Aerographer's mate	12	136	14
	Aviation machinist's mate	21	957	68
	Control-tower operator	6	230	28
	Link-trainer instructor.......	10	232	43
	Parachute materiel..........	12	147	4
	Recognition instructor.......	1	12	0
Marine Corps:				
Officers.........	Aviation materiel............	12	17	0
Enlisted Women..	Aviation supply.............	12	278	10
	Link celestial navigation.....	7	25	0
Civilian Contract:				
Officers.........	Bendix turret maintenance....	3	1	0
Enlisted Women..	Aircraft instrument repair....	15	145	18
	Bendix turret maintenance....	3	5	0
Total: Officers and enlisted women...................			2,193	187 (*8%*)

As was the case in all the women's services, recruits in the MCWR were first sent to "boot camp." While at the recruit depot they took a series of classification tests to determine their military aptitudes. Upon completion of basic training, they were divided into two groups—general duty and aviation. The latter group did not form a separate corps. Recruiting, uniforms, discipline, basic training, and so forth, were alike for all MCWR personnel.

The Division of Aviation of the Marine Corps selected qualified women reservists for training, prescribed the types of specialist courses, handled its own detailing of personnel, and developed its own enlisted promotion policies. The distinction between the women assigned to aviation and those assigned to general duty or training in nonaviation specialties was more a matter of organization than of specific aptitudes. With the exception of a large number of mechanics and those on a comparatively few "glamour jobs," most women reservists on air stations performed the same duties as those on other posts of the Marine Corps—clerical, communications, quartermaster, post exchange, motor transport, and the mess-hall assignments—and the training courses for such jobs were not particularly different in the Division of Aviation from those elsewhere in the Marine Corps.

From May 1943 to November 1944 there was a separate Women's Reserve Unit working under the head of Aviation Personnel in coordination with Aviation Male Enlisted and Officer Detail, with the responsibility for training and detailing aviation women reservists. All specialist school training was planned by this unit, school quotas were filled, and the maximum number of women reservists aboard (8,153) was detailed to aviation. In November 1944 this work was transferred to the detail section of male officers and enlisted men, because by that time no school quotas were filled and there was only an occasional request for a few women reservists to be trained in a civilian or Navy school. No recruits were taken into aviation from August 1944 to February 1945, after which time only a few small replacement quotas were available for detailing.

PLATE III

—Official U. S. Marine Corps Photo

AN AVIATION MACHINIST'S MATE AT THE MARINE CORPS AIR STATION,
CHERRY POINT, N. C.

A considerable amount of personnel classification occurred at Cherry Point, North Carolina, to which women reservists were assigned while waiting for the completion of housing at their duty stations. Their classification cards were checked and the aviation opportunities made known to them. Voice tests were given for control-tower operators' school and Link-trainer operators' school; the radio-code operators' tests were given; and short-hand and typing tests were given. The history of the Women's Reserve of the Marine Corps indicates that some assignment officers later disregarded the recommended assignments, but it was believed that "generally women reservists were assigned to billets requiring the specialist training they had received." However, in the same history the statement appears that it was "the impression" of the director, MCWR, that there were really great inconsistencies between the training and subsequent use of personnel, and that too many storekeepers and machinist's mates were trained.

Inasmuch as no women had ever been members of the Marine Corps before, their usefulness in aviation was not at first realized. While the stations were being organized and built, complete plans for the assignment of women had not been made, and at first there was no uniformity in their assignments. Later, fairly arbitrary plans were made in order that housing might be requested and built. In December 1942 a training program was planned based upon the need—as estimated by the Division of Aviation—for 476 officers and 8,618 enlisted women. These estimates were later reduced to 357 officers and 7,130 enlisted women, largely because of housing conditions. Changes in training quotas were frequent as the use of women personnel developed.

The comparison between the number of women whose main civilian occupations were in the field of aviation (126) and the number assigned to aviation duty (1,312) confirms the statement made earlier that the women's services could not depend upon recruitment of women trained in aviation skills to meet wartime needs and that it was necessary to provide training courses for nearly all aviation personnel. Also, the data demonstrate that relatively few women were classified for assignment to military duties which were in the field of aviation proper. Data are not available to exhibit exactly the correlation between the previous civilian experience and military assignment of women reservists, because they were ordered to their respective commands as "basics" and the command was responsible for their proper assignment.

Table 11 contains data which are of interest from two standpoints.

TABLE 11

CIVILIAN OCCUPATION OF 21,051 MARINE CORPS WOMEN RESERVISTS, COMPARED WITH THE MILITARY CLASSIFICATION OF 17,666 WOMEN RESERVISTS IN COMPARABLE CATEGORIES

Type of Job	Main Civilian Occupation	Primary Military Occupational Specialty
Professional and managerial................	2,008	1,342
Clerical and sales........................	13,734	11,020
Agriculture and service...................	373	587
Mechanical:		
Aviation.............................	51	1,086
Nonaviation..........................	109	285
Skilled trades:		
Aviation.............................	60	83
Nonaviation..........................	700	261
Semiskilled:		
Aviation.............................	15	143
Nonaviation..........................	1,368	1,162
Unskilled and general duty...............	2,122	1,662
Students...............................	511	35
Total.............................	21,051	17,666

Many of the 17,666 women reservists observed in Table 11 were assigned to the Division of Aviation to perform professional, clerical, and other nonaviation types of services. The military classifications of 6,987 of them are shown in Table 12, which presents a breakdown of classifications of women reservists assigned to the Division of Aviation, by primary duty assignments. Only 1,578 are classified under headings which indicate without doubt that the duties were specifically in the field of aviation.

As to the appropriateness of the various aviation billets to which women were assigned in the Marine Corps, the history of the MCWR offers an interesting evaluation. The first plan-

TABLE 12

DISTRIBUTION OF 6,987 MARINE CORPS WOMEN RESERVISTS IN AVIATION AS GROUPED
UNDER BROAD OCCUPATIONAL CATEGORIES

Type of Job	Number	Percentage
Professional and managerial................	617	8.83
Clerical and sales.........................	3,496	50.03
Agriculture and service....................	259	3.71
Mechanical:		
Aviation.............................	1,041	14.90
Nonaviation..........................	86	1.23
Skilled trades:		
Aviation.............................	86	1.23
Nonaviation..........................	97	1.39
Semiskilled:		
Aviation.............................	451	6.46
Nonaviation..........................	135	1.93
Unskilled and general duty................	719	10.29
Total...........................	6,987	100.00

ning for an "all-out" war provided that women would be employed in "any duties publicly approved for civilian women."

Actually, there were at all times enough able-bodied men ashore in the Marine Corps to make it unnecessary for women reservists to perform the less appropriate duties. The women were very enthusiastic and would have done anything asked of them. Their assignments were determined on two bases—the physical location of the work, and the physical aspects of the duty. In the Division of Aviation, they worked into the following jobs which were considered to be not suitable for women:

1. Mechanics on the flight line. This involved dangerous work around moving planes; ladders and fire extinguishers were too heavy for continuous handling; and some types of planes taxi too fast for women to keep up with them for signaling.

2. Heavy truck driving (dump and garbage).

3. Auto mechanics and auto servicemen. Some personnel prejudice may have operated in these cases, but as long as men are available, it seems unsuitable to have women handling heavy truck tires, climbing over motor equipment, and being covered with grease.

The women reservists were all assigned to duty in the United States, except 387 who were sent to the Marine Corps Air Station at Ewa, and 614 who were on duty at Pearl Harbor. Their duties in connection with aviation did not in any case involve assignment to flight duty.

SPAR

On account of the fact that Coast Guard stations were usually small, with limited housing facilities, and concerned almost wholly with outdoor and mechanical work, very few members of the women's reserve in the Coast Guard could be utilized in the aviation duties of that service. Eighteen enlisted women were trained as parachute riggers at the Lakehurst Naval Air Station in 1943, 22 were trained to operate Link trainers, and 12 were trained as control-tower operators. The total number (52) is too small to have importance in the present study.

THE WOMEN'S ARMY CORPS

The women in military aviation who were most widely known by the public (with the exception of the Wasps) were the "Air-Wacs"—those members of the Women's Army Corps who served with the Army Air Forces. The reason for this probably lies in the very extensive recruiting campaign carried on during 1943 and 1944, when the AAF used every means to obtain desirable publicity concerning the participation of women in their program.

Table 13 presents certain pertinent facts concerning the numbers of women assigned to the AAF, both in continental United States and abroad. At the peak, early in 1945, nearly 40,000 Wacs were on duty—approximately 32,000 in the United States and over 7,000 abroad. Recruitment figures indicate that 27,047 women enlisted specifically for service in the AAF during the fifteen-month period (October 1943-December 1944) in which this type of enlistment was open. The rest of the Wacs in the AAF came in after enlistment for general duty in the Women's Army Corps. The first WAC unit to serve with the Air Forces abroad landed in England in July 1943 for assignment to the Eighth Air Force.

No separate statistics or command histories are available which present descriptions or evaluations of the training of women in the Army Air Forces. The explanation of this lack

PLATE IV

—U. S. Coast Guard Photo

A Spar at the U. S. Coast Guard Air Station at Elizabeth City, N. C.

PLATE V

—*Air Transport Command Photo*

Air-Wacs in "Abandon Ship" Drill, in Preparation for Transportation Overseas

TABLE 13

WACS ON DUTY WITH THE AAF FROM JULY 1943 TO JULY 1945, BY SIX-MONTH
INTERVALS

	July 1943	December 1943	July 1944	December 1944	July 1945
In continental U. S.:					
Officers.................	545	1,758	1,787	1,579	1,522
Enlisted women.........	16,094	16,082	26,468	29,931	27,449
Total..............	16,639	17,840	28,255	31,510	28,971
Overseas:					
Officers......................			184	267	316
Enlisted women.............			4,034	6,505	6,666
Total......................			4,218	6,772	6,982
Total:					
Officers......................			1,971	1,846	1,838
Enlisted women.............			30,502	36,436	34,115
Total......................			32,473	38,282	35,953

(NOTE: Peak strength in continental U. S. was in January 1945, with 32,008 officers and enlisted women; peak strength for total AAF was in the same month, with 39,323 officers and enlisted women; peak strength overseas was in April 1945, with 7,601 officers and enlisted women.)

is a very simple one. In the first place, WAC basic training, as well as cook, clerk, driver, and medical training, was done by the Army Service Forces at a WAC Training Center before the women arrived at the Army Air Forces. The AAF kept no record of this training except on the individual's service record. In the second place, the AAF did not ordinarily maintain separate or regular specialists' courses for women. They were allowed to attend any Army schools as individuals if they were qualified (the qualifications were the same as for men) and if they could be utilized in that field. The training of women was thus completely integrated with the entire AAF training program, and in many cases separate records were not kept for women trainees. This procedure insured that women had to be as well qualified as men to be assigned to a course and to be graduated.

In order to supplement the historical material dealing with WAC assignments in the AAF, information relative to their training was obtained through conferences with WAC officers. Comparison between the training given to Wasps and the training given to Wacs in the AAF presents an important consideration which should be remembered in evaluating results. Wasps were trained at a separate flying school, they were given modified tests, and their course at the AAF School of Applied Tactics was different from the men's course. These courses were said to be much like those for men, but there is no proof that women did not require more time, more individual attention, and different progress rates. Statistics of graduation from separate men's and women's schools thus have undetermined elements of unreliability. On the other hand, after Wacs had completed basic training in a separate school, their further training was carried out in Army schools established for men. After training, Wacs were required to replace men on a one-for-one basis. As a result of this latter method of training Wacs can be compared with male personnel with reasonable validity.

There was another important difference between the WAC program and that of the WAVES. The WAC did not plan to train women in fields in which they are not dominant in civilian life, but the WAVES did train large numbers in such fields. Women in civilian life have all but taken over certain clerical duties in the business world—telephone operators, typists, etc.— and the WAC consequently planned to enlist many women with such training. On the other hand, the Army did not object to using a woman in a man's field if she had been trained for it in civilian life or if she was obviously so well qualified for training that she could learn such a job faster than a clerical one. When shortages of men developed in certain fields, small numbers of qualified women were sought out and trained. There never was a situation in the WAC program like that in the WAVES in which large classes of women just out of basic training were sent regularly into training for work not usually in a woman's field.

Air-Wac graduates from basic training were sent, not to specialists' training requiring weeks or months, but directly to an air station. There the effort was made to put them to work on the basis of their civilian experience, or to teach them a technical skill by on-the-job training while they were working at the station. If they could not be utilized in these ways, or if they had special qualifications for attendance at a school, the station could send them to any school (combat courses excepted) which the Army ran for men, provided that housing could be arranged for them. After training, the station received them back. This prevented training waste in that (1) women were not trained if they already had a usable skill, and (2) they were not trained in jobs which a station could not use. At various times the AAF broke this rule and set up regular classes when a shortage seemed imminent. The AAF also received numbers of women who had been trained by the Army Service Forces as clerks, cooks, drivers, and medical technicians, but the AAF preferred to train its own personnel.

From the standpoint of the present study, possible implications for the training of civilian women in aviation will have to be based largely upon the duties to which Wacs were assigned in the AAF, rather than upon their experiences during the training period. Tables 14 and 15 show limited data on the duty assignments of WAC officers and enlisted women in September 1945 in continental United States. Because of the large number of different assignments—more than two hundred—selection has been made of the duties to which a considerable number of assignments were made.

TABLE 14

Types of Duty in the AAF to Each of Which 30 or More WAC Officers Were Assigned, in Continental United States, September 1945

Duty	Number
Administrative officer	328
Unit officer, nontactical	235
Adjutant or adjutant general	76
Military personnel officer	70
Personal affairs officer	67
Special services officer	44
Supply officer, general	40
Mess officer	38
Air technical supply officer	35
Civilian personnel officer	30
Priorities or traffic officer	30
Total	993 [a]

[a] The actual total of WAC officers on duty was 1,264 in 65 different types of duty assignments. Of these officers, 22 were Negroes, of whom 17 served as unit officer, nontactical; 3 as administrative officer, and 2 as adjutant.

TABLE 15

TYPES OF DUTY IN THE AAF TO EACH OF WHICH 200 OR MORE WAC ENLISTED
WOMEN WERE ASSIGNED, IN CONTINENTAL UNITED STATES, SEPTEMBER 1945

Duty	Number
Clerk-typist	4,437
Clerk, nontypist	4,339
Auto equipment operator	1,188
Medical technician	1,055
Stenographer	998
Medical corpsman	933
Supply clerk	860
Basic duty	761
Cook	729
Photo laboratory technician	692
Teletype operator	450
Surgical technician	410
Administrative specialist	363
Tabulating machine operator	321
Airplane engine mechanic	299
Radio mechanic, AAF	266
Telephone switchboard operator	243
Synthetic trainer operator	240
Air operations specialist	212
Weather observer	201
Total	18,997 [a]

[a] The actual total of WAC enlisted women on duty was 23,805, in 145 different assignments. Of this total, 1,088 were Negroes, serving in 24 different assignments.

The most striking conclusion to be derived from the data in these tables is that, although 25,069 Wacs, as of September 30, 1945, performed duties in continental United States in the aviation branch of the Army, a very considerable proportion of that number actually performed functions which had relatively little relation to aviation. Approximately 2,500 of the enlisted Wacs were medical or surgical technicians, or medical corpsmen. More than 11,000 of the enlisted women were employed as clerks and in other clerical capacities. More than 800 enlisted women were cooks. These three groups alone total over 14,000 of the 23,000 enlisted women. It would be difficult to classify accurately all the duties performed by WAC officers and enlisted women on the basis of the degree of relationship to aviation. Inspection of the lists upon which Table 15 is based leads to the conclusion that less than half of the duties performed by Wacs in the AAF were in aviation specialties and, consequently, we have not much evidence as to their capacities in such fields.

An important study on the subject is the document entitled "The WAC Program in the Army Air Forces." This was prepared by an officer in the WAC Branch, Military Personnel Division, Assistant Chief of Air Staff-1, AAF Headquarters, in November 1945. The study includes the history of the various preliminary plans and early experiments in the assignment of Wacs to the AAF, the special recruiting programs for such personnel, their duties in the continental United States and overseas, and certain conclusions as to the merits and the problems of the entire program. Very little is included which relates to the training of these women because, as was stated above, there was no separate training program established for them. The following paragraphs summarize the relevant portions of the study.

It may surprise the average citizen to know that there was a widespread interest among the men who pioneered America's development of military air power in the possible use of women soldiers—"an innovation almost as revolutionary as the introduction of the airplane as a weapon of war." From 1917 through the 1920's and 1930's, several plans were made. After World War II began, the AAF showed increasing interest in the proposals for using women personnel, and their plans for the WAAC and later for the WAC became increasingly ambitious. The earliest plans centered around the use of women to man stations of the Aircraft Warning Service, and the first Waacs reported at the AWS in Albany, New York, in September 1942.

The next duty assignments for women in the AAF were in the clerical field. In November 1942 request was made for 42,000 women to serve as clerks, typists, telephone operators, radio operators, and as mechanics, photo laboratory technicians, and weather observers. The largest figure ever suggested by the AAF indicated that over 370,000 assignments then available in the Zone of the Interior (early in 1943) were considered suitable for women. The maximum total on duty in January

1945 was 39,323—approximately 10 percent of the 1943 estimated utilization.

At the height of the AAF-WAC program, there were 10 Negro WAC units in the AAF representing about 1,100 women, "and most of the Negro Wacs were performing the same type of clerical, hospital, and flight-line jobs as were the white Wacs. In several cases their efficiency and cooperative spirit were highly praised by base commanders." After October 1943 a unit of Negro Wacs was sent to each command, and the command designated the station to which the unit was assigned. About one-fourth of the Negro Wacs in the AAF, chosen from eight air bases in this country, were sent as a unit to the European theater to operate a postal-directory service there. Many of these women were skilled stenographers and clerk-typists. At all times there were strict headquarters directives that Wacs be assigned to jobs and schools on the basis of their qualifications, regardless of race.

After conduct of the Aircraft Warning Service was turned over to civilians in March 1943, Waacs began to arrive at air bases throughout the country, and within a few weeks they were formally assigned to AAF units in which they were serving. By the end of the summer there were 171 air bases which had WAC personnel as a part of their permanent complements. A WAC officer was sent to the headquarters of each of the major air forces and commands, charged with staff supervision over all Wacs assigned to the commands.

After some difficulty with respect to the procedure for assignment of Waacs, a satisfactory plan was established late in 1943. The AAF simply provided that Wacs might occupy any appropriate military jobs and grades within the command's allotment. This system apparently resulted in greater freedom in utilizing Wacs and greater equity between men and women doing similar jobs. WAC headquarters gave to AAF headquarters a weekly "availability report," by military occupational specialty, as to the total number of women available to AAF under its quota of 43 percent of all WAC recruits. These women were distributed among the commands on the basis of the greatest current need existing for their military occupational specialties.

Publication of this regulation represented a landmark in the progress of the AAF-WAC program. Thereafter commands and bases, which had been wrestling with such elementary problems as the provision of housing . . . could turn their attention to more individual and more constructive problems (such as) the up-grading of WAC personnel to positions of responsibility, training of Wacs for highly specialized jobs, thorough integration of Wacs into the military program, etc.[2]

In spite of numerous operating problems, interest in receiving women personnel remained high. The Technical Training Command was ordered to give a course for photographic laboratory technicians and several hundred such specialists were trained at Lowry Field, Colorado. Radio operators were arriving in AAF already trained, and the Weather Wing began in-station training of weather observers. Additional women officers were needed in the various commands to handle the increasing number of women personnel.

Full Army status was granted to women on July 1, 1943, and the WAAC became the WAC, a component of the Army of the United States, in September 1943. About 80 percent of the members of the original organization re-enlisted in the new corps, and the Air Forces which had over 16,000 Waacs assigned to them in July still had fewer than 15,000 Wacs in September. By the end of 1943 the WAAC-WAC change was completed, women soldiers were members of the Army, and the basic problems concerning their assignment and administration in the AAF had been worked out. A whole new program for the utilization of WAC personnel was developed, and the AAF obtained War Department approval for a plan to recruit its own Air-Wacs.

In November 1943, the Army Air Forces ruled that Wacs were eligible to attend any suitable (noncombat) training course or school to which AAF men were sent, provided the training would render them more efficient in their jobs or would make it possible to utilize them in some higher skill for which aptitude or civilian training had already partially fitted them.

The basic guide to AAF administration of Wacs (AAF Regulation 35-44) was published later in November. During the same month, the office of the Air-Wac Officer was made a divi-

_____

[2] "The WAC Program in the Army Air Forces," mentioned herein on p. 103.

sion with three branches: research, staff inspection, and exempted activities.

On November 4, 1943, the War Department approved an AAF recommendation that the Air Transport Command be allowed to send its WAC personnel to its stations anywhere in the world, just as it did its male personnel, provided the appropriate theater commander concurred. Airways Communication System received a quota of 1,450 Wacs as radio operators, control-tower operators, and clerical personnel in November; and in December the Weather Wing, in equal need of weather observers and forecasters, received a quota of 500 Wacs. At the same time, the first Wacs were brought to the Military District of Washington, and very soon weather observers and statistical control machine operators were assigned to Washington.

Provision was made in December 1943 for WAC air inspectors in all echelons of AAF commands. After January 1944, Air-Wacs were officially authorized to wear the wings and propeller of the AAF as the branch insignia on their uniforms. In March 1944 plans were crystallized for training and utilization of 1,000 Wacs in the AAF statistical control units throughout the country, and a six-week course was established at the AAF Tactical Center in Orlando, Florida. At the same time, Wacs were placed at the three AAF redistribution centers, and these women later became the nucleus of the WAC group in the new Personnel Distribution Command of the AAF.

In discussing various proposals for the future status of Wacs in the AAF, the study titled "The WAC Program in the Army Air Forces" contains the following statement:

Everything that had been done in the WAC program during the previous three years had pointed toward less specialization of Wacs and greater integration of WAC personnel into all commands and organizations of the Army. Consequently WAC officers were performing every type of officer job, from that of WAC squadron commander to that of Judge Advocate or Quartermaster Officer. . . .

The AAF, as its last suggestion in its long campaign to simplify the mechanics under which WAC personnel could be assigned to any and all appropriate Army jobs, made the counterproposal that WAC personnel be considered eligible, not just for a WAC officer-candidate school, but for any officer-candidate school in the Army which trained people to do the types of jobs which WAC officers were assigned to. Under this plan only those Wacs who were being selected for officer training with the view of preparing them to be WAC squadron officers would attend the WAC officer-candidate school—primarily a school for administrators of women. Wacs destined to become Air Corps administrative officers would attend the AAF Administrative Officer-Candidate School; Wacs destined to become Adjutant General officers would attend the Adjutant General Officer-Candidate School, et cetera. The boards which selected male officer candidates for the various schools would select WAC officer candidates for the same schools. There would be no WAC quotas (except to the WAC officer-candidate school), but commands would have the right to send the best qualified people, men or women, to fill any officer-candidate quota they received, just as they sent the best qualified men or women to AAF's own specialists' schools. This proposal was receiving its first detailed study in the War Department when the Japanese surrender put an end to the recruiting of WAC personnel. The plan was therefore tabled.

Further in the study, a question related to the problem above was discussed:

When the mechanics for placement of women in the Army have been so completely integrated into the mechanics for placement of men, as they would be under a system such as that described . . . the question arises as to whether it is necessary or desirable to continue to enlist women in a special women's component of the Army and administer them as WAC units, or whether it would be better simply to enlist them in the branch of the Army (AAF, etc.) in which they are destined to serve. The WAC during World War II has had only one corps mission—the administration of women in the Army. As men have become more and more familiar with the WAC program, there has been less and less need for special WAC directives, channels of communication, tables of organization, etc. However, it has been apparent throughout the WAC program that the WAC squadron commanders have been extremely important factors in the program, and their importance seems in no way to be diminishing as the WAC draws toward the close of its World War II career.

After citing illustrations, the following conclusion was reached:

A good WAC commander, however—one who knew that, with women even more than with men, it was impossible to drive but essential to lead; one who recognized that Wacs were adults and did not "mother" them like adolescents; one who realized that women must know "the reason why"; one who worked well with other officers on the base—such a commander could and often did increase the actual job efficiency of an entire WAC unit, even though she had no direct connection whatever with the jobs the individual women held or the sections in which they worked.

As to the assignment of women officers as WAC staff directors at higher headquarters, it was said:

So long as a condition exists, as it did in World War II, in which women represent only about 3 percent of the total strength of any command, it is probable that the presence of a staff officer in the headquarters of the command to devote her time exclusively to the problems and progress of the women's group will result in better utilization and administration of that minority.

The contribution of the Women's Army Corps was well summed up:

All in all, there can be little doubt that, even though the recruiting of women volunteers was an expensive process and even though the number recruited was only a very small part of the AAF's strength, women did contribute many critically needed administrative and clerical skills—not generally possessed by men—to the AAF at a time when there was a very great need for such skills. The intangible things which the WAC program contributed—heightened esprit because of friendly rivalry between men and women at a certain post, or because of the presence of American girls who were "like the girl next door" at some battle station overseas; development of the women themselves in job skills, self-assurance, poise, etc.—these things cannot be assessed until the program can be viewed from the judicious and impersonal distance of the future. Even now, before the full value of the program is known, it can be said with assurance, however, that the WAC program in the Air Forces during World War II was a part of the natural evolution toward full utilization of women's skills and full recognition of their place as citizens, just as it was a part of the natural evolution toward the full employment of a nation's manpower during a modern war.

VI. THE FUTURE OF WOMEN
IN AVIATION

AFTER THE cessation of fighting in World War II, interest in
civilian aviation is perhaps as great as was the interest
in military aviation during the war. New routes for air travel,
new transport and private passenger planes, increases in the
numbers of planes and of licensed pilots are accompanied by an
expansion in the facilities of civilian aviation schools and by the
appearance of new schools, departments, and courses in aviation in all parts of the educational system.

Undoubtedly the effects of the development of aviation during the war and the service of so many young men in aviation
branches of the armed services are major factors in the current
expansion. The implications of the armed services' aviation
training programs for civilian education are of great significance
because the scope of those programs during the war was so
tremendous that the progress in training methods which might
have taken decades in time of peace was accomplished in less than
five years.

IMPLICATIONS FOR EDUCATION AND TRAINING

What of the position of women in civilian aviation? What
women and how many of them can be trained, and what methods
are suitable for their training? The experiences of the women in
the several women's military services are probably the best
source of indicative information. Preceding chapters have described that experience in some detail.

1. *Women in military aviation were relatively few, but the
results of their pioneering are nevertheless far-reaching.*

It is perhaps rather surprising to realize how few women,
relatively speaking, were connected with military aviation. If
all members of the WASP, those members of the four military
services (WAC, WAVES, SPAR, and MCWR) who were on
duty in aviation, and the members of the Army and the Navy

Nurse Corps who were on flight duty are included, the total is not large. Because of differences in the methods of compiling records exact data cannot be presented to determine such a total, nor can subtotals based on different types of training or assignment be compiled.

Many of the women assigned to aviation actually performed clerical, medical, and other types of duties not properly classifiable as "aviation," as pointed out in earlier chapters. Admittedly, the available evidence is far less extensive than could be desired. There was so much publicity, desirable and otherwise, about "women in aviation" during the war that the public has attached more drama to their record than is warranted by the objective facts. While this situation must be recognized, it is nevertheless true that such information as we have is valuable to a degree far beyond its extent. Before the war very few women were engaged in any activity connected with aviation, and the addition to their number of a few tens of thousands during the war years furnishes us with more information than would have been produced in a much longer period of peace. Furthermore, the variety of their experience during the war was greater than would have been the case during an equal length of time in peace.

Even though the period from December 1941 to VJ Day in 1945 seemed longer than a lifetime, it was in fact a very short period from some standpoints. Military aviation itself went through the most far-reaching changes during those four years. In 1941 and 1942 the first plans were made to recruit and train and use women in the aviation services, and these plans had to be prepared from the very foundations. The few thousand women who were trained and were on military duty as pilots, mechanics, instructors on training devices, control-tower and radio operators, flight orderlies, and flight nurses were as truly pioneers in the history of women in aviation as the first women who, only a few years earlier, had dared to learn to fly a plane.

At the beginning of the war, the attitude toward women in aviation, both on the part of the public and the military services, was curiously reminiscent of the attitude toward women who wanted to learn to drive automobiles in the earlier years of the twentieth century. Aviation was a "man's job" and a woman would become "unfeminine" as a result of working at it. Furthermore, men would not like and respect her, particularly if her work necessitated the wearing of slacks or overalls, and if she had to "climb all over a plane" or "get covered with grease working on the engine." Even if women were willing to run such a risk, their "instability" and "emotionalism" and "lack of physical strength" were cited as reasons why they should not fly planes. Women would have to work as members of teams, and "men will not take orders from a woman" and "women are not cooperative." Aviation was somewhat dangerous, and the public which could bear the idea of young men being killed as pilot trainees could not extend this toleration to women. To be sure, a few women such as Nancy Harkness Love and Jacqueline Cochran who played principal roles in the story of the WAFS and the WASP were actually doing the aviation jobs in question, but they were conveniently classified as exceptional.

Further, the situation was complicated by an attitude on the part of many young women, encouraged by the press and radio and motion pictures. This group attached so much glamour to the position of women in aviation that the principal qualifications for service appeared to be a combination of the qualities of a first-class combat pilot and a Powers model. It was the latter attitude which influenced some of the 25,000 young women volunteers who offered themselves for the WAFS and the WASP. Both attitudes probably prevented many competent women from venturing into aviation.

The stimulation of a two-front war, with its actual and threatened manpower shortages, was required to make the services willing to include women in their personnel. The experimental nature of their utilization as pilots was legally recognized in the case of the WASP, and was a strong influence in the programs for women in other types of aviation service, except in the traditional and accepted clerical and similar jobs. Recognizing this fact, it is important to evaluate any changes in attitude which occurred during the war years.

2. *Traditional attitudes toward women's limitations have been changed by experience.*

After careful consideration of AAF reports on the WASP, and conferences with many persons who knew their history thoroughly, it seems fair to conclude that the reasons for their deactivation in December 1944 were not based upon deficiencies due to their sex. The oversupply of trained pilots in the AAF and the difficulties of arranging on-duty training for women noncombat pilots and men combat pilots without hampering the program for the latter group were the fundamental reasons for discontinuing the training of women as pilots. The conclusions stated in chapter iv are based upon judgments of the AAF officers who understood the total situation in the Air Forces and who knew the WASP program well. These conclusions indicate very definitely that women can be trained successfully to fly military planes in the same way that men are trained, if due consideration is given to their physical size and strength, and if proper classification procedures are used.

Precisely the same statement can be made for men as prospective pilots. A man who is only 61 or 62 inches tall, or who has no great physical stamina, or who cannot achieve a reasonably high rating on standard aviation tests will have the same difficulties in flying a given type of plane that a woman will have. This indicates that, if we ever run short of men and women who can be trained to fly the kinds of planes which are being manufactured, we shall have to produce new plane types with necessary modifications to permit shorter or weaker or less competent people to operate them. This is exactly what happened in the case of the automobile. Manufacturers who wish to employ women frequently produce machines to be operated by shorter people with a shorter "reach" and less strength. Furthermore, extensive experimentation is now going on in the field of aviation to produce planes which are easier and safer to fly. Even if not many women could qualify to fly C-54's and B-29's, the field of aviation is not closed to them. The WASP has a very respectable record of achievement in learning to ferry difficult types of planes, particularly if one considers that most of the women pilots had only brief backgrounds of training and experience.

The prewar uncertainty with respect to training women pilots cannot occur again, because of the record of the WASP program. The carefully collected physical and psychological data, and their evaluation in terms of later performance, are of the highest value, even though based on relatively small numbers of cases and covering a comparatively brief period of time. The data presented in chapter iv of this book will be of value to women who are considering for themselves the occupation of aircraft pilot, as well as to those who would select them for training and plan curriculums and employ teachers, and to prospective employers of women pilots.

The evidence indicates no support for a belief that women as a group are less capable of being taught to pilot a plane than men as a group, or that different or higher qualifications should be set for women pilots.

3. *There are many nonpilot jobs in aviation in which women have demonstrated capacity.*

Turning from the training and employment of women as pilots, we look next at their position in other phases of aviation—a much less clear-cut situation. Aside from piloting a plane, aviation is a very complex activity which includes jobs based upon a wide range of abilities and interests. The present study, dealing only with women in aviation in the armed services during the war, necessarily omits their experiences in the aircraft manufacturing industry and in commercial and private phases of civilian aviation. Furthermore, the sole consideration in the training and employment of women in the armed services was the successful prosecution of the war, and not the best interests of aviation or of men or of women in the service. Based upon this consideration, women were found useful as teachers, radio and control tower operators, administrative personnel, clerical workers, mechanics, flight orderlies, and in small numbers as various other kinds of workers. They were not trained and employed in large numbers, but it is most important to note that the numbers of women in aviation services, the variety of positions which they filled, the numbers of stations at which they served, and their acceptance by male personnel steadily increased during the course of the war. This can be assumed to express the satisfaction of the services with the work of women and all evidence confirms this assumption. From a military point of view, women were found to be more useful for some kinds of work than for others, for a wide range of reasons—including their size and strength, their backgrounds of education and experience, the attitude of women toward different jobs, the attitudes of commanding officers and the men with whom the women worked, and the places in which different duties were to be performed.

The statement in the preceding paragraph is quite different from saying that women were better qualified or not so well qualified for these particular positions, because so many other factors than personal ability enter into availability from a military standpoint. If the Army and Navy and Coast Guard and Marine Corps had been ordered, as the Army Air Forces were, to consider the utilization of women as an experiment which was to be evaluated, we should have better evidence to answer the question as to their qualifications. As it was, they were so well integrated into their respective services that it is difficult to separate either their individual or group records. Probably the women were least successful in aviation jobs involving mechanical skills, and most successful as radio and control tower operators, as teachers on the various synthetic trainers, in various administrative and clerical jobs, and as flight nurses and orderlies. There were not infrequent cases in which women were conspicuously successful in other types of aviation jobs. If there had been a more drastic manpower shortage during the war, leading to the drafting of women for military service, there is every reason to believe that many more women could have been found to be trained and employed by the aviation services. Experience in England furnishes strong evidence to support this belief.

4. *Not only attitudes, but also economic conditions and employment prospects must be considered.*

One important consideration in planning aviation education for the future is the attitude of women toward work in this field.

It will be recalled that 25,000 young women applied for admission to the WASP although no recruiting campaigns were conducted, and that the AAF-WAC campaign for recruits was very successful although it was conducted at a time when business, government, industry, nursing, and the other women's services were competing strenuously for available womanpower. At present, too, many women are applying to the commercial aviation companies to enter their training schools, and many are taking out pilot licenses from the Civil Aeronautics Administration. Young college women are asking for pilot training courses, even though academic credit is not usually granted for such work.

At least one college for women is developing a considerable program of work in aviation, including flight training and aviation mechanics. In the course of conferences during the first half of 1946 no competent person who discussed the matter with the writer even suggested that women might *not* desire to be employed in the various business and professional jobs connected with aviation. One WAC officer who had served in the AAF in a position which had given her wide experience with the Air-Wacs, said that it would make a temporary difference to women if, in the immediate postwar period, they should encounter difficulties in finding occupations in this field but that "women are going to fly" and that fact was hardly worth discussion. In fact, this assumption seems to be the prevailing opinion, and those who are concerning themselves about education and employment in aviation certainly should base their plans upon it until there is sufficient experience to confirm or to correct it.

The persons with whom this question has been discussed—and they include women who are competent in the field—believe that the one great hindrance to the future of women in aviation lies in postwar conditions and not in women's ability or desire to enter aviation. Two postwar conditions in particular will affect the situation of women. So many men were trained as pilots, mechanics, and other types of aviation personnel by the armed services that there is a great supply of trained people already on the market. Aviation is expanding rapidly and this supply, while large, may not be more than can be absorbed. But the opportunities for more young men and women to start training in aviation now are obviously curtailed as a result of the existing number of people who can be put to work with little or no further training.

In the second place, the general economic conditions during the first years following the war will have an important effect upon aviation as an industry which will be reflected in training and employment aspects. If there is a long period of prosperity, more planes will be manufactured, more pilots will be trained, more orderlies and hostesses and ticket-sellers and control-tower operators and other types of employees will be needed, and there will have to be more teachers and supervisors and administrators. No one knows whether we shall have prosperity or depression, or both, or in what order of succession. Yet this is possibly the most important determining factor in the future of women in aviation. Questions as to their ability or desire to enter aviation can be answered with reasonable certainty, but the problem of opportunity for them is far from solution.

5. Sex distinctions need not be overstressed in the planning and organization of training programs.

There apparently is no reason to think that any important differences in training methods for men and women will be required if the same physical and other requirements are established for trainees of both sexes. As the war continued, more and more women were trained in the courses and schools that were operating for male trainees. Practically the only significant differences in the training of men and women were those arising from the fact that relatively few women were trained for duties related to aviation in combat areas, and in no cases were they trained for combat duty.

Even though the Wasps were trained in basic flying skills at a separate training station, their course was fundamentally like the parallel courses for male pilot trainees. After women pilots were assigned to duty they continued on-the-job training in order to ferry faster and heavier planes, but were not trained in combat flying skills. In short, the differences in training were almost exclusively such as arose from the fact of women's exclusion from *combat* flying, but not from flying as such, nor from flying in occupations not traditionally closed to women through cultural attitudes.   It will be recalled that there were many Russian women pilots who flew in combat in World War II, because in Russia it was fairly well accepted that women could join men as active members of fighting forces.   This acceptance was not a part of American culture in the decade of the 1940's and it resulted in the difference in women's training for aviation duties with the armed services described above.   With this exception noted, the general statement can be made that men and women were trained by the same methods for the same duty assignments, and that the implication for training of civilians in aviation jobs and professions is that no differences need to be made in the preparation of men and women.

Part Three

WOMEN IN MEDICAL, NURSING, AND RELATED SERVICES

VII. WOMEN IN THE MEDICAL DEPART-MENT OF THE ARMY

ALTHOUGH the present chapter discusses only the training of women in the Medical Department of the United States Army, it may help the reader in following this rather complex program to have an understanding of the organization of the Medical Department's whole training program.

MEDICAL DEPARTMENT'S ORGANIZATION FOR TRAINING

At the beginning of the war, the organization of training in the Medical Department was affected by the prevailing rule that the chiefs of the armed services act as immediate advisers to the War Department General Staff on training matters peculiar to their particular arm of the service. Thus, the Surgeon General was the adviser on the technical training of Medical Department personnel. His office prepared master program guides, approved manuals and instructional aids, and, in general, established the basic policies under which Medical Department personnel everywhere were trained. However, the degree to which the Surgeon General exercised control over training depended upon the location of personnel. Certain exempted Medical Department installations were under his direct jurisdiction, but the greater number was under the jurisdiction of the commanders of the nine corps areas and four overseas departments and of the post commanders within each. There was a surgeon of the area in each corps area, and subordinate surgeons were stationed in each post. The commanders were in control of the training programs in their respective areas under the Army doctrine that "training is a function of command." However, the surgeon in each area was adviser to the commander in all technical matters pertaining to the Medical Department, including training, and all basic policy in such matters emanated from the Surgeon General. No precise definition of responsibility for training under this organization could be offered to which there would not be exceptions. Numerous shifts occurred as the war programs of training were initiated but, from the War Department's standpoint, these programs were basically uniform regardless of the agency immediately responsible for their conduct, because of the Surgeon General's responsibility for them.

After the reorganization of the War Department in March 1942, training, as a function of command, became the responsibility of the Army Ground Forces, the Army Air Forces, and the Army Service Forces. The last named had much the largest training responsibility because of its control over all numbered general hospitals, station hospitals, hospital trains, and similar facilities. The Surgeon General was the agent of the Army Service Forces, and for this reason his relationship to the Service Forces was more direct than to the Ground Forces or to the Air Forces. However, it is important to remember that the Surgeon General remained the ultimate source of training doctrine for Medical Department personnel in all three major forces. The Training Division of Operations Service in the Office of the Surgeon General was ultimately responsible for programs and doctrine, with the actual process of training carried out as a function of command.

PHYSICIANS

For the first time, women were commissioned as officers in the Army Medical Corps during World War II. A few women doctors, under an act of Congress of April 16, 1943, were directly commissioned into the Medical Corps without any special orientation. Beginning in October 1943, all newly commissioned women doctors were oriented into the Army by a four-week course at the Medical Department Replacement Pool at Lawson General Hospital. Approximately seventy-two women physicians were commissioned and 55 of this number attended the orientation course. In addition, four women enrolled at the Army Medical School, one in the course on anesthesiology and three in tropical and military medicine; four took the course in military neuropsychiatry at Mason General Hospital; and five enrolled in the anesthesiology course at New York University.

"Women doctors have shown they can justify their place in the profession in war as well as in civilian practice," said Maj. Gen. Norman T. Kirk, Surgeon General of the Army (New York *Times,* April 23, 1946). "The seventy-two so commissioned in the Army built up an enviable record of exceptionally high professional standards in their respective specialties," he said. "In the face of considerable prejudice women have demonstrated their skill and fitness and all the qualities necessary for the successful physician."

NURSES

American women had served as nurses to care for wounded soldiers in every war since the American Revolution, but they first became a definite component of the Army when the Army Nurse Corps was created by Congress in 1901. Legislation in 1920 provided the status of officers for members of the corps, but their pay and allowances were not the same as those of the men. In 1944 they were given full military rank for the duration of the war plus six months, and an act of April 16, 1947, established this status permanently.

Since the establishment of the corps in 1901, more than 100,-000 nurses have been members. Immediately before the first World War there were 403 nurses in the corps. This number was increased to 21,480 as peak strength during that war, and more than 10,000 nurses served overseas. By 1939, however, the enrollment had decreased to 625. During World War II more than 57,000 nurses (including approximately 600 Negroes) were in the corps at the peak, and upwards of 30,000 served overseas.

Registered nurses less than forty-five years old were eligible for membership in the corps during the war. A nurse was appointed to the Army Nurse Corps as a second lieutenant and after eighteen months of service she could be promoted to first lieutenant. The superintendent of the corps held the rank of colonel.

Training for all nursing personnel was the responsibility of the Training Division, Operations Service, in the Office of the Surgeon General. Although several very extensive training programs for nurses were conducted during World War II, the basic plan in use before the war was not changed. The Army had previously recruited nurses who were graduates of civilian nursing schools and colleges, and had given them on-the-job training in Army nursing procedures, with more or less formal indoctrination into military service. During the war, the task of indoctrination became more important because large numbers of new members were constantly being inducted, and particularly because so many nurses were sent overseas for duty in the different theaters of operations. It also became necessary to set up training for nursing specialties.

FIELD MEDICAL UNITS

In May 1942, field medical units were being organized. Doctors, nurses, and other assigned personnel were given training as functional groups before being sent into the field, in the Zone of the Interior or in overseas theaters of operations. Responsibility for developing programs for the nurses newly appointed and assigned to such units was local, and there was no guide approved by Army Service Forces for such training. The manual prescribing training procedures for field medical units which received enlisted personnel direct from reception centers contained no provisions specifically applicable to nurses. Certain units, designated by the Director of Training, Services of Supply, Army Service Forces, were located at named Army general hospitals and direct responsibility for their training was vested in the Surgeon General. Corps area commanders were responsible for training other units located in station hospitals, as designated by the Director of Training; the commanders were directed to make the facilities of station hospitals available for the administrative and technical training of individuals belonging to the units, and the maximum facilities in medical enlisted technicians schools were to be utilized in the training of dental, x-ray, pharmacy, medical, laboratory, and surgical technicians in the units.

A major difficulty soon became apparent in the plan described above. The shortage of nurses was so serious that frequently nurses were kept on duty with the hospital to which they were

PLATE VI

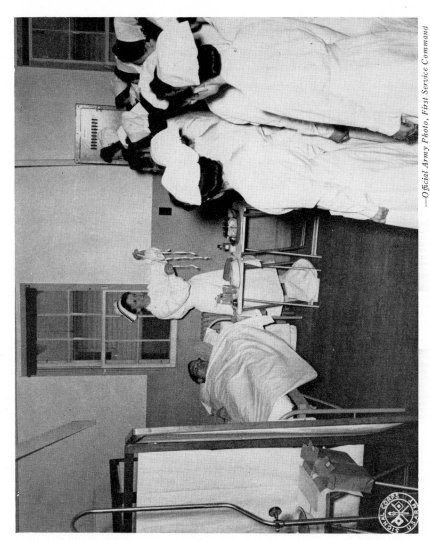

—*Official Army Photo, First Service Command*

A GROUP OF ARMY NURSES RECEIVING INSTRUCTION AT FORT DEVENS, MASSACHUSETTS

first assigned, until the unit which they had been ordered to join was almost ready to be activated; consequently, they had little or no training with their respective units. In many cases they received no Army indoctrination at all.

In October 1942 a new training program for nurses was prepared by the Training Division for the purpose of correcting the difficulty. Every nurse-member of a field medical unit was required to take a course which insured adequate indoctrination, and this was to be given to her in a field unit prior to commitment. The suggested four-week course of 176 hours included:

64 hours of employment on duty assignment

37 hours of general subjects:

Orientation lecture, military courtesy and customs of the service, wearing of the uniform, care of clothing and equipment, dismounted drill, physical training, individual defense against chemical, air, parachute, and mechanized attack, military training (methods, aids, programs, schedules, standards, inspections, techniques of instruction and testing).

16 hours of administration:

Military law, military correspondence, safeguarding military information, national service life insurance, ward management, operation of clinics within the Army hospital.

6 hours of sanitation:

Control of respiratory diseases, housing and barracks sanitation; control of intestinal diseases, general and fly control; food inspection and mess sanitation; field water supplies and purification; waste disposal and control of insect-borne diseases.

20 hours of nursing and care of patient:

Principles of first aid, emergency treatment, routine hospital procedures, treatment of chemical casualties, hospital diets, care of the seriously ill, isolation and care of communicable diseases, care and management of mental patients, oxygen therapy, disinfection of wards and equipment, physical examinations.

8 hours of organization, function, and operation of the unit:

Organization of the Army, of the Medical Department, of the Army Nurse Corps, of the unit; evacuation of the wounded; standard operating procedure for the unit.

5 hours of conferences and round-table discussion

4 hours of inspections and tests

16 hours of unscheduled time

In January 1943 the superintendent of the Army Nurse Corps suggested to the chief of the Training Division certain changes in the indoctrination program described above. Since all nurses under a specified age were eligible for foreign duty, the superintendent believed that all of them should receive the minimum training provided in the indoctrination program. The absence of quarters and mess facilities in stations where the numbered units were in training made it impossible for nurses to train with the units to which they were assigned, and they were placed on temporary duty in their home stations pending the shipment of units. Consequently, they were not receiving the training considered essential for personnel going overseas. Furthermore, the superintendent believed that all nurses newly inducted would benefit greatly by receiving the training as soon as practicable after entering upon active duty. She suggested a program of training lasting from six weeks to two months for nurses other than those assigned to medical units.

A new program for the training of Army nurses, based upon the foregoing recommendations, was made effective in June 1943. Since all nurses less than forty-five years of age were eligible for foreign duty in numbered medical field units, it was required that all nurses then in service, or to be appointed in the future, should have a satisfactory knowledge of basic military subjects. Commanding officers of hospitals in the Zone of the Interior which had 250 or more beds were to provide training, as prescribed in the new program, to all nurses under the age of forty-five who were not thoroughly familiar with its contents. The new program consisted of one-half classroom work and one-half ward duty, and covered a four-week period of 48 hours a week. The courses in administration, organization, and nursing and care of patient were reduced by a few hours, and 24 hours were added to employment on duty assignment. In August 1943 it was provided that this program of training could be carried out in hospitals of less than 250-bed capacity by extending the course of instruction over a period of time longer than the prescribed four weeks. At about the same time the requirement was made that all nurses must be assigned to numbered medical units at least thirty days prior to their movement overseas.

SERVICE COMMANDS RESPONSIBLE FOR BASIC MILITARY TRAINING

During 1943 the War Manpower Commission had allocated procurement objectives for nurses for each state, the total for the year having been set at 28,000. The nine Army service commands were notified of these quotas and were made responsible for meeting them. In October 1943 the Surgeon General changed the plan of basic military training of nurses by removing the responsibility from the commanding officers of individual hospitals in the Zone of the Interior (as provided four months earlier) and establishing schools under the jurisdiction of the nine service commands. A majority of the commands desired to conduct the basic military training of the nurses they procured and had, in fact, been doing so for some time. Each command was now instructed to set up a school of sufficient size to accommodate the command's monthly procurement objective. This plan also obviated the necessity of transportation to one central school. Newly commissioned nurses were to be trained under the new program, but the program of June 1943 continued in effect for the training of nurses who had been in Army service for some time but who had had no basic military training. The commanding general of each service command was instructed to report within a month as to the location and capacity of each training center.

The program of October 1943 prepared by the Training Division, Office of the Surgeon General, continued in effect until June 1945. One week of the training period was allotted to processing, equipping, and deprocessing. Three weeks of 48 working hours each were allotted to instruction. The purpose of the program was to furnish a general guide for the instruction of newly commissioned nurses in the principles and methods of medical field service and Army nursing, and to orient these nurses by giving them a general background of information concerning the Army and its organization, and in particular the organization and function of the Medical Department and the Army Nurse Corps.

Although the subjects included in the new program were, in general, like those in the earlier program, the distribution of time was considerably changed. The total of 144 hours of work (as contrasted with 176 hours in the earlier program) included increased hours of instruction in all courses, but the 64 hours of employment on duty assignment were omitted, and 14 hours of routine visits to clinics and various types of medical and surgical wards for group instruction were substituted.

White nurses were given the basic military training course in one or two installations in each service command. Fifty colored nurses were trained at Fort Huachuca, Arizona. After September 1944, colored nurses received their training at the basic training schools in the several commands.

The scope of the basic military training program for nurses is indicated by Table 16.

TABLE 16

SERVICE COMMAND CAPACITIES FOR TRAINING NURSES, AS OF APRIL 10, 1945

Service Command	Location of Training Capacity	April Capacity	May Capacity
First............	Fort Devens, Mass.	800	2,000
Second..........	Tilton General Hospital, Fort Dix, N. J.	500	500
Third...........	Fort George G. Meade, Md.	250	Closed
Third...........	Camp Lee, Va.	400	300
Fourth..........	Camp Rucker, Ala.	500	500
Fifth............	Billings General Hospital, Fort Benjamin Harrison, Ind.	100	100
Fifth............	Fort Knox, Ky.	150	....
Sixth...........	Camp McCoy, Wisc.	300	300
Seventh.........	Camp Carson, Col.	300	300
Eighth..........	Brooke General Hospital, Fort Sam Houston, Texas	300	300
Eighth..........	Camp Swift, Texas	....	....
Ninth...........	Madegan General Hospital, Fort Lewis, Wash.	300	300
Total monthly capacity		3,900	4,600

Recruits in excess of the stated capacities in any service command were to be assigned to adjacent commands or to Fort Devens. It was expected that capacities named for May would represent the peak of recruitment and that the centers would be maintained at the May capacities. No changes were made in the basic military training of nurses for more than a year and a half. On June 16, 1945, a new program at hospitals in each of the nine service commands became effective as a means of orienting all newly commissioned nurses in the Army and in its medical and nursing service, both in the field and in the Zone of the Interior. One week of the five-week training program was devoted to processing, and the remaining time to actual training. The ward duty (28 hours) was scheduled for the last week of the period, and was arranged for five mornings of four hours each and one full day of eight hours. This was defined as "on-the-job" training under regularly assigned duty nurses, and not as relief for duty nurses. Time allotted to road marches, tent pitching, camouflage, defense against chemical attack, field water supply, field sanitation and waste disposal, and malaria control was to be utilized in part for instruction in the field when practicable.

General training notes for each course included a statement of the course objective, listed references and training aids, and in some instances suggested methods of instruction. The training manual stated, "Nothing in succeeding paragraphs is intended to limit the initiative and ingenuity of the training personnel in the manner of presentation. . . . The objective given must be attained and the mandatory requirements in the general training notes complied with."

Gradually, as the war came to an end, basic training for Army nurses was discontinued. In September 1945 the course was given in only three hospitals, and it was discontinued entirely by the end of that month. At that time a total of 27,330 nurses had taken the basic military training courses.

COURSES FOR SPECIALISTS

In three specialist categories—anesthesiology, operating room supervision, and psychiatric nursing—the Army Nurse Corps found that the shortages of qualified nurses were so extensive that special courses would have to be set up to provide adequate personnel.

Anesthesiology

A program of instruction for applicatory training of nurse anesthetists was prepared in August 1944 by the Training Division, Office of the Surgeon General. It set forth the requirements to be met by the named general hospitals in the Zone of the Interior which furnished instruction. The course lasted for 26 weeks, with 48 hours of work a week. Clinical experience of 920 hours was the largest item in the total of 1,248 hours of instruction. The other subjects were a summary of technical training, principles of anesthesiology (160 hours), anesthesia equipment, shock and transfusion, clinical conferences, review of literature, quiz sections, review, and make-up. By December 1945, 580 nurses had been graduated from courses in anesthesiology which were provided in 55 different hospitals.

Neuropsychiatric nursing

Beginning early in 1944, Mason General Hospital offered to its duty personnel a course in neuropsychiatric nursing which was operated in connection with the School of Military Neuropsychiatry for medical officers. In addition to nurses on duty in Mason General Hospital, other nurses were assigned to temporary duty there for the purpose of taking the twelve-week course. Instruction was provided for 10 hours a week, and 38 hours were spent in supervised ward activity. The subjects taught were all in the fields of neuropsychiatry and neuropsychiatric nursing, including hydrotherapy, shock therapy, Army reconditioning programs, occupational therapy, new treatments, and new drugs.

A different plan was offered for nurses who were already skilled in neuropsychiatric nursing and who wished to take advanced work. For the purpose of coordinating their knowledge of nursing care with a knowledge of patients, clinical diagnosis, and disposition, the nurses were given selected lectures from the officers' course, scheduled clinical conferences, and disposition-board sessions. It was considered desirable but not necessary that, after completing their course, the nurses who had received training in this specialty should assist with teaching other groups of student nurses, and several nurses postponed overseas assignments for a few months for this purpose. A total of 722 nurses completed the course by December 1945.

Operating-room technic

The courses in operating room technic, basic and advanced, were not established on a War Department level. Each service command was permitted to determine the scope and content of these courses. They varied in length with classroom work of 75 to 87 hours, and clinical experience or applicatory training of from 294 to 419 hours. The Office of the Surgeon General prepared suggested programs of instruction. The courses were conducted in general and in large station hospitals in the United States and in numbered hospitals in the theaters of operation. There is no record of the total number of nurses trained, but 88 completed the course in the United States subsequent to 1943. No record of the number trained overseas is available.

CLASSES AT REDISTRIBUTION STATIONS

To complete the description of the Medical Department's training programs for nurses, two classes which were offered at certain redistribution stations should be mentioned. The mission of such a station is to obtain maximum utilization of Army personnel who have returned to the United States from overseas stations for reassignment. This is accomplished through occupational and physical classification, mental and physical reconditioning, orientation, and indoctrination for the purpose of assigning individuals to appropriate positions to further the war effort, in accordance with their civilian and overseas combat experience.

First Lieutenant Dorothy E. Lopnow of the Army Nurse Corps described such a station in her article "Our Nurses and Redistribution Stations" which appeared in the March 1945 issue of *The Army Nurse*. It was based on her experiences as a staff member. That particular station processed approximately 1,000 returnees every two weeks, all of them personnel of the Army Ground and Service Forces from fifteen western states. Lieutenant Lopnow stated that the reactions of these men and women varied from confusion and bewilderment to frank belligerency.

Women who had served in other countries with climates and environments not unlike our own returned in better condition than, for example, those back from the South Pacific and China-Burma-India theaters who required the greatest adjustment. They had lived under most difficult conditions in an unfamiliar environment, but the writer said, "The final consideration is the manner in which the individual reacts to her personal problems and her ability to adjust to them, regardless of theater and whether or not she has been in a combat zone. In some areas living, alone, is a challenge, without being under fire."

Medical examination, orientation classes, and reclassification were completed within a few days, and during the remainder of the nurse's stay the time was given to rest and play. The average stay was ten to fourteen days. Special Services arranged splendid programs of sports, tours, movies, and shows. Afternoon coffee, orchestras at meals, and other niceties and comforts were arranged.

The first reaction of nurses was that they wished to go back overseas immediately, not realizing how much they needed change and relaxation. After two weeks, it was a satisfaction to see how these nurses had relaxed and to observe their change of attitude. One nurse wrote, "We arrived there in an unsettled and confused state after traveling here and there with nothing definite to look forward to—but you just seemed to settle all that."

From an educational standpoint two orientation classes described by Lieutenant Lopnow have considerable interest. One called "Home Front" was a discussion conducted by an officer, well equipped with statistics to explain what had been occurring at home. She said:

Naturally, our service people have heard many rumors, and he [the discussion leader] supplies actual facts concerning War Bonds turned in, blood donors, strikes, and allied subjects. Many nurses have expressed the wish that they could have attended these classes before going home to family and civilian friends. Whether or not we wish to recognize it, there is a cleavage in ideas which must be bridged. "Sound off" or the gripes-and-cheers session gives them an opportunity to tell of good or bad features of their experiences. These stories are consolidated into a report which goes through channels to proper authorities. This is a vital factor in creating changes for the benefit of nurses and troops now going overseas.

After classification, an evaluation was made of the physical condition, experience record, and ability of the nurse, and her new assignment was usually to a general or a regional hospital where the wounded return from overseas and thus receive care from nurses who have had similar experiences.

NURSING AID FROM CIVILIANS

Both paid and volunteer civilian graduate nurses offered a supplementary source of nursing personnel. These nurses could do the same, or practically the same, work that an Army nurse could do, without the necessity of more training or more supervision than the Army nurses needed.

Volunteer and paid civilian nurses' aides performed the duties taught in the Red Cross nurses' aides course. They were required to have completed the 80-hour course and to have 150 hours of supervised practice in approved hospitals. Both the Army and the Red Cross required close supervision of the work of nurse's aides by a registered professional nurse. Although no provision was made for formal on-the-job training, in many cases it was furnished to increase the usefulness of the aides.

On March 26, 1945, Headquarters, Army Service Forces, published ASF Circular No. 108, Part II, Section V of which summarized existing provisions for civilian nursing care of patients in Army hospitals. The purpose of the publication was not to set up training programs but rather to name the groups authorized, to describe their qualifications and duties, and, in general, to define in detail all conditions surrounding the employment of civilian and, in many cases, of nonprofessional and volunteer nursing aides. The most important general characteristic of the use of such aides from a civilian standpoint is the total pattern of nursing care which the Army developed as a result of the acute shortage of fully qualified graduate nurses who could meet the standards of admission to the Army Nurse Corps.

DIETITIANS

For many years before World War II, the Medical Department of the Army employed women as dietitians. A postgraduate dietitians' course for civilian women was offered at Walter Reed General Hospital after 1922, and other civilian women took similar postgraduate courses in civilian schools and colleges in preparation for appointments to the Army.

At the beginning of the emergency, the course at Walter Reed was twelve months long and involved both didactic and applicatory training activities. In November 1942 this course was modified so that all basic didactic material was covered in the first six months. This part of the course was taught at Walter Reed. The second six months of applicatory training was carried out at several other Army hospitals. In effect, the plan doubled the output of trained dietitians. As the need for dietitians increased, the six-month student dietitian course was offered at four Army general hospitals and at selected civilian hospitals, and the apprentice dietitian course was also offered at 36 hospitals. By December 1945, 332 students had completed the student and apprentice courses, and 88 students were still in training.

The women who attended the Army's courses for dietitians were selected under Civil Service regulations and were civilians throughout the training period. In 1943 dietitians were accorded rank equivalent to that of officers in the Medical Department, and after June 1944, upon completion of the 12-month course, they were commissioned as second lieutenants with exactly the same status as male officers. Although in fact the course remained one for civilian student dietitians, it was designated an officer-candidate course by Headquarters, Army Service Forces. Actually, training for student dietitians in Army hospitals, both before and during World War II was professional training on a Medical Department level, by agreement between the Surgeon General and the United States Civil Service Commission.

REQUIREMENTS FOR ADMISSION TO DIETITIAN COURSES

Women between the ages of twenty and forty were admitted to the student dietitian course if they were graduates of four-year college courses with majors in food and nutrition or in institutional management. Later the educational requirement was changed. Provision was made for the substitution of certain types of experience for some academic courses. The student was required to have completed 36 semester hours in college (including a specified number of hours in chemistry, biology, foods, nutrition, and diet in disease and institutional management) and to pass a written examination containing both general and technical questions. Students were required to meet physical standards specified by the Army.

Six alternative requirements for admission to the apprentice dietitian course made it possible for women to enter who had not been students in the student dietitian course: (1) completion of a full six-month training program in an approved course for student dietitians, including specified courses; or (2) one year of experience as a dietitian in a hospital of at least 200-bed capacity including all types of work mentioned under plan (1); or (3) two years of experience in college teaching of food, nutrition, or institution management; or (4) two years of experience in high school teaching of food and, in addition, management of school lunchroom or school cafeteria serving 200 or more people at each meal; or (5) two years of experience in management or direction of a school lunch program, or an industrial or commercial food service serving 200 or more people at each meal; or (6) two years of experience in nutrition work with a social service or public health agency.

Students who entered the apprentice dietitian course under plans (2) to (6), inclusive, were given appropriate parts of the student dietitian course and the apprentice dietitian course, depending upon their previous experience. To facilitate instruction, entrants with similar backgrounds of training and experience were grouped for their work in the apprentice course. Maj. Helen C. Burns, Director of Dietitians, AUS, comments upon the success of many dietitians who came into the service under certain of the alternative plans, particularly of those who had previously directed school or industrial cafeterias and lunchrooms.

STUDENT DIETITIANS COURSE DESCRIBED

Curriculums of the student dietitians course at the four general hospitals were practically alike. A detailed description of the course at Fitzsimons General Hospital, written by Capt. Mildred Allbritton, who was in charge of that course, appeared in the *Journal of the American Dietetic Association* for December 1944.

A student's first week is spent in taking physical examinations, orientation and lectures. Throughout the remaining 6 months, lecture periods are scheduled from 1 to 3 P.M., for 4 days a week. Two afternoons are devoted to clinics. Mornings and the hours from 3 to 5:30 P.M., 6 days a week, are devoted to practical assignments under the supervision of 9 staff dietitians.

The article follows the student on each of her practical assignments throughout the six-month course.

She spends ten weeks in the administrative section—four in one of the large messes which serves 1,800–2,000 enlisted patients and civilian employees, and three weeks in a small mess where about 250 officer patients have table service. Here, among other things, she writes menus; figures costs; requisitions staple and canned foods from the central storeroom; writes the daily order for dairy products, the twice-weekly order for perishable fruits and vegetables, and the weekly order for meat; and follows the 50 hours of lectures on meat and dairy hygiene by trips to observe how these foods are checked and stored. She spends a week in the bakery, working with the pastry crew in the morning and with the bread crew in the afternoon. Two weeks are spent in the storeroom and office, where she learns how orders are filled, familiarizes herself with the inventory system used for foods and equipment, obtains prices, goes to market with the mess officer, and on her last trip is allowed to do the buying.

During the ten-week therapeutic training, she spends four weeks in the consolidated diet kitchen where approximately 45 varieties of diet are prepared. Here she writes the standard special-diet menus (light, soft, convalescent ulcer, bland, low-residue, low-salt, fat-free), figures their costs, orders supplies, watches and supervises the preparation of food, and learns to use gram scales and to visualize portions of food so weighed. She spends time on surgical wards, heart and kidney wards, and in the gastrointestinal and diabetic section where she learns to figure diabetic menus and to calculate carbohydrate substitutions for unconsumed food on the diabetic's tray.

A month is spent on pediatrics—two weeks of this time in the milk formula laboratory, where the student learns to sterilize equipment, and to prepare and cap the formulas. Twice a day she delivers the formulas to the nursery and feeds the babies. She also works with older children—writes the menus, prepares the food, serves the trays, and actually feeds the smaller children. Once a week, during this period, the student participates in the well-baby and prenatal clinics, and three times a week in the postnatal clinic. Captain Allbritton continues:

> At this point the student becomes an apprentice dietitian. As such she follows much the same routine in the administrative section but she is granted much more authority. For instance, she relieves the staff dietitian when off duty or on leave, and acts in a supervisory capacity on the wards where one staff dietitian is covering a number of wards. She is in charge of the milk formula laboratory, and does the postnatal clinic teaching. In fact, the apprentices do all the teaching in the very active training program for civilian mess and ward attendants, and they are doing an excellent job.

Specific rating scales were set up at Fitzsimons General Hospital to measure the progress of trainees. The student was graded on eight professional subjects, and on her personal and professional qualities. The rating sheet included space for comments on her outstanding characteristics and for suggestions for improvement. The student herself, the supervising dietitian, and the chief dietitian all signed the rating sheet to indicate that there was full understanding of her status. For each of the nine items to be rated (as, for example, "Storeroom and Purchasing" or "Personal and Professional Qualities"), a statement was prepared giving in precise detail the factors to be considered, and containing a definite explanation of what was meant by a rating of 1, 2, 3, or 4.

At Walter Reed General Hospital, the chief dietitian filed a monthly report for each student. The efficiency record was based upon grades in food standards, standards of cleanliness and order, supervising ability, knowledge of diet therapy, accuracy, ability to teach, reliability, judgment, ability to adjust, interest, initiative, cooperation, tact and courtesy, professional attitude, leadership, attitude toward criticism, poise, friendliness, voice, personal appearance, physical fitness, and progress, and students were required to average not less than 80 percent.

BASIC MILITARY TRAINING

Basic military training for dietitians commissioned in the Medical Department was initiated in October 1943. All dietitians less than forty-five years of age and physically qualified were eligible for assignment to overseas duty in numbered medical units. It was therefore considered essential that those already in service, or to be appointed in the future, should have a satisfactory knowledge of basic military subjects and be thoroughly familiar with the types of food used in overseas rations, methods of preparation, and types of equipment used. Dietitians were to attend the Service Command Nurses Basic Training Centers to receive this basic training, and all dietitians commissioned directly from civilian life received the training immediately after processing at their first station of duty. The basic military training course was modified for the dietitians by replacing 23 hours of the training with the same number of hours in their professional field: expeditionary and overseas hospital ration, food inspection and sanitation, meat and dairy hygiene, waste disposal, organization and functions of Medical Department dietitians, mess management, hospital messes, ward food service, waste control, field rations (11 hours).

All Medical Department dietitians selected for service overseas were required to complete course K, Cooking of Dehydrated Foods, at a station designated by the service command. This one-week course for commissioned and enlisted personnel was offered at bakers-and-cooks schools in several commands. The course was planned to offer instruction in the cooking of all dehydrated foods to mess supervisors, mess officers, and rated cooks.

On June 16, 1945, the basic training program for dietitians was once more revised and the following courses substituted for the 53 hours deleted: expeditionary and overseas hospital ration, food inspection and mess sanitation, meat and dairy hygiene, organization and functions of Medical Department dietitians, mess management, diet planning, and diet kitchen duty, including main kitchen duty (36 hours). Prior to assignment overseas, dietitians were still required to take course K, cooking of dehydrated foods.

Between October 1943 and September 1945, 802 dietitians had attended the Service Command Nurses Basic Training Centers. At the peak in the summer of 1945 there were approximately 1,600 dietitians in the Medical Department.

PHYSICAL THERAPISTS

Beginning in 1922 a course for student physical therapists was offered by the Medical Department at Walter Reed General Hospital, Washington, D. C. All physical therapists assigned to Army hospitals during the period 1932 to 1940 were graduates of this training course, which was conducted annually. Students for these courses were selected under the provisions of the United States Civil Service Commission regulations. The course, which was originally of six months' duration, was lengthened to twelve months in 1934 and subsequently changed to a ten-month course in 1940 and a nine-month course in 1941.

NEW PHYSICAL THERAPY COURSE FOR CIVILIANS

In April 1941 the Surgeon General with the approval of the American Medical Association inaugurated a new course. This was offered to qualified college graduates with majors in physical education and biological sciences, and it included a six-month professional course offered in selected Army hospitals and approved civilian hospitals, to be followed by six months of applicatory training under supervision in Army hospitals. The first part of the course was offered at a number of different Army hospitals during 1942, 1943, 1944, and 1945.

PHYSICAL THERAPY COURSE FOR WACS

The course described above did not attract enough students to meet the increased demand for physical therapists, and an additional emergency course was set up in the fall of 1943. This was opened to enlisted Wacs who wished to qualify as physical therapists in the Medical Department. Upon successful completion of the course, they were discharged from the WAC and commissioned as Medical Department physical therapists with the rank of second lieutenant in the Army of the United States. An applicant for admission to the course had to meet the following qualifications: completion of basic training at a WAC training center, graduation from an accredited school of physical education or two years in an approved college with emphasis on biological and physical sciences, age less than thirty-eight, an AGCT score of not less than 110, and ability to meet the physical requirements for a commission as a Medical Department physical therapist.

The program of instruction for WAC personnel was twenty-six weeks in length, with 48 hours of work each week. The 1,248 hours of instruction were divided as follows:

Concurrent basic military training .... 156 hours
Physical conditioning 78
Technical courses:
  Human anatomy 200
  Bandaging 35
  Dermatology 5
  Electrotherapy and electrophysics 75
  Hospital ethics 5
  Hydrotherapy 35
  Massage 90
  Muscle and sensory tests 35
  Neuropsychiatry 20
  Pathology 25
  Physical therapy and orthopedics 65
  Physiology 30
  Phototherapy 40
  Principles of general medicine 15
  Principles of general surgery 15
  Therapeutic exercise and measurements ... 100
  Clinical practice (under the direct supervision of a Medical Department physical therapist) 200
  Open and make-up time 24

After three months of instruction, if the student demonstrated unsuitability or if she could not meet the scholastic or physical requirements, the situation was reported to the Surgeon General with the recommendation that she be returned to her original post.

An apprenticeship period of twelve weeks (as contrasted with the twenty-six-week period required for the civilian trainees enrolled in the program which had been in operation since 1941) followed the six months of professional training. During apprenticeship, both WAC and civilian students had practice in the actual treatment of patients who had received war injuries such as amputations, peripheral nerve injuries, burns, and fractures with complications. Students attended selected ward rounds and professional conferences.

The course for civilians was conducted on a Medical Department level by agreement with the Civil Service Commission, and the course for Wacs was cleared through, and approved by, the Division of Military Training, Army Service Forces. After June 1944 the course for Wacs led to a commission and it was listed as an officer-candidate course; but in the same publication, the course for civilians was not so listed even though commissions were granted to its graduates who were accepted by the Army.

By January 1946 a total of 190 civilians and 581 Wacs had been graduated from the student-level courses and had qualified for apprenticeship training prerequisite to appointment as commissioned physical therapists in the Medical Department. After 1944 courses were discontinued at several Army hospitals as the procurement needs for physical therapists were met.

TRAINING FOR OVERSEAS DUTY

In April 1944 when physical therapists in the Medical Department began to be assigned to overseas duty in considerable numbers, a special order directed that all such officers who were less than forty-five years old and who were physically qualified for overseas duty in numbered medical units should attend the basic training centers for Army nurses. The nurses' course was modified by the deletion of 23 hours of professional training useful only to nurses and the substitution of an equal number of hours in courses in the field of physical therapy: organization and functions of physical therapy service, physical therapy equipment, special records and charts, and clinical practice and study (15 hours).

On June 16, 1945, a modification of the basic training program for physical therapists eliminated 43 hours of nursing training and substituted the following: organization and functions of Medical Department physical therapy service, clinic instruction and duty (41 hours).

All newly commissioned physical therapists received this training. The 43 hours of professional work were given by or under the supervision of a Medical Department physical therapist. The training time allotted to "clinic instruction and duty" was devoted to actual on-the-job training in the physical therapy clinic of the hospital, because the small number of trainees involved made that type of training possible.

By September 1945, 439 physical therapists had attended the basic training courses. At the peak in the summer of 1945 there were approximately 1,300 physical therapists in the Medical Department.

During the months of May through July 1945, groups of enlisted Wacs were trained in twelve Army general hospitals in the duties of physical therapy technicians. Requirement for attendance was satisfactory completion of not less than two months in a Medical Department training course for surgical and medical technicians. This four-week course did not lead to a commission; the students who completed it were qualified only to serve as aides to trained personnel. Four hundred and two Wacs took the course.

TECHNICIANS

Medical Department schools first accepted enlisted women as students in September 1943. Five technicians' courses were offered—laboratory, X-ray, dental, medical, and surgical. They varied in length, were given at many hospitals, and in general were identical with the technical courses provided for enlisted men, although in most cases separate classes for Wacs were conducted. Some six thousand women completed the courses. The graduates served as replacements for male technicians needed to staff general hospitals for overseas service.

In 1944 some Negro Wacs were trained as Medical Department technicians at the station hospital in Fort Huachuca, Arizona. Eighty-five women completed the courses. At the end of the year, however, the technical training for Negro Wacs at Fort Huachuca was discontinued, and after that date colored and white personnel were trained without separation.

WAC enlisted medical and surgical technicians were used in large numbers in Army hospitals. Their formal training was concluded before assignment to duty, but a considerable amount of on-the-job training was carried on. The duties of technicians were strictly limited, and they were under the direct supervision and control of graduate nurses.

In the early months of 1945, spurred by critical shortages of trained hospital personnel to care for the battle casualties pouring into the general hospitals in this country, the WAC began a recruiting campaign to enlist women for training as medical technicians and medical clerks to be assigned to ward duty in Army general hospitals in the United States. Army Service Forces provided the training program which was carried out at the Third WAC Training Center, Fort Oglethorpe, Georgia.

Administration, discipline, supply, mess, and all functions of the training center except actual instruction in the medical and surgical technician course, were performed by the training center staff for medical trainees in exactly the same manner as for other WAC trainees. The training center staff provided basic military training and medical clerical training for the whole group. A special staff of 41 Medical Department officers, 25 Army nurses, 54 Medical Department enlisted men, and 84 enlisted women provided training in the medical and surgical technician course. A special intensive ten-day instructor-training program was provided for all instructor personnel during the initial operation of the program while the training load was light. Three days were used for briefing on medical subjects to be taught, and for indicating objectives and points of emphasis. The remaining time was used for instruction in teaching techniques, preparation of lesson plans, use of training aids, and practice instruction. In the practice instruction 5- to 15-minute presentations were conducted by individuals and were recorded and used in critiques.

Over six thousand recruits underwent this training; 4,969 completed the medical and surgical technicians' course and 1,304 completed the course for medical clerks.

The medical technician's training course consisted of four and one-half weeks of basic military training, one month of technical training, and on-the-job training in the general hospital of assignment. The technical training consisted of the following:

Anatomy and physiology	35 hours
Emergency medical treatment	35
Hygiene and prevention of disease	26
Public property	3
Ward procedures	67
Mathematics and materia medica	24
Ward management	8
General training in hospital procedures	38

The course for medical clerks took the same length of time, and the training consisted chiefly of the following:

Touch typing	60 hours
Correspondence and filing	25
Company records	14
Medical records and reports	45
Personnel administration	20
Finance	11
Organization and administration of general hospitals	7
Company supply	6
Medical supply	15

ORDERLIES

An "opportunity" school conducted at the first WAC training center for WAC enlisted personnel with low AGCT scores was discontinued in August 1944. At that time, Headquarters, Army Service Forces, requested the Surgeon General to provide a course of predominantly applicatory training in hospital orderly duties for such personnel. The Training Division, Office of the Surgeon General, developed a program consisting of 48 hours of concurrent basic military training, 48 hours of training in basic technical subjects, and 288 hours of essentially apprentice-type training designed to qualify the student to assist nurses in routine ward duties. The program was assigned to two general hospitals, and each hospital graduated only one class. The students were found inept for hospital duties and they could not replace male hospital orderlies on the wards. The total number of students completing the course was 140.

WOMEN IN THE SANITARY CORPS

During the last three months of 1944, a small group of enlisted Wacs was commissioned in the WAC and immediately detailed to the Sanitary Corps for duty in the Medical Department laboratories.

These women had been biochemists, serologists, and bacteriologists in civil life. A special two-week orientation program was offered, and 31 newly commissioned WAC second lieutenants completed the course. The program, which was written in the Training Division of the Office of the Surgeon General, devoted the first week to a miscellany of lectures on almost thirty subjects bearing upon Army organization and the functions and duties of officers. The second week was devoted almost exclusively to instruction in approved methods and procedures for operating Medical Department laboratories and performing laboratory tests and analyses. The women officers in the Sanitary Corps were usually assigned to duty as laboratory superintendents.

RECONDITIONING COURSES

The Army's training courses in occupational therapy and educational reconditioning were part of a comprehensive reconditioning program in the Office of the Surgeon General. The program was under the immediate control of the Reconditioning Consultants Division which was organized in three branches— educational reconditioning, occupational therapy, and physical reconditioning. In a particular hospital this organizational pattern was repeated through a chief of reconditioning service as the head of three functional branches.

The Surgeon General, in describing the mission of this service, stated:

. . . the purpose of the reconditioning program is to accelerate the return to duty of convalescent soldiers in the highest state of physical and mental efficiency consistent with their capacities and the type of duty to which they will be assigned. Or, if the soldier is disqualified for further military service, the reconditioning program must provide for his return to civilian life, conditioned to the highest possible degree of physical fitness, well oriented in the responsibilities of citizenship, and prepared to adjust successfully to social and vocational pursuits. The mission is accomplished by a coordinated program of educational reconditioning, physical reconditioning and occupational therapy.

He defined the specific missions of the three branches as follows:

Educational reconditioning is the process of exciting, stimulating and activating the minds of convalescent patients through education, orientation, and information, thereby encouraging mental attitudes conducive to health and normal activity. . . . Physical reconditioning is the process by which physical and psychological fitness is maintained and restored through participation in progressively graded physical activities during convalescence. . . . Occupational therapy is that form of treatment characterized by assignment to purposeful physical tasks and prescribed by a medical officer.

Its principal values lie in physical, mental, social, and economic results.

In December 1944 three War Department Technical Manuals (TM8-290, TM8-291, and TM8-292) were published. They describe in detail, respectively, the programs of educational reconditioning, occupational therapy, and physical reconditioning. They are well written and well illustrated and would be of real interest to a lay reader.

The extent of participation by women in the three branches of the reconditioning program varied widely. No women were trained or utilized as personnel in physical reconditioning.

EDUCATIONAL RECONDITIONING

At the School for Personnel Services at Washington and Lee University, Lexington, Virginia, enlisted and commissioned men and women were given training in educational reconditioning. The course was four weeks long and was open to women from August 1944 to October 1945. During that period 298 enlisted Wacs and 59 WAC officers completed the course. This was an Army Service Forces school which was in operation at the time when the Office of the Surgeon General determined to initiate a course in educational reconditioning, and through coordinating activities the Surgeon General was enabled to use the school staff and facilities for the training of this special group.

The course included instruction in educational methodology; orientation activities; recreational activities, including dramatics, radio programs, and music; and the philosophy and methodology of guidance and prevocational counseling. Preparation was planned for officer and enlisted personnel who would be working in a program of wide scope.

The educational reconditioning of convalescent soldiers involved consideration of current conditions at home and abroad, including reviews of the progress of the war, refresher military training, and general informational and cultural courses, as well as more specific training and study. The necessity of offering education suited to the needs, abilities, and desires of the soldiers was constantly emphasized, and the effort was made to "create in the hospital, through every possible means, occasions and an atmosphere where learning is inescapable." Cooperation with the chaplain, ward officer, personal-affairs officer, Red Cross aides, information and education division, Army off-duty educational agencies, and various civilian government agencies was necessary during all phases of the program. The patients were carefully screened in order that opportunities available to them might be fitted to specific interests, ambitions, abilities, and physical conditions.

OCCUPATIONAL THERAPY

Although they retained their civilian status, it has seemed suitable to include women who served as occupational therapists in Army hospitals because in other respects their training, work, and status were like that of servicewomen in the Medical Department.

The process of training women as occupational therapists was somewhat complicated. Three different types of courses were offered in this field—two for civilian women and one for enlisted Wacs. The number of occupational therapists in the employment of the Medical Department increased very slowly during 1942 and 1943. These civilian women had been recruited by the

Civil Service Commission, certified to the Surgeon General for selection, and then assigned to work in Army hospitals as civilians. The first formal provision for their orientation into military service began in October 1943 when the commanding generals of the nine service commands assigned all newly appointed occupational therapists to attend one of the three orientation courses (at Lovell General Hospital, Fort Devens, Massachusetts; Lawson General Hospital, Atlanta, Georgia; and Letterman General Hospital, Presidio of San Francisco, California). The two-week course was planned to make newly appointed personnel familiar with the organization of the Army, the Medical Department, and Army hospitals, and with the particular problems of the care and treatment of sick and wounded military personnel. Occupational therapists who had been assigned before October 1943 were also required to take this course. Upon its completion, personnel reported to the general hospital of permanent assignment. The course was discontinued in July 1944. By that time all heads of the service in Army hospitals had been trained, and they in turn could train newly appointed members of their own staffs. Approximately 150 civilian women took this course.

By June 1944 it had become impossible to recruit a sufficient number of trained women to fill the need for occupational therapists, and an emergency training course was initiated. In order that this course could be relatively short to meet the urgent need, the qualifications provided that students must be graduates of an accredited college or university, with a major in industrial, fine, or applied arts, and that they must have knowledge of at least three manual skills. The training consisted of two parts: four months' attendance at one of eight civilian schools which had contracted with the Surgeon General to provide such instruction, followed by an eight-month assignment to an Army general hospital for a period of practical experience under trained supervision. At the end of the twelve-month training period the student took the examination for professional registration with the American Occupational Therapy Association and was qualified for appointment as an occupational therapist. The course of instruction was prepared by the Training Division of the Medical

Department; the first four months of training were under staff supervision by the Office of the Surgeon General, and the clinical training program was supervised at the command level.

The curriculum included the following subjects:

Organization and administration

Orientation and indoctrination:

> Organization of the Army and the Medical Department; evacuation of sick and wounded; the functions, organization, and operation of ASF hospitals; military courtesy and discipline; safeguarding military information; professional and hospital ethics; Army regulations and other directives; directives pertaining to the occupational therapist; organization and operation of the reconditioning program; staff procedure and interdepartmental relationships; organization and administration of an occupational therapy department; civilian personnel in military hospitals.

Interpretation of volunteer diversional programs:

> Red Cross, including arts and skills; function of volunteer activities; arts and skills shop; other uses of volunteer service; administration and supervision of volunteers; exploration of craft techniques.

Treatment procedures:

> Occupational therapy in the fields of physical function, incoordination, neuropsychiatry, and industrial (work) therapy.

Specialization:

> During this period the student received further instruction and training in a given field, according to her demonstrated aptitude and ability: orthopedic, neuropsychiatric, industrial therapy, general medicine, amputation, blind, tuberculosis, neurosurgery, plastic surgery.

By December 1945, 605 students had completed the four-month didactic course, and 225 had completed the entire twelve-month course.

From December 1944 to October 1945 a four-week course of training for assistants in occupational therapy was offered at Halloran General Hospital for women who had been recruited into the WAC for the special program. Other qualified enlisted women could request assignment to the course. Qualifications consisted of teaching experience plus some knowledge of a handicraft, or expert ability in some handicraft plus a high school education and some aptitude for teaching.

The course was developed in the Training Division, Office of the Surgeon General, and it included 162 hours of essentially applicatory training in crafts and skills useful in the rehabilitation of convalescent patients, 12 hours of calisthenics and supervised recreational-type conditioning exercises, 3 hours of make-up work, and 15 hours of lectures on the function of occupational therapy in Medical Department hospitals. The 265 Wacs who completed the course successfully were assigned as assistants to civilian occupational therapists in Army hospitals and convalescent centers.

VIII. WOMEN IN THE NAVY NURSE CORPS AND THE HOSPITAL CORPS

THE Navy Nurse Corps and the Hospital Corps were administered directly by the Surgeon General, chief of the Bureau of Medicine and Surgery. The Training Branch in the Professional Division of this Bureau delegated large powers over their respective training programs to these two corps during the war, and it is correct to state that the development of these training programs was their own responsibility. The Navy Nurse Corps training program had two phases—the indoctrination of civilian nurses who joined the corps, and the specialist training of members of the corps. In the Hospital Corps the program involved the training of members of the Women's Reserve in various specialties to serve as technicians and assistants to fully qualified professional personnel.

THE NAVY NURSE CORPS

The first trained nurses in the Navy, though they did not constitute an official unit, were a group of women employed at the Naval Hospital, Norfolk, Virginia, in 1898, to care for the sick and wounded of the Spanish-American War. They served for fifty days and were eventually paid for their services, but they were neither enrolled nor enlisted, nor even sure of payment during the time of their service. At various later times the Navy employed nurses on a contract basis to meet nursing needs in certain naval facilities. Upon the establishment of the Nurse Corps as an integral unit of the Navy in 1908, nurses were assigned to duty in the Naval Medical School Hospital in Washington, D. C. Within a few years they were also receiving orders for duty in other naval hospitals in the United States, the Philippine Islands, Guam, Honolulu, Yokohama, Samoa, the Virgin Islands, Haiti, and Guantanamo Bay, Cuba. As the only women in the Navy, the nurses were a unique group. They were neither officers nor enlisted personnel, yet they had a military rather than a civilian status. They were legally recognized as members of the naval service and were amenable to naval discipline.

During World War I, 1,224 Navy nurses served in hospitals in the United States and 327 nurses served in England, Ireland, Scotland, France, Japan, and our island possessions. With the general reduction of American military forces after the war, the size of the Navy Nurse Corps was reduced, and there were only 332 members in 1935. Throughout this period of retrenchment no nurses were enrolled in the Reserve corps.

In 1939, shortly after war began in Europe, military preparation began in the United States. Under the authority of the Naval Reserve Act qualified nurses were recruited, and the membership of the Regular Nurse Corps was increased. On July 31, 1945, a fortnight before the surrender of Japan, the grand total of nurses was 11,021, of whom 1,799 were in the Regular corps and 9,222 were in the Reserve.

Shortly after the end of the war (September 30, 1945) the following statistics were published. The total number of Navy nurses was 10,914. Those serving ashore, in continental United States, numbered 9,121; outside continental United States, 1,495; with Air Evacuation Service, 108; on hospital ships, 298. The number of stations at which Navy nurses were serving was 318; of these, 263 were in continental United States, 43 were outside continental United States, and 12 were hospital ships. Nurses served outside the United States in the Admiralties, Africa, Alaska, Australia, Bermuda, Brazil, Cuba, England, the Hawaiian Islands, the Marianas, New Caledonia, New Guinea, Newfoundland, Okinawa, the Panama Canal Zone, the Philippines, Puerto Rico, the Russell Islands, Samoa, and Trinidad.

In the Navy Nurse Corps during World War II there were opportunities for the exercise of many different skills and abilities. The teaching and supervision of young men from the Navy who were assigned as hospital corpsmen, of young women from the WAVES assigned to the Hospital Corps, and of senior cadets from the Cadet Nurse Corps, formed a most important part of the work of the Navy nurses. To assist the medical officers in carrying out complex modern surgical and medical procedures, the corps provided nurses with the most advanced training and experience in such specialties as surgery, orthopedics, physical therapy, occupational therapy, dietetics, anesthesia, and psychiatric nursing.

Special courses were provided in teaching and ward administration and in operating-room technique and management. The schools for training native nurses on Samoa and Guam were in existence before the war and, in spite of interruptions during the war, they continued to furnish a valuable service. A considerable number of Navy nurses received special training to serve in the Air Evacuation Service. Transcontinental trips with the wounded were made and in early 1945 teams were sent to the Pacific area. Nurses were assigned to three main flights of air evacuation planes: from target areas to forward hospitals, from these hospitals to Pearl Harbor, and from Pearl Harbor to the United States. Navy nurses were also assigned to hospital ships. The military awards to Navy nurses, as of May 1, 1946, totaled 184.

The requirements for admission to the Navy Nurse Corps were that the candidate should be an American citizen of good character, unmarried, a high school graduate, a graduate of an accredited school of nursing, and registered in her profession. For the Regular corps the age limits were twenty-two to twenty-eight years, and for the Reserve corps twenty-one to forty years. The candidate was required to pass a physical examination.

Further recognition came to the corps through legislation which improved its status in the service. In 1942 Congress granted nurses the permanent relative rank of commissioned officers and corresponding base pay and, with some exceptions, allowances. In 1944 the latter omissions were corrected, and Congress provided that during the war and for six months after, Navy nurses should have actual commissioned rank. Legislation was proposed in May 1946 and enacted April 16, 1947, to make commissioned rank permanent after expiration of the wartime legislation.[1] The nurse in the Navy organization is invested with authority next after commissioned officers of the Medical, Dental, and Medical Services Corps in all medical and sanitary matters.

[1] Public Law 36, Chap. 38, 1st Sess. 80th Cong., known as Army and Navy Nurses Act of 1947.

The policy of the corps at all times has been to enlist only fully qualified graduate civilian nurses and no modification of the policy occurred during the war. The corps had always conducted "orientation" or "indoctrination" courses for newly enlisted nurses, to acquaint them with procedures in naval hospitals and with Navy customs and etiquette. The only changes which occurred during the war were the results of the rapid increase in nurse personnel and the necessity of handling a greatly increased case load in naval hospitals. Indoctrination courses became more formal, and the training of nurses in various specialties was made necessary when such specialists were needed in increased numbers and could not be made available through recruiting. In turn, the nurses themselves were called upon to do more teaching and training as the numbers of male corpsmen, WAVES corpsmen, and senior cadets increased.

During the first part of the war newly enlisted nurses who were assigned to east coast stations first went to the Norfolk Naval Hospital at Portsmouth, Virginia, for an intensive orientation period of three weeks. Naval hospitals in other parts of the country conducted similar courses for nurses assigned to them, and after December 1943 the Norfolk hospital indoctrinated only its own nurses. In January 1945 a new plan of initial assignment to the indoctrination course in one of nine hospitals was inaugurated, and the effort was made to standardize these courses in all hospitals. A description of the course at the Norfolk hospital will serve as explanation of the type of program set up in the various hospitals during the war period.

INDOCTRINATION COURSES

Every three weeks a new class of nurses was received at the Norfolk hospital and, after a two-week program of instruction and certain formal processing they went to their respective duty posts. The course of instruction included drill (20 hours), lectures (22 hours), and ward management lectures and demonstrations (21 hours).

The lectures were planned to familiarize newly inducted officers in the corps with Navy customs and traditions and they covered the following subjects: introduction to the program, introduction to and historical survey of the Nurse Corps, uniform regulations, rules and regulations regarding the Nurse Corps, military customs and traditions, subversive activity, chemical warfare, government insurance and allotments, dependent's unit and sick officers' quarters, status of Officer of the Day and Master-at-Arms as related to nurse and patient, Hospital Corps School, and nurses' quarters.

These lectures were given by different members of the staff of the hospital. The course in ward management was planned to familiarize the new members of the corps with policies and routine regarding medical and nursing care of the sick in naval hospitals, and correlation between lectures and actual ward work was managed in so far as possible. The course included the following subjects: lectures on ward management, including the keeping of reports, demonstrations of nursing procedures as carried out in naval hospitals, model sick call on selected wards, central dressing room and operating room demonstrations of preparation and administration of various treatments and medications, linen room, diets, medical storeroom, ward duty (six hours) on selected wards, and four of the compound and various departments of the hospital.

The indoctrination course for all newly inducted nurses who were assigned to the naval hospital in Philadelphia for permanent duty lasted for three weeks, and included all nurses on day duty. The course was similar to that offered in Norfolk hospital, described above, with some variations. Drill occupied twelve hours and swimming lessons began one month after reporting for duty. Classes included ward supervision and management (twelve hours), Navy forms and records (six hours), Navy etiquette and traditions in the Nurse Corps (six hours), special departments in the hospital (six hours), chemical warfare and fire control (six hours), psychiatric nursing (five hours), ward supervision and ward conferences. Many films were used in this program, including "The Teacher," corpsmen's instruction films, eight films on Navy etiquette and tradition, films on chemical warfare, fire control, psychiatry, combat fatigue, swimming, and castaway.

It is impossible to give accurate figures as to the numbers of nurses who took indoctrination courses similar to the two described above, during the war period. The number of Navy nurses processed during World War II was 13,325, and it is safe to assume that all, or practically all, of them took indoctrination courses.

NURSING SPECIALTIES

Modern medicine and surgery have made necessary the training of nurses in various specialties, and the Navy has provided such training, both in its own and in civilian hospitals, for many years. The variety of training in nursing specialties in the Navy before, during, and after World War II embraced those of flight nurse, air evacuation; anesthesiology; dietetics; occupational therapy; operation-room technic and management; physical therapy; psychiatric nursing; and teaching and ward administration.

In most cases a need arose for a special type of nursing and, in the absence of personnel trained in the particular specialty, a quota of nurses, selected because they were judged to be competent, was given intensive training, very often "on the job," in a naval or civilian hospital.

After 1941 approximately thirty Navy nurses a year were given a four-month course in psychiatric nursing in St. Elizabeth's Hospital in Washington, D. C. In the summer of 1943, twelve nurses took a three-month course in anesthesiology at the Lahey Clinic in Boston. Beginning in 1941 a separate unit of nurses (from ten to thirty) was trained in dietetics each year by the faculty of George Washington University. These examples will serve to illustrate the manner in which specialist nursing training was conducted.

An indoctrination course for flight nurses was begun in January 1945. Such nurses formed part of a squadron complement assigned to an Air Evacuation Squadron of medical personnel operating in the Naval Air Evacuation Service. Wounded men who were brought to the United States from the Pacific war theater and who were then transported within the United States to suitable hospitals, were brought in Navy planes in those cases in which speed of transportation was necessary. Each "flying ambulance" squadron had its complement, and women nurses were assigned to duty in this service in 1945 for the first time. A complement consisted of a flight surgeon, a hospital corps officer, twenty-four flight nurses, and twenty-four male pharmacist's mates. Nurses first completed an indoctrination course of basic classroom instruction followed by practical flight indoctrination, and were then assigned to duty in the continental United States aboard regular hospital flights of the Naval Air Transport Service, and eventually they went to the Pacific to serve in the newly formed Naval Air Evacuation Service. One hundred and eight nurses were on duty with this service in September 1945. The flight nurse in charge was Lt. (jg) Mary Ellen O'Connor, who had joined the Nurse Corps in 1943. She had been a stewardess for seven years, and a flight instructor for three years, with United Air Lines, and she held the record for American women for miles in the air (2.5 million) and hours in the air (8,800).

The syllabus of instruction for training of an Air Evacuation Squadron complement provided classroom lectures and demonstrations with audio-visual aids relating to the medical aspects of the air transport of patients; survival training and preparation for overseas duty; and flight indoctrination training in connection with the air transport of patients.

The one great change in the training program in nursing specialties after the war is that of emphasis upon full accreditation for all courses offered to the Navy's nurses in well-qualified civilian institutions—hospitals and universities. The nurses will be recognized specialists upon successful completion of any one of the courses among those continued after the war. Flight training, as above described, is being continued, though on a much smaller scale than in wartime.

THE HOSPITAL CORPS

In the introduction to the present chapter a brief mention was made of the position of members of the Women's Reserve (WAVES) in the training program of the Hospital Corps of the Navy Bureau of Medicine and Surgery. It would be difficult, if not impossible, to describe the training of women in this corps without describing the training for men because there was no separation of the two groups in the training program. Such an apparently simple matter as determining the number of Waves who took particular courses is difficult because even the records of admissions, grades, and completions were made up without classification on the basis of sex. In June 1945 a comprehensive questionnaire requesting data on Hospital Corps WAVES personnel was prepared, the results to be used in allocating an increased number of Hospital Corps Waves to be procured during the coming year. A medical officer of the Women's Reserve was assigned to duty in the Bureau of Medicine and Surgery as adviser to the chief, in connection with problems involving WAVES personnel, and she was to act as liaison officer between the Bureau and the director of the Women's Reserve in the Bureau of Naval Personnel. The end of the war, however, brought the suspension of the training program for Waves, and the questionnaire study was cancelled.

THE TRAINING AND USE OF WAVES CORPSMEN

The organization of the training program of the Hospital Corps was set forth in the revised (1944) *Catalog of Hospital Corps Schools and Courses,* published by the Bureau of Medicine and Surgery, Navy Department. Women did not enter the courses directly from civilian life. All Waves enlisted as apprentice seamen, to serve for the duration of the war and six months after. If a candidate was considered qualified by her civilian experience and training, she was accepted as a technician in the Hospital Corps and she then spent six weeks in recruit training. Upon completion of basic training she was rated as hospital apprentice second class, and oriented through the department of her specialty in a naval hospital, before assignment to duty. Applicants without previous training were accepted under the designation "regular service" and, upon completion of basic recruit training, they were rated as hospital apprentice second class, and given a special Hospital Corps course in anatomy, physiology, first aid, minor surgery, hygiene, sanitation, and nursing. After this course they were rated and assigned to duty.

The ratings for both groups of women were hospital apprentice second class, hospital apprentice first class, pharmacist's mate third class, or pharmacist's mate second class, depending upon age, professional qualifications, and suitability for service. Further advancement to pharmacist's mate first class, and chief pharmacist's mate was possible. After proper service, Waves who possessed appropriate qualifications were eligible to enter one of the special advanced courses maintained for the purpose of expanding the professional capacities of the personnel of the Hospital Corps. Advanced courses for officers in the Hospital Corps were also open to WAVES officer personnel.

Table 17 indicates the courses to which Waves were assigned and the numbers of women who completed the courses successfully.

TABLE 17

NUMBERS OF WAVES COMPLETING NAVY HOSPITAL CORPS SPECIALIZATION COURSES, V-10

Courses	Graduates
Acrylic eye illustrating	9
Clerical procedures (6 months)	158
Clinical laboratory technology (6 months)	380
Commissary assistant (6 months)	13
Dental technology general (10 weeks)	1,007
Dental technology prosthetic (6 months)	4
Electrocardiography and basal metabolism	91
Electroencephalography	18
Fever therapy (3 months)	2
Low-pressure chamber (3 months)	197
Neuropsychiatry nursing (4 months)	64
Neuropsychiatric clerical procedures (4 months)	218
Occupational therapy (3 months)	253
Operating-room technic (6 months)	222
Photomicrography	5
Physical therapy (3 months)	290
Property and accounting (6 months)	145
Spectacle dispensing	22
X-ray technique (5 months)	101
X-ray and photofluoroscopy	6
Total	3,205

The 1944 *Catalog* of the Hospital Corps listed four advanced courses for officers: office administration, commissary administration, property and accounting administration, and a special war emergency course in hospital administration. Specialization courses open to enlisted personnel were also listed. Upon completion of a course the graduate was awarded a certificate and was carried on the rolls of the Hospital Corps as a technician or qualified assistant.

On June 30, 1945, 42 officers of the WAVES had been assigned to the Medical Corps, 409 to the Hospital Corps, and 2 to the Dental Corps in the Bureau of Medicine and Surgery. On the same date about 13,000 Waves were in the Hospital Corps and, in addition, about half of the 2,000 new recruits enlisted each month were selected to enter the Hospital Corps after completing recruit school.

TRAINING AT A LARGE NAVAL HOSPITAL

A most interesting article (unpublished) on training WAVES corpsmen was written by Lt. (jg) Margaret H. Wolff (NC), USNR, who described the program as she saw it in operation in the naval hospital in Philadelphia. It was said that the program of instruction which was sent from Washington seemed an almost impossible undertaking, because to expect untrained women to assimilate and later be able to use, without confusion, so much nursing information "would seem to defy all the principles of education. It was a fearsome challenge."

The daily schedule for trainees was planned, and unused space at the top of a hospital wing was converted into a classroom. For illustrated lectures and demonstrations the hospital auditorium was used. She continued:

Our biggest task, by far, was the setting up of our educational program. Before making plans for the classes, we paused to define our objectives. Just what did we want these young women to do? What was to be considered essential and what could be deleted in this accelerated program for WAVES trainees? For our ultimate aim, we chose the following: "To develop in these young women the ability to observe closely, report intelligently, and carry out simple nursing procedures with consideration of comfort and safety to the patient." The objectives, to so train her, are that she shall have the ability to: (a) care for the environment of the patient; (b) make neat and comfortable beds, both routine and emergency; (c) admit patients, care for their gear, bathe and render physical and mental comfort; (*d*) take and record temperature, pulse, and respiration; and (*e*) assist the nurse in administration of drugs, take blood pressure, collect specimens and deliver them to the laboratory, give treatments ordered, chart, transport patients with comfort and safety, and discharge or transfer patients.

Appreciating how very carefully we should have to plan our work in order for these WAVES trainees to derive a clear understanding of the work, we felt it would be helpful to present this mass of subject matter in the same chronological order in which the corpsmen would be called upon to admit, care for, and then discharge a patient on the wards. On this basis, the nursing classes were arranged as follows:

Unit One: The Environment; Ward Routines
Unit Two: Admission of the Patient
Unit Three: General Care and Treatment of Medical Patients
Unit Four: Diets in a Naval Hospital
Unit Five: Demonstration and Review
Unit Six: Nursing Consideration in the Administration of Drugs
Unit Seven: Care of the Surgical Patient
Unit Eight: Discharge of the Patient
Unit Nine: Final Demonstration

Methods of instruction included lectures, study guide sheets, demonstrations, educational films from the Bureau of Medicine and Surgery, and trips to various hospital departments. A short written review was given four times a week and the corrected papers were returned the next day. Individual demonstration reviews were arranged, and members of the class other than the demonstrator criticized the work.

Although the Waves received supervised ward experience during the course, it was not considered to be enough to be satisfactory because so much was to be learned in so short a time.

It was felt that a dramatization of work covered would enable the student to see the segregated parts presented together, giving unification to her studies. It is no mean task to plan a series of demonstrations in this manner for twenty-some girls, and work each part into a unified whole. There is, admittedly, much to criticize about our method, yet I am convinced that good results are obtained, and for that reason we use this arduous form of review.

The article contains a copy of the three-page instructions given to students to enable them to prepare for the group demonstrations. Students wrote their own plays and rehearsed them, making training in teamwork one of the products of the project. The dramatized demonstrations were presented to the commanding and executive officers, and the medical and nursing staffs. Members of the class wrote group criticisms of the dramatizations and chairmen of the groups gave the summaries to all the trainees.

Nineteen films on various aspects of nursing and first aid were used. These films and one on weights and measures were prepared by the Bureau of Aeronautics, Photographic Section, Training Film Unit. Examinations were given on the films which were shown in the first-aid course.

Ward practice periods were held four afternoons each week. The class was divided into groups of five to eight and each group was assigned to a designated nurse. They tried to choose nurses for this teaching who had had ward teaching experience, but the teaching program continually suffered because of frequent changes in personnel. To remove part of the undesirable results of such changes an instruction sheet for ward teachers was prepared, and a considerable amount of assistance was given to them in the effort to maintain the quality and the uniformity of instruction.

Lieutenant Wolff's article concluded with a discussion of the values of the teaching program and its effect on the profession of nursing in the postwar period. This discussion is quoted in chapter x of this book.

TRAINING AT NATIONAL NAVAL MEDICAL CENTER

An article entitled "Hospital Corps WAVES" by Annabelle R. Decker, PhM 1c (W) USNR, in the magazine *Hospital Corps Quarterly* for June 1945 contains a good brief account of the work of WAVES corpsmen:

In September 1942 the Bureau of Medicine and Surgery recommended that Waves be enlisted in the Hospital Corps in order to relieve male technicians for assignment to sea duty and to medical department activities beyond the continental limits of the United States and with the U. S. Marine Corps. It was also recommended that 50 percent of the qualified technicians in medical department specialties be replaced by personnel of the Women's Reserve.

In December 1942 approximately 100 professionally qualified women technicians in the fields of clinical laboratory, dental technology, both general and prosthetic, X-ray, physical therapy and occupational therapy, who had enlisted as apprentice seamen were ordered to report to the State Teachers College, Cedar Falls, Iowa, for their indoctrination period of approximately five weeks. After successful completion of this indoctrination period the group was divided equally and transferred to the Naval hospitals at San Diego, California, and the National Naval Medical Center, Bethesda, Md., for a further period of approximately four weeks orientation in the duties of their rating.

Upon completion of this course, they were given a suitable rating and assigned to active duty in shore establishments. In February 1943 the Bureau of Medicine and Surgery requested that approximately 600 women be enlisted each month for assignment to duty in the Hospital Corps. It became necessary to train Waves to replace approximately 25 percent of male corpsmen on duty within the continental limits. Women who had any training or experience in civilian life which would give them special ability were urged to enlist. After recruit training they were rated and ordered to naval hospitals for a four-week training course in the general duties of the Hospital Corps. Training of Hospital Corps Waves was conducted at seventeen different naval hospitals and 6,000 Navy women were trained and placed on duty in the Hospital Corps.

The curriculum for the first special Hospital Corps School for enlisted Waves included the following courses:

	Classroom Hours	Supervised Study	Total Hours
Anatomy and physiology......	16½	2	18½
First aid and minor surgery....	16½	2	18½
Hygiene and sanitation........	16½	2	18½
Weights and measures........	8¼	1	9¼
Materia medica..............	8¼	1	9¼
Nursing (including use of 11 films on nursing procedures).	57	6	63
Total..................	123	14	137

In January 1944 the first special Hospital Corps School for enlisted members of the Women's Reserve was commissioned at the National Naval Medical Center, Bethesda, Md. A four-week course in anatomy and physiology, first aid and minor surgery, hygiene and sanitation, nursing, metrology and pharmacology, plus three weeks active ward duty, constituted the basic professional training. Until recently a quota of 240 enlisted women entered the Hospital Corps School every two weeks. (At the present writing the course has been extended to sixteen weeks.) Those women who were already qualified by civilian experience as technicians, laboratory assistants, or nurses aides were sent directly from "boot camp" at Hunter College, N. Y., to the St. Albans or San Diego naval hospitals, for special courses.

There are two references to be consulted if the reader wishes to study in more detail the Hospital Corps schools and courses of the war period. The 1944 revised edition of the *Catalog* of the corps, an 83-page document, includes an explanatory foreword, summary tables of the various courses, and full description of the basic course leading to a Hospital Corps Certificate, and the intermediate, specialization and advanced courses. At least half of the *Catalog* is used for outline statements of all courses in the thirty departments of the corps. In the foreword, responsible officers were directed to insure that instruction in all courses described in the *Catalog* conform to the minimum outlines provided. All the courses were established on a peacetime basis but some had been accelerated to meet wartime needs (these are indicated in the *Catalog*). When acceleration was indicated the scope of the course was not changed but the required hours of instruction in all subjects were to be modified proportionately. Of the thirty-one courses listed, approximately half were accelerated for the war period. Outlines of courses were considered to be minimum coverage but it was expected that the actual instruction would elaborate and expand upon the outlines as indicated by the needs of the personnel under instruction. It was further desired that pertinent audio-visual and other appropriate teaching aids be utilized to the extent practicable to achieve the maximum efficiency of instruction. These orders were issued over the signature of the Surgeon General of the Navy.

The June 1945 issue of *Hospital Corps Quarterly* was a special education number, and some fifty pages were devoted to numerous short articles on various aspects of the schools and courses of the Hospital Corps. The issue is well illustrated. One article dealt specifically with training of corpsmen from the WAVES.

IX. THE CADET NURSE CORPS OF THE PUBLIC HEALTH SERVICE

ALTHOUGH the United States was not an active belligerent in World War II until December 1941, planning for an increase in the national supply of nurses was recognized in 1940–41 as a necessity in view of the strong possibility that we would be participants in the war.

PREWAR INCEPTION AND POSTWAR EXPANSION

A national inventory of nursing personnel in 1940–41 revealed an imminent shortage and, in June 1941, Congress appropriated more than a million dollars to be administered by the United States Public Health Service as assistance to schools of nursing in training additional nurses for national defense. Under this act, 15,500 student nurses in 380 schools received aid in 1941–43; equipment, supplies, and salaries for instructors were provided; 3,800 nurses received scholarships for postgraduate education in special fields essential to the war effort, and 2,300 inactive nurses were given refresher courses. The state-accredited schools admitted 9 percent more students in 1941 than in 1940, the 1941–42 enrollment of 45,000 falling short by 5,000 students of the estimated need. The National Nursing Council for War Service, Inc.,[1] began organized recruitment and drew up a statement of principles to guide the schools in keeping high standards while expanding their programs.

The federal appropriation was almost doubled in 1942 ($5,300,000 was appropriated for the biennium 1941–43) with the need for nurses increasing at an unparalleled rate. The

---

[1] The Nursing Council on National Defense was organized in July 1940 by six national nursing agencies to coordinate war activities: American Nurses' Association, National League of Nursing Education, National Organization for Public Health Nursing, Association of Collegiate Schools of Nursing, Association of Colored Graduate Nurses, American Red Cross Nursing Service (and, by liaison, the federal nursing services). In April 1942 the name was changed to the National Nursing Council for War Service, Inc., and the council became incorporated in July of that year. In 1943 representation was expanded to include hospital administrators and nonnurse members-at-large, both white and Negro. In January 1946 the name was changed to the National Nursing Council, Inc.

Army and Navy issued a call for 2,500 graduate nurses each month in 1943, in addition to the 35,000 already in the military services. The schools of nursing were urged to admit students three times a year, and it was estimated that 55,000 new students would be needed in 1942–43, and 65,000 in 1943–44. The National League for Nursing Education worked out suggested programs for accelerating the three-year training courses.

The proposals for rapid expansion made necessary increased scholarship aid. Recruiting for nursing was difficult in competition with recruiting for well-paid jobs in industry or the women's military services, and offers of free training in industry. Plans for a much more comprehensive program of federal aid culminated in the act of Congress known as the Bolton Act which was approved June 15, 1943. This act received strong support of professional medical and nursing groups, the American Red Cross, the Army and the Navy, the United States Public Health Service, Veterans Administration, and other federal agencies, the American Hospital Association, and hospital superintendents from all parts of the country.

The general purpose of the act was the authorization of federal grants-in-aid to approved schools of nursing meeting certain scholastic and curricular requirements, for the purpose of assuring a supply of nurses for the armed forces, governmental and civilian hospitals, health agencies, and war industries. The act set up the United States Cadet Nurse Corps in the United States Public Health Service, with provision for federal funds to compensate nursing schools for tuition and fees for students; it provided costs of maintenance of the first nine months of the course, as well as outdoor uniforms and the payment of monthly stipends to students; the schools accepting such aid were to offer approved, accelerated programs, lasting from 24 to 30 months; the students receiving aid under the act were required to promise to remain in essential military or civilian nursing service for the duration of the war; and provision was made for a senior cadet internship period in various essential civilian and military hospitals. The act also provided aid for postgraduate and refresher courses.

The Cadet Nurse Corps was not militarized. When the plans were made it was considered advisable to keep the corps a civilian organization in order that the schools would be left free to select their own students, and that students could select their own schools. The use of a uniform for the corps was a recruiting measure in keeping with wartime psychology. Although the wearing of the uniform was optional, during the major portion of the war, cadet nurses wore it extensively.

The effects of the act and of an intensive recruiting campaign were immediate. The quotas established for the 1944 and 1945 fiscal years were 65,000 and 60,000, respectively. New admissions in all schools in these fiscal years were 65,521 for 1944 and 61,471 for 1945, of which numbers 50,827 and 54,396, respectively, were enrolled as members of the Cadet Nurse Corps. In the 1946 fiscal year, the quota was 60,000 but corps recruitment stopped as of August 20. The admissions to the corps between July 1, 1945, and October 16, 1945, were 28,220 students. Since it requires three years to produce a graduate professional nurse, increasing the student nurse enrollment in the country was the quickest means of increasing the nurse power, because student nurses serve while they are learning. Approximately 30,000 of the cadet nurses had completed their training by December 21, 1945.[2]

THE BOLTON ACT AND ITS RESULTS

The basic act establishing the corps (Public Law 74, 78th Congress, Chapter 126, 1st session, approved June 15, 1943) is usually referred to as the "Bolton Act" because it was actively sponsored by Mrs. Frances P. Bolton, Congresswoman from Ohio. The purpose is stated in the act as being to assure a supply of nurses for the armed forces, governmental and civilian hospitals, health agencies, and war industries. Funds appropriated for the purpose were to be administered, without discrimination on account of race, creed, or color, through schools of nursing or other institutions which submitted plans for nurses' training to

[2] An excellent source of information about the Cadet Nurse Corps is *The Cadet Nurse Corps News,* published by the Division of Education, U. S. Public Health Service, Federal Security Agency, Washington, D. C. First issued in April 1945; four pages, six issues yearly.

the Surgeon General of the Public Health Service for approval.

Section 2 of the Bolton Act set forth requirements applicable to the plans for training. Courses might be for student-nurse or postgraduate or refresher training. A plan submitted by an institution would be approved only under the following conditions:

(a) That no student or graduate nurse will be included under the plan unless in the judgment of the head of the institution such nurse will be available for military or other federal governmental or essential civilian services for the duration of the present war, and such nurse so states in her application for inclusion under the plan;

(b) That nurses under the plan will be provided courses of study and training meeting standards prescribed by the Surgeon General;

(c) That the institution will furnish student nurses under the plan (without charge for tuition, fees, or other expenses) courses of study and training, uniforms, insignia, and maintenance in accordance with regulations of the Surgeon General;

(d) That the institution will pay student nurses under the plan a stipend at not less than the following monthly rates: $15 for the first nine months of study; $20 for the following fifteen to twenty-one months of combined study and practice, depending upon the curriculum of such institutions;

(e) That the institution will either afford student nurses under the plan an opportunity to complete their course of training until graduation at such institution and will pay such student nurse a stipend at a monthly rate not less than $30 for the period following the period of combined study and practice and prior to graduation, or will transfer such student, after completion of the period of combined study and practice and prior to graduation, for training in some other institution, but only if such training may be credited toward graduation, and the institution to which the nurse is transferred agrees to pay her a stipend at a monthly rate of not less than $30 until graduation; and

(f) That where extramural credit toward graduation can be given under the law of the state in which the institution is located, such institution will make transfers to federal hospitals, under the conditions specified in subsection (e), in any case where a student nurse desires such transfer and appropriate request for such transfer is made on behalf of such hospital.

Section 3 of the Bolton Act provided for payment to each institution whose plan had been approved under the provisions of Section 2, for the following expenses incurred in training student nurses—(1) reasonable tuition and fees for courses of study and training; (2) reasonable maintenance for the first nine months of their course of study and training, to the extent that such maintenance was not compensated for by the value of their services during this period; (3) costs of uniforms and insignia; and (4) the minimum rate of stipend specified in Section 2 for periods prior to completion of the course of combined study and training. Compensation for items furnished graduate nurses, in amounts to be determined by the Surgeon General, was authorized to repay the institution for reasonable tuition and fees for postgraduate and refresher courses of study, and reasonable maintenance for graduate nurses undertaking postgraduate courses. With the approval of the Federal Security Administrator, the Surgeon General was authorized to enter into agreements with nonprofit organizations for the recruitment of student and graduate nurses for training and courses under plans approved under the Bolton Act, and he was authorized to compensate the organizations, but such compensation could not exceed the necessary cost.

The authority to promulgate rules and regulations to carry out the purposes of the act was vested in the Surgeon General after conference with an advisory committee of not less than five members consisting of representatives of the nursing profession, hospitals, and accredited training institutions. The Federal Security Administrator was directed to appoint these members, who served without compensation.

Finally, the act was declared to be ineffective upon the date of termination of hostilities in the present war as determined by the President, or upon an earlier date if Congress or the President designated one. Payments for obligations incurred prior to such date would be made, and also payment to permit the continuance after such date, of training and courses by graduate or student nurses who were receiving training or courses ninety days prior to the date.

FISCAL AND ADMINISTRATIVE PLANS

On July 9, 1943, the Surgeon General published regulations governing payments to provide training for nurses (Title 42, *Public Health*, Chapter I: Public Health Service, Federal Security Agency, Part 28). The regulations contained definition of several terms used in the act and in the regulations. In three separate sections there were very specific requirements which a school of nursing had to meet to be eligible for participation in the student nurse training program, the refresher program, and the postgraduate program. Other sections provided exact procedures for approval of plans and determination of allotments, methods of payment for the three types of programs, cancellation of allotments, and accounting for funds.

As a supplement to the formal regulations an excellent summary of the position of the school of nursing in the new program was prepared and sent to the schools in July 1943. The purposes of the program were said to be the recruitment of more young women into nursing through the establishment of the Cadet Nurse Corps, and the acceleration of essential instruction and experience in the nursing school curriculum to 24 to 30 months (32 months were allowed for students admitted during the year 1941). This further statement appeared:

This legislation is not to be interpreted as an attempt to standardize schools of nursing. Although the federal government assumes substantial financial responsibility for nurse training, this plan in no way alters the present relationship between the school and the individual student. The student will continue to meet the admission and graduation standards of your school. Students eligible for admission to your school who do not wish to become members of the U. S. Cadet Nurse Corps are not affected by this legislation either as to its benefits or as to its requirements.

The proposed intensive recruitment drive was described. National, state, and local nursing councils for war service, the United States Public Health Service, and the schools of nursing were to cooperate in presenting a unified, vivid appeal through radio, newspapers and magazines, and posters and recruitment materials for prospective students were in preparation. It was expected that a large proportion of nursing students presently in the schools would wish to join the corps and these students would be the best recruiters of others. Clear interpretation of points of emphasis was to be given to parents as well as to candidates, and a list of such points was provided.

An extremely important section was headed "Acceleration of Curriculum." Concentration of essential instruction and experience ordinarily requiring 30 or 36 months into 24 to 30 months would prepare students to assume responsibility at an earlier date. The regulations of the Surgeon General referred to two periods in the accelerated curriculum—the precadet period (first nine months) and the junior cadet period (15 to 21 months following). If a school could not graduate its students at the end of these periods, because of state law or school requirements, a senior cadet period up to twelve months could be added to meet the remaining time requirement. Assistance in planning an accelerated program would be given by several named agencies. Acceleration would achieve its purpose if the precadets and junior cadets filled the extended capacity of a school, leaving the senior cadets free to replace graduates in military, other federal, and civilian hospitals. The increased use of affiliations for the first two periods would also permit the enrollment of more students, and furnish wider background of experience. The schools were urged to plan for as liberal an allowance for vacation periods as could be arranged in the accelerated program.

The schools of nursing which were approved by the state boards of nurse examiners and which offered accelerated programs of required courses in 24 to 30 months were declared to be eligible to apply for federal funds and, if a school's plans were approved, its students were eligible for membership in the Cadet Nurse Corps. All details of the requirements which schools had to meet were stated in four sections of the Surgeon General's regulations (28.2–28.5), forming a considerable part of that document. These requirements included specifications as to faculty, educational and living facilities, admission requirements, curriculum, and health and welfare of students.

A new student in a school of nursing, to be eligible for membership in the corps, had to be a graduate from an accredited high school, she must have fulfilled all other requirements for admission to the school of nursing which she planned to attend, and she was required to agree to make her services available for military, or other federal hospitals, or essential civilian nursing service, for the duration of the present war, and so state in her application for admission to the corps. Special provisions were made for those students already in schools of nursing who were admitted after January 1, 1941, including a 32-month period in which to complete the required instruction and experience, plus a four-month senior cadet period. Students admitted after January 1, 1942 were to be enrolled in a curriculum in which essential training and experience were completed in 24 to 30 months, with a six-month senior cadet period. There was no prohibition against marriage, either before or during training, although many schools continued the policy of not admitting or retaining married students.

Three forms (an application, a supplement to an application, and a budget) were submitted to the schools of nursing. A request for funds could include (1) reasonable tuition and fees, (2) maintenance for the first nine months of the basic nursing program at $45 a month, (3) stipends for precadet and junior cadet nurses, and (4) the cost of outdoor uniforms ($100 was allowed for each outdoor ensemble). Upon approval by the Surgeon General of the plan and budget proposed by the school, application forms for membership in the Cadet Nurse Corps would be sent. The budget was to be based upon the number then in the school and the estimated number to be admitted, who would wish to enter the corps. Further details of procedures of allotment and payment were described in the directions sent to the schools of nursing.

The senior cadet period was defined as that part of the training period following the 24-to-30 month accelerated program of combined study and practice for precadets and junior cadets. It might be considered a period of internship for those students who, because of requirements of state law, could not be graduated at the termination of the junior cadet period. Senior cadet nurses could be assigned to a hospital connected with the "home" school, to other civilian hospitals, including psychiatric institutions, to selected community agencies, such as public health nursing agencies, and to federal hospitals under the Army, the Navy, the Public Health Service, the Veterans Administration, and the Indian Service. Opportunities for assignment to such hospitals would be made known to the school of nursing, and the home school was responsible for arranging assignments for senior cadets in much the same manner as they arranged affiliations for other students. All experience during the senior cadet period had to meet the requirements of the home school for graduation and of the state board for registration.

On July 12, 1943, funds to carry the act into effect became available. Within a week application forms and instructions were mailed to some 1,300 accredited schools of nursing which might be eligible to participate in the new program. At the same time a Division of Nurse Education was established in the office of the Surgeon General of the United States Public Health Service, Federal Security Agency, and Miss Lucile Petry was appointed director of the division and director of the Cadet Nurse Corps.

On March 4, 1944, an amendment to the Bolton Act (Public Law 248, 78th Congress, Chapter 83, 2d session) provided for full participation of federal hospitals in the continental United States, exclusive of Alaska, in the training of senior cadets who were to be paid a stipend at a rate to be determined by the President (subsequently set at $60 a month), and other details of compensation and living expenses were provided. The last section clarified earlier provisions relating to insignia and uniforms.

Congressional appropriations for fiscal 1944 were $55,200,-000; for 1945, $63,000,000; and for 1946, $44,400,000.

COOPERATION BY SCHOOLS OF NURSING .

It is not difficult to realize the tremendous responsibility which was imposed upon American schools of nursing by the provisions of the plan for training a Cadet Nurse Corps. More than a thousand of the approximately 1,300 schools qualified for participation during the first year after the initiation of the plan, and in an undetermined number of cases, probably constituting a large majority, the basic curriculums of the schools had to be reorganized to furnish the accelerated program required by the Bolton Act. They received able assistance in solving this problem and those resulting from other legal provisions and the effects of the war, from the National League of Nursing Education. A series of bulletins was published by the league (fourteen issues) each under the title of "Nursing Education in Wartime," between November 1942 and June 1945.[3] The titles of the bulletins indicate the scope of assistance rendered by the league:

1. *Curriculum Adjustments*
2. *Faculty and Facilities*
3. *More about Curriculum Acceleration*
4. *Cooperative Planning by Schools of Nursing*
5. *Selection of Students in Wartime*
6. *The Supervised Practice Period*
7. *Analyzing Your Clinical Facilities*
8. *Analyzing Your Clinical Facilities* (continued)
9. *Expansion of Pediatric Facilities*
10. *Expansion of Medical and Diet Therapy Facilities*
11. *Developing a Master Plan—For Rotation of Student through Clinical Assignments*
12. *Clinical Instructional Program*
13. *Student Personnel Practices*
14. *Administrative Budget in the School of Nursing*

It will be noted that Bulletin No. 1, *Curriculum Adjustments*, was published in November 1942, and that the purpose of the adjustments suggested was in the direction of acceleration. This movement preceded the enactment of the Bolton Act by approximately eight months, indicating that consideration and even concrete planning of accelerated programs were at an advanced stage before the federal government stimulated the movement toward accelerated programs in nursing schools.

The National League of Nursing Education sent the following recommendation to all state-approved schools of nursing:

The Board of Directors of the National League of Nursing Education in this critical period when there is unprecedented demand for graduate nurses of both military and civilian services believes that all those concerned with nursing schools should give immediate consideration to making adjustments in their educational programs. In making these adjustments, it is important that the essential elements of a sound preparation for nursing be maintained. The responsibilities that are being placed on nurses were never greater and according to all indications these will be greatly increased in the postwar period.

A special curriculum committee of the league was responsible for preparing concrete suggestions for carrying this principle into

[3] Available from National League of Nursing Education, 1790 Broadway, New York 19, N. Y.

effect. The purpose was not to set up a hard-and-fast program, which would be neither possible nor desirable. In wartime, as in peacetime, it was the responsibility of the individual school to build a curriculum which would give a sound preparation for professional nursing and which utilized the school's facilities to the best advantage.

Bulletin No. 1 carried a quotation from an address by the chairman of the league's Committee on Educational Problems in Wartime as an introduction to a specific treatment of means of curriculum adjustment to produce a shortened training program. The necessity for insuring high quality as well as increased numbers was strongly emphasized.

CURRICULUM ADJUSTMENTS

Three concrete curriculum plans (for a 30-month training period followed by a six-month internship, a 28-month period for students with two or more years of college education, and a 24-month period for mature students who were college graduates) were presented in Bulletin No. 1. The accompanying text made six important points, as follows:

1. Flexibility would have to be a characteristic of the program. Differences in teaching facilities, clinical resources, state board requirements, and other varying factors would influence curriculum planning, and each school would have to set up its own sequence of courses and plan its own time allotment.

2. Schools should analyze the content of instruction and experience in all courses with a view to eliminating overlapping and repetition, bearing in mind the fulfillment of state nursing board requirements. In the 28-month and 24-month programs for students with college preparation plans should be made to eliminate repetition in the nursing curriculum of courses already carried in college.

3. The proposed plans for accelerated courses did not include time allotments and each school would have to make time adjustments on the basis of its own conditions. More class hours might be necessary in each week in an accelerated program; with such an increase more hours for study would have to be provided. Again, state nursing boards in different states imposed varying requirements as to length of particular courses and this fact would affect total time distribution.

4. The readjustment of clinical courses was made necessary in an accelerated program. The plans proposed by the League placed general medical and surgical nursing, including both theory and practice, in the

first year as basic courses. The second year was divided into four periods of twelve weeks each, with concurrent classes and experience in medical specialties, surgical specialties, obstetrics and pediatrics. Through careful planning, students in the 24-month course could also be given short periods of experience or guided observation in psychiatry, nursing and health service in the family, tuberculosis nursing, et cetera. The third year provided 24 weeks in the 30-month plan, and 17 weeks in the 28-month plan, for psychiatry and other specialties.

5. Adjustment in teaching methods would be necessary, if courses were to be condensed and students carried a larger share of the service load, and instruction at the bedside would become increasingly important. Planning for such instruction must insure that the student had a suitable spread of clinical experience. The clinical instructor must use demonstration, discussion, conference, evaluation of nursing care, and other teaching methods. No reduction, therefore, could be made in the number of minutes of instructional time per student in the clinical division. A new type of instruction would have to be given in hospitals in which volunteer nurse's aides and other auxiliary workers were used to a considerable extent. Students would need instruction in delegating tasks to such workers and in supervising them.

6. The recommendation to accelerate the organized instruction of the basic curriculum presupposed a faculty capable of analyzing the current program and making the necessary adjustments. It was considered imperative that faculty members who could not readily be replaced remain in their positions, and that promising young graduates be prepared for teaching. Schools of nursing would have to have well-prepared faculty members who had the vision and ingenuity to carry on sound learning programs, even under difficult conditions.

THE NATIONAL PICTURE

The success of the Cadet Nurse Corps program was due in large part not only to the efforts of the professional organizations described above, but also to the professional staff of the Division of Nurse Education consisting of twenty-two nurse education consultants. They guided schools in the preparation of plans for participation in the program and in the preparation of budgets, and they interpreted the regulations in concrete, constructive terms and evaluated school applications for annual approval for participation in the program. Each school plan was scrutinized in great detail and suggestions for improvement to produce better compliance with the Bolton Act were given each school annually, with considerable follow-up during the year.

Schools reported improvements as they were made. Nine of the consultants on the professional staff were stationed in the United States Public Health Service districts throughout the country, and they visited all schools in their districts. These consultants advised the directors and faculty of the schools regarding the administration of the corps program, interpreted the regulations constructively, and interpreted the program to cadet nurses themselves. Since the regulations of the Surgeon General involved qualifications of the faculty, curriculum, admission standards, selection and guidance of students, their health and welfare, and their living and learning conditions, the interpretation of the provisions gave a comprehensive function to the consultants.

In describing this program, the director, Miss Petry, said:

We shall perhaps never be able to measure by any objective criteria the value of this consultation service. I am convinced from our records, however, that it had a marked effect on educational programs. The Division carried on a continuous program of staff education for its consultants to guarantee that the content of their consultation service was in line with the provisions of the Act and as practical and usable as possible to the schools. The emphasis on the student health program is an example of addition to the content of consultation service. The bulletins of the Committee on Education Problems in Wartime and publications and reports of the Division of Nurse Education served as source material for these consultants. The consultants who remained in the Washington office reinforced all this consultation service through correspondence and the evaluation of school reports. One of the implications for nursing in this consultation service is that appropriate professional organizations, national or state, or the Public Health Service itself, might well continue to offer this service to schools. On the whole, the service was extremely well received and appreciated. Of course, when it is disconnected from a program of allotments of funds, consultation service can be more comprehensive. At the same time, it would lose some of its "leverage."

The duration of the Cadet Nurse Corps program was from its inception in July 1943 to October 15, 1945, on which date all admissions ceased. It will terminate on a date in 1948 upon which the last of this group of students will complete her work. Recruitment of cadet nurses was assisted by the Office of War Information and the War Advertising Council which donated an estimated $13,000,000 of publicity for the program. An interesting comparative figure is the $4.95 which represents the per capita cost of recruitment by the government itself. Local recruitment committees were assisted by community action groups who understood community needs. These committees were voluntary and were organized by the Division of Nurse Education, Public Relations staff, in cooperation with the National Nursing Council for War Service, Inc., and the American Hospital Association. All recruitment was stopped immediately after the Japanese surrender and only those students previously recruited were admitted on dates already scheduled up to October 16. During the first six calendar months of 1946 only about one-third as many students were admitted as had been admitted in the corresponding six months of the previous year. Tables 18 and 19 throw additional light on the extent and character of the program:

TABLE 18

STUDENTS AND GRADUATES OF THE CADET NURSE CORPS,
JULY 1, 1943 TO JUNE 30, 1946

Fiscal Year Ending	New Students	Graduates
30 June 1944 [a]	50,827	1,206
30 June 1945	54,396	15,248
30 June 1946	28,220	13,589 [b]

[a] Prior to this fiscal year 43,561 "old students" were already in the program.
[b] Figure is for the fiscal half-year July 1, 1945, to December 31, 1945, only.

TABLE 19

UTILIZATION OF CADET NURSE CORPS SENIOR CADETS
DURING FISCAL YEAR ENDING JUNE 30, 1945

Type of Institution	Number of Senior Cadets Assigned
Home hospitals	14,181
Other civilian hospitals	2,778
Army hospitals	3,901
Navy hospitals	717
Other federal hospitals	1,110
Public health nursing agencies	583
Total	23,270

In addition to the students who joined the Cadet Nurse Corps, federal aid was furnished to graduate nurses (23,542 in number) who took postgraduate courses. A considerable number of

PLATE VII

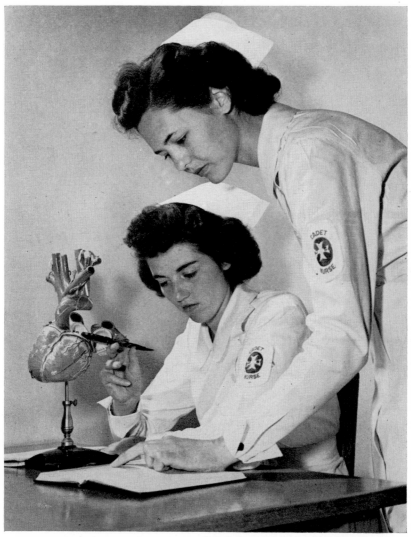

—*U. S. Public Health Service, Federal Security Agency*

CADET NURSES STUDYING THE ANATOMY OF THE HUMAN HEART

the courses were of the intensive on-the-job type, and they were also accelerated. Before the war postgraduate courses usually consisted of professional content (such as methods of teaching in schools of nursing or supervision in public health nursing or maternal and child hygiene) and considerable general education, the latter usually fulfilling requirements for a bachelor's or master's degree. During the war period the requirement was made that graduate nurses, accepting federal scholarships, should choose at least 50 percent of their course credits from professional offerings and prepare as quickly as possible for nursing positions beyond the first level.

For peacetime this would be a shortsighted arrangement, but during the war it resulted in producing more teachers and more specialists, more rapidly, than if the conventional programs had been maintained. During the fiscal year 1944–45, the postgraduate program provided for instruction of five hundred so-called trainers, who were carefully selected and prepared by universities with well-established graduate programs. These trainers during the year taught 5,000 graduate nurses employed in hospitals, schools of nursing, and public health nursing agencies to improve their nursing skills. The trainers travelled to the students, rather than the reverse, and the courses were consequently called "in-service" courses.

THE SENIOR CADETS

In December 1943, Bulletin No. 6 of the series, "Nursing Education in Wartime," was published under the title *The Supervised Practice Period.* In January 1944, *The American Journal of Nursing* contained an article by the director of the Division of Nurse Education, Miss Lucile Petry, entitled "Planning the Senior Cadet Period." These two publications presented to hospitals, military and civilian, and to the nursing schools a clear explanation of the purposes of this period and the responsibilities of all interested parties—the senior cadet, the various federal agencies, the home nursing school, the hospital in which the cadet served her senior internship, and the state boards of nurse examiners.

The bulletin, *The Supervised Practice Period,* stated very concisely the underlying premises to be considered in planning such a period:

1. That an accelerated program is in operation and that the basic instruction and experience required by the school will have been completed prior to the supervised practice period;

2. That, while nursing service is the primary objective during this period, the plan will provide for the development of the educational values inherent in the experience from the practical standpoint;

3. That good standards of supervision, of working, and of living and recreational conditions will be maintained during the supervised practice period;

4. That schools will make assignments in the light of current nursing service needs but that students, with faculty advice, will have the opportunity to indicate the experience in which they would like practice;

5. That only in case of serious emergency or a great need will students be made available for services other than those included in the plan made for the student in advance; and

6. That the experience during the supervised practice period is in accord with the general requirements of the school for graduation and that it meets with the approval of the state board of nurse examiners.

Miss Petry's article opened with a discussion of the advantages to the cadet of the senior cadet period—namely, that it offered opportunity to try out a field of nursing in which she might later elect to serve; that she had the advantage of previous orientation if she chose, as her first postgraduate position, the type of nursing which was practiced during the senior cadet period; that the senior cadet period offered opportunity to supplement experience received in her precadet and junior cadet periods; that she had the advantage of practicing in a different type of community; and, finally, that the senior cadet was afforded the advantage of increased responsibility sooner than would otherwise be possible.

One point was given particular emphasis—that the senior cadet period was not an affiliation, nor was it an opportunity for advanced study. Affiliations were to be completed in the junior cadet period.

The planning of the senior cadet period lay entirely with the school of nursing in all instances except where senior cadets were transferred to federal hospitals. It was hoped that, in making such plans, the schools would assign senior cadets where the need for them was greatest, and that they would plan the period first for its service value, taking also into consideration the possible educational values of the experience whenever possible. It was also desirable that the school of nursing, the receiving institution, the state board, and if possible, the nursing council, should participate in making the final plans.

The school of nursing had the responsibility for guaranteeing the quality of the supervision provided in the institution utilizing senior cadets, whether it was the home hospital or another agency. Most institutions would probably plan six-month assignments, but it was considered desirable that some plan assignments of varying lengths (three, four, and six months). The school of nursing also was responsible for guaranteeing that senior cadet experience met its own requirements for graduation.

The responsibility of the state board of nurse examiners lay in guaranteeing that the cadet upon graduation would be eligible to take state board examinations. The responsibility of the receiving institution was the maintenance of good working and living conditions, providing supervision, and the payment of a stipend of at least $30 a month in addition to full maintenance.

The Division of Nurse Education was responsible for urging schools to participate in the plan, and for encouraging students to enter and to continue in the corps. The division was the source of information, and it had taken the initiative in calling together the heads of the various federal nursing services to assist in preparing uniform plans. The Public Health Service was required to verify the facts submitted by the directors of nursing schools who made application for funds from the federal government to pay the monthly stipends and maintenance costs of senior cadets, and to see that the certified statements were carried out.

Junior cadet nurses, under the Cadet Nurse Corps provisions, had the privilege of requesting a senior cadet period either in a civilian hospital or in a federal nursing service (Army, Navy, Veterans Administration, Public Health Service, Marine Hospital, or Indian Service). Applications for the latter were processed by the Medical Division of the United States Civil Service

Commission. After a roster of qualified applicants was established, assignments were made based upon the expressed desires of the students, and the quotas in the various federal services and, in turn, the quotas in their respective hospitals.

SENIOR CADETS IN NAVAL HOSPITALS

As of December 31, 1945, student nurses in training under the program of the United States Cadet Nurse Corps who had chosen to spend their senior cadet periods in naval hospitals, and had been so assigned, numbered 1,149. On the same date, 868 of this group had completed the six-month training period and 58 of them had joined the Navy Nurse Corps. It must be remembered that by the time the student nurses were ready to choose permanent work, the acute necessity for recruiting military nurses was at an end and there was little opportunity to enter either the Army or the Navy Nurse Corps.

The Navy carried out its program of training for senior cadet nurses in nine large naval hospitals. Early in 1944, Vice Admiral Ross T. McIntire (MC) USN, as chief of the Bureau of Medicine and Surgery, promulgated a four-page directive entitled "General Policies in Relation to Senior Cadet Nurses in Naval Hospitals." The aims were summarized therein as follows: To offer supervised nursing practice in the various clinical fields; to supplement the student nurses' previous preparation by means of a teaching program consisting mainly of clinics and conferences; to offer instruction and practice in case of conditions and injuries peculiar to the Navy in wartime; to augment the nursing care of Navy personnel by using the services of the senior cadet nurses; to provide experience in Navy ward administration for those senior cadet nurses with proven ability and interest along that line; to familiarize senior cadet nurses with Navy customs, traditions, discipline, and etiquette, and with the fundamentals of military drill; and to give the Navy Department an opportunity to evaluate the student nurses in their senior cadet period with a view to their acceptability into the Navy Nurse Corps upon graduation from the home school.

Most of the instruction was directed to be given during supervised practice on wards by Navy medical personnel; required were three hours weekly of clinics and conferences under the direction of the supervisor of cadet nurses and with the assistance of the medical officers on the staff; and a course of lectures in Navy history, traditions, etiquette, custom, and discipline. Standard calisthenic practice of the Navy was to be carried out; and all teaching facilities available to other student personnel on the station (library, classrooms, etc.) were to be open to cadet nurses; and the hours indicated were to be included in the usual 48 hours of duty expected of government personnel.

Cadet nurses were to be supplied with medical and hospital care in naval hospitals and dispensaries, free of cost, dental service being limited to that of emergency nature only. Cadet nurses in naval hospitals were to be paid the same monthly stipend as cadet nurses in other federal services (this amount was established at $30 a month) with no overtime pay of any kind allowed.

The program at the Norfolk Naval Hospital illustrated the concrete application of the directive just summarized. At this hospital 158 senior cadets were assigned to duty, 153 of whom completed the period successfully. The first group was assigned on June 1, 1944. The number of cadets in a group varied from 24 to 78.

The senior cadets lived in their own quarters. The dormitory contained twenty-three double-decker bunks and individual lockers. The quarters contained a living room and recreation room, writing room, library, bag rooms, toilets and showers and washrooms, offices for the directors, and room for the cadet director in residence. A cadet officer of the day was regularly assigned for one week to act under the guidance of the director in residence, with responsibility for order in quarters and for supervision of the housekeeping. The general cleaning was done by men on outside detail. Meals were served in the officers mess cafeteria. There was provision on the station for participation in thirteen different sports, and for dramatics, music appreciation, choir, and movies. The monthly reports of the director indicated that there were many parties to which cadets were invited, and that cadets frequently took advantage of the privilege of spending short leaves at the Virginia Beach Nurses Rest Home. The students elected a student council to serve as a medium of expression of their interests as a group and to assume responsibility for student activities, both professional and social. Provision was made for complete health service for the cadets and medical histories were kept to form a part of their records. Time lost from duty due to illness up to two weeks was not made up, nor was the stipend discontinued for time lost less than two weeks. At the end of the senior cadet period each nurse decided which nursing service, military or civilian, she wished to join in fulfillment of her promise upon enlistment to continue in essential nursing service for the duration of the war.

Although changes were made from time to time in the educational program offered at the Norfolk Naval Hospital, it was not essentially altered and a description of its contents as of January 1945 indicates its nature:

Orientation—one week

A. Compliance with entrance regulations—physical examinations, immunization, endorsement of orders, etc.

B. Naval hospital organization and administration—16 hours. Introduction of personnel and program, history of Nurse Corps, U. S. Navy, general plan of hospital organization with trips to various departments, demonstration of technique of nursing procedures in use in a naval hospital, the Hospital Corps with a trip to advanced school on station.

C. Ward administration—16 hours.

D. Military instruction—62 hours. Military customs and traditions, military drill, athletics, inspections.

Program proper—23 weeks

A. Clinical practice. Each student was assigned for periods of not less than one month to the clinical service needed to supplement her previous experience. Students worked an eight-hour day, six days a week. Classes were held during time on duty. The day off was alternately Saturday and Sunday. Emphasis was placed on care of patients with illnesses and injuries resulting from combat conditions:

(*a*) Medical (general medicine, tropical diseases, gastrointestinal diseases, respiratory diseases, dermatology). The majority of students were found to need experience in the care of medical patients.

      (*b*) Surgical (general surgery, orthopedics, neurosurgery, burns, dental surgery, general traumatic surgery, genito-urinary conditions).

      (*c*) Psychiatry.

      (*d*) Eye, ear, nose and throat clinic.

      (*e*) Central dressing room.

      (*f*) Blood bank.

      (*g*) Physical therapy.

      (*h*) Special duty nursing with acutely ill patients.

B. Clinical instruction—clinics and conferences—60 hours. Clinics were given by the ward medical officer and followed by a conference when indicated. Following topics are typical of clinical material utilized:

      (*a*) Medical. New therapies (sulfonamides, penicillin), rheumatic fever and arthritis, tropical diseases, dermatological conditions, neuropsychiatric conditions with emphasis on combat fatigue.

      (*b*) Surgical. Care of trauma and shock in the field, orthopedics, burns, neurosurgery, genito-urinary conditions, eye, ear, nose and throat conditions, dental surgery, particularly fractures, traumatic surgery, plastic surgery.

      (*c*) Field medicine. Battle aid stations ashore and afloat, evacuation facilities, mobile hospitals.

C. Naval customs and traditions. Organization of the U. S. Navy, naval personnel, training and services, military law, decorum of Naval personnel, history and development of Navy traditions.

D. War orientation. Given by Educational Services Officer with aid of movies.

E. Military drill and athletics—four hours a week for two weeks, and two hours a week thereafter.

SENIOR CADETS IN ARMY HOSPITALS

The active work of the Cadet Nurse Corps began in the last months of 1943. By June 1944, senior cadets were being received at twenty-five different Army hospitals. Between June 1943 and September 1943, a total of 4,571 cadets was sent to forty-eight different Army hospitals from 856 schools of nursing in continental United States and Puerto Rico. This included twenty-two Negro cadets who were sent to six different hospitals, four Japanese-American students, and a considerable number of Puerto Ricans. Less than seventy senior cadets assigned to Army hospitals failed to complete the period. The reasons for precompletion termination were marriage (against school policy), ill health, unprofessional conduct, inefficiency and unsuitability, home conditions, and absence without leave.

When the program commenced, the Army considered senior cadets in the class of officer candidates and it was thought that the great majority of those choosing to spend this period in Army hospitals would seek commissions in the Army Nurse Corps. This was, in fact, the expressed intention of the senior cadets in Army hospitals. By the time that they were ready for commissions, the quotas of the Army Nurse Corps had been met. After VJ Day, consideration was given to terminating the program. It was, however, continued because the nursing schools had planned on it as one important type of affiliation and because additions to the nursing profession were still needed. The number of senior cadets in Army hospitals decreased markedly in 1946.

Army Service Forces Circular No. 108 (March 26, 1945) contained a complete description of the senior cadet program. In order to supplement nursing service provided by Army nurses for patients in Army hospitals the assistance of several groups was authorized—paid civilian graduate nurses, volunteer civilian graduate nurses, senior cadet nurses, WAC medical and surgical technicians, male medical and surgical technicians, volunteer nurse's aides (from the Red Cross), and paid nurse's aides (certified by the Red Cross).

The section of the circular dealing with senior cadet nurses contained provisions on their admittance, status, procurement, assignment, stipend, tour of duty, duties, hours of duty, subsistence and quarters, supply of furniture and linens, laundry, travel expenses, disability or death benefits, leave, personnel actions, termination of training period, final physical examination, uniform, and appointments to the Army Nurse Corps. A comparison of the provisions of ASF Circular No. 108 with the Navy directive mentioned in the preceding section of this chapter indicates that the programs in the two services were similar in all essential respects and even in respect to most details.

The senior cadet nurse program was considered by the Army as a supplementary experience for nursing students who had not completed their course, and approval of the courses offered them had to be obtained from the state boards of nurse examiners. To facilitate this process, the boards sent representatives to each Army hospital for a survey, and all the hospitals were approved by the boards of the states in which they were respectively located. Transfer of students from one state in which a nursing school was located, to a different state in which the Army hospital was located to which they were transferred, was approved by all state boards, except the board in Texas.

It was planned originally to use the senior cadet period as an affiliation to supplement a basic program completed in the civilian school. Directors of schools of nursing submitted a report for each student, stating (1) the courses which she had completed, and (2) those which she was required to complete. Early in the program, it was evident that such requests could not be met. The various schools of nursing were given time to complete the process of accelerating their courses and then the detailed reports were omitted. Instead each director stated that the cadets had completed the basic course required to meet state regulations. Thus the Army program became an elective type of experience, rather than a required supplement.

Senior cadets were assigned to large hospitals with complete medical and surgical services. Assignment to a department of one of the services was for a minimum period of one month, but for operating-room or psychiatric experience the period was from six to twelve weeks. At least two hours a week of instruction were required in the form of lectures, demonstrations, or ward conferences. Most of the instructors were well-prepared Army nurses, a majority of whom had previously been educational directors, instructors, or supervisors in schools of nursing. The director of cadets, her assistant, and supervisors, head nurses, and some medical officers did most of the teaching. Student government was established and operated with varying degrees of success, depending largely upon what proportion of the cadets had come from schools where there was strict supervision and little self-government.

In June 1944, Army Service Forces Circular No. 168 directed that senior cadets should take physical examinations at Army installations. This produced revealing data on the health education at the schools of nursing from which the cadets came. Over 13 percent of cadets applying were physically disqualified, in many cases for cardiac conditions, tuberculosis, and other conditions which should have been noted earlier. ASF Circular No. 75 (February 28, 1945) provided that reports of physical condition should be submitted by private physicians, and the result was that very few disqualifying defects were reported prior to assignment.

The revelations concerning unsatisfactory health conditions, described above, as well as other indications, encouraged the Public Health Service to undertake a study of the prevailing practices in health programs of schools of nursing participating in the Cadet Nurse Corps, and to formulate a recommended health program. In October 1944 the Surgeon General appointed a working committee to evaluate health programs in one hundred of the eleven hundred schools concerned.

Findings of the study made by a widely representative committee, including representatives of the American Medical Association, American Hospital Association, American Dental Association, American Student Health Association, nursing schools, and many others resulted in the following recommendations: (1) the admission of students in as good physical condition as possible and possessing potential capacity and aptitudes for nursing; (2) all possible measures for the prevention of infection; (3) maintenance of a balance between work and recreation conducive to physical and mental health; (4) formal instruction in personal and community health; (5) provision for the care of students who become ill; (6) provision of a safe and healthful environment; and (7) provision of an organized health and guidance program under direction of qualified persons and representative committees.

The recommended program was distributed to all schools of nursing as well as allied professional groups, and was published in professional journals. The recommendations were adopted in May 1945 by the Advisory Committee to the Surgeon General on Nurse Education and were subsequently used as content of the nurse education consultation service.

A description of the senior cadet program in one Army hospital was published in the *American Journal of Nursing* (Louise M. Schmitt, R.N., and Joseph J. Michaels, M.D., "How We Planned for our Affiliated Students," Vol. 46, No. 1, January 1946). Miss Schmitt was director of cadets at Newton D. Baker General Hospital. The writers reported that staff cooperation was excellent for several reasons: (1) there was need for the services of the senior cadets, (2) the program was well understood by the staff before it was put into effect, (3) it was regarded as "an investment toward an ideal of nursing in Army hospitals," and (4) "it expanded opportunities of adult education in the understanding of the returned veteran."

Orientation of the hospital staff which preceded the arrival of the first cadets included in-service staff conferences to evaluate nursing duties, educational experience, and the service of each ward unit. A fact-sheet on the program was prepared and circulated. One week before the cadets arrived, the director of cadets personally explained the objectives of the program at a weekly meeting of all officers.

Orientation for the cadet nurse included a general explanation of over-all functional and physical relationships, with a later, more specific orientation to the special services and the ward unit. The commanding officer and the chief nurse addressed the cadets. Explanation was given to them of the organization of the Army Medical Department, and the care and treatment of the wounded soldier in the line of evacuation from the theater of operation to the Army hospital nearest his home, unless specialized treatment was needed, including the part played by each department of the hospital. Newton D. Baker General Hospital specialized in neurosurgery, plastic surgery, ophthalmologic surgery, and neuropsychiatry.

The authors reported that the cadets were very enthusiastic; that there were no disciplinary problems and little, if any, friction; that officers of the hospital were seeking assurance that a second group would follow the first group (fifty-three senior cadets from eighteen schools of nursing); and that there was "apparent satisfaction from a needed service well administered."

WHAT SOME CADET NURSES THOUGHT OF THEIR TRAINING

It is of some importance to record the opinions of the senior cadets themselves as to the values of their training period in an Army hospital. In August 1945 a group of forty-three senior cadets completing their training at O'Reilly General Hospital were asked to write statements of their reactions to the program, in connection with a recruiting drive for the Cadet Nurse Corps. These statements indicate a variety of aspects of the program which seemed to the cadets to be worthy of being called to the attention of prospective students.

Many cadets emphasized the value of their work from a patriotic standpoint. They were helping to cure sick and wounded soldiers and to boost their morale. Nursing the boys was "fun" because they were so gay and so cooperative—in fact, the morale of the patients was so high that in itself it was a morale-builder for those who cared for them. The experience made the cadet nurse realize the horrors and the meaning of war, and it gave the opportunity to do one's own part in the war effort. As one cadet wrote, "The best we can give, the most we can give, is still minute in comparison to this freedom which they are giving us."

The professional advantages of the cadet program were strongly emphasized in the statements. The cadet nurses were taught to use the newest and best techniques, with the best equipment, by the best personnel. Excellent lectures and a medical library were available. An opportunity was offered for many girls to receive nurse training who might otherwise have found it impossible. Many of the cases under care were unusual and interesting and would seldom be seen in a civilian hospital. Many students mentioned the uses of physical and occupational therapy and the fact that they had not previously realized the importance of reconditioning.

The working and living conditions were excellent, with plenty of recreational facilities, and from the moment the cadet arrived she was treated as "a part of it" in the hospital. Finally, the period in an Army hospital gave the cadet an opportunity to determine whether she wished to join the Army Nurse Corps, and, if she did, it placed her in a better position with respect to acceptance.

A number of more general advantages were listed which might be considered as those having general educational or personal values. Students enjoyed the opportunity to travel and they gained a new conception of Army life as actual participants. A cadet wrote, "We are young enough to see life the same as a young soldier who must confront it with a handicap. We will be better prepared to care for these veterans . . . medically and psychologically, as well as socially. They are like brothers." Another cadet said almost the same thing in different words, in stating her belief that she had gained a "newer and more complete understanding of 'G. I. Joe' and a profound respect for American boys and American ways." A third cadet believed that her experience had made her aware of the greatness of the international conflict and of the urgent need for complete cooperation among all nations toward securing a lasting peace.

The real enthusiasm, great enjoyment, and appreciation of opportunity voiced in the letters were even more apparent than the foregoing brief summary indicates.

X. THE FUTURE OF NURSING EDUCATION

IT IS encouraging to be able to report that the nursing profession has given careful consideration to the effects of the war and the effects of other changed conditions upon the status of its members, and that as early as July 1945 the National Nursing Council for War Service, Inc. through its National Nursing Planning Committee was able to publish a comprehensive program for future action. This appeared under the title *A Comprehensive Program for Nation-Wide Action in the Field of Nursing.* The National Nursing Planning Committee includes representatives from fifteen professional and governmental agencies, and the publication of its program represented realization of the need for coordinated action in the postwar period similar to such action which had been most effective during the war.

CURRENT PROGRAM OF THE NURSING PROFESSION

Ten objectives were approved in principle, in September 1944, as the basis for a five-year program for nation-wide action in the field of nursing. One of the objectives was the "education of nurses to give the best service which current scientific knowledge makes possible." The committee further defined five areas in which programs for study and action should be developed: (1) maintenance and development of nursing services in all fields, (2) a program of nursing education (professional, basic and advanced, and practical), (3) channels and means for distribution of nursing services, (4) implementation of standards (including legislation) to protect the best interests of the public and the nurse, and (5) information and public relations program.

The composite program takes into consideration the increase in responsibilities shouldered by professional nurses as a result of the war emergency and the effective use which has been made of practical nurses, other paid workers of various types, American Red Cross volunteer nurses' aides, other volunteers, Wacs and Waves.

The report further recognized the probable results of the expansion of hospital and health facilities proposed by the United States Public Health Service, the Children's Bureau, and the Veterans Administration, and it pointed out "the need for study to overcome the gaps and inadequacies in prewar service and nursing education which war demands have highlighted."

The report continued:

Some projects are national in scope as, for example, accreditation, curriculum revision, and the study of selected aspects of nursing education. Others, like the counseling and placement bureaus, will be developed nationally, regionally, and locally. The nursing service bureaus and the community nursing councils are primarily community projects, to be stimulated and guided by the national organizations.

The main headings under "A Program of Nursing Education (Professional, Basic and Advanced, and Practical)," are as follows:

A. Study of selected aspects of nursing education.
B. Study, evaluation, and continuous development of curricula for schools of professional nursing.
C. Study, evaluation, and development of curricula for schools of practical nursing.
D. Program of curriculum interpretation and promotion.
E. Establishment of a single professional accrediting body with specified functions.
F. Educational counseling to individuals, organizations, and agencies.
G. Financial aid for students in nursing education.
H. Recruitment program.
I. International nursing problems.
J. Cooperation with state boards of nurse examiners.

In other parts of the comprehensive program there are many items which indicate the intention to profit by wartime experiences, and there is every reason to believe that the National Nursing Planning Committee as the representative of the nursing profession is taking a most constructive attitude toward its problems including those which were caused or magnified by the war.

The Division of Nurse Education, United States Public Health Service, accumulated a large amount of information about the eleven hundred schools of nursing which participated in the

Cadet Nurse Corps program, as a result of the data on application blanks, of the visits by consultants, and of required enrollment and fiscal data. This was to be compiled into a comprehensive report which will be of great value in the studies proposed by the National Nursing Planning Committee.

OPINIONS OF LEADERS IN THE PROFESSION

At the request of the writer, Capt. Nellie Jane DeWitt, superintendent of the Navy Nurse Corps, prepared a statement in reply to the question, "What are the implications for civilian education of the wartime nurse training programs?" This statement is quoted in part below:

The military nursing services have a somewhat different approach to the problem of education within their ranks than that of the nursing school. The members of the military services come to their duties already prepared in their profession. The question becomes not "How shall we train them?" but "How well were they trained for our purposes?" Also, "How shall we keep them trained?"

The very nature of the nurse's education in itself—the discipline which goes with it—stands the nurse in good stead in military service, where that quality is quite essential in the individual.

One lack we have seemed to find in the nurse, however, has been in that some training schools have made certain departments of nursing electives instead of requirements. Outstanding among these electives are psychiatric nursing, tuberculosis nursing, communicable disease nursing, teaching, and ward administration. In the Navy, the nurse is called upon for all these types, as well as all the others which are generally required by schools, and many nurses have had difficulty because of lack of such foundations. This, too, delayed the program within the service somewhat.

Training in citizenship, also, would seem to be of prime importance—the training which gives a nurse self-confidence, a picture of the function of the nursing profession in the country as a whole, the responsibility of nurses to the country as a whole as well as to their patients, the responsibility of the nurse for keeping informed concerning what goes on in political, economic, and social life as a whole and how the nursing profession can best serve in that picture. So many times, in the armed services, we received nurses who were good professionally so far as actual nursing care went, yet had been so beaten down, as it were, in their training that they were completely lacking in self-assurance and the ability to think for themselves. A certain measure of self-assurance is necessary in military service, where emergencies so often demand just that, and where the clinical teaching and supervision of corpsmen is so much a part of the nurse's duty, as well as good administration of a ward, for the best care of patients.

Training in the proper quality of supervision would also seem to be of great importance, and this we found somewhat lacking in a great many nurses who came to us. The conception of the supervisor as one whose function was to detect derelictions seemed to predominate over that of teacher and assistant with difficult problems and that of representative of the nursing administration in the testing of the soundness of administrative policy and its carrying through in an integrated whole.

Might there not also be, in the Navy Nurse's training of hospital corpsmen and Waves, some implication for the training of vocational or practical nurses by trained professionals in civilian life?

We are mindful in all these implications, however, of our great debt in the Navy Nurse Corps specifically, and, may it not also be said in the military nursing services generally, to the civilian nursing schools which responded so nobly to the needs of wartime and which put forth, on the whole, such a remarkably good product. We trust that whatever implications we may have set forth in the foregoing will not be construed as criticism but merely as directed toward furthering to some slight extent the profession's constant search for improvement in service.

At the request of the writer an officer of the Army Nurse Corps commented on the foregoing statement, with which she agreed in general. The desirability of making neuropsychiatric and communicable disease nursing required rather than elective courses was re-emphasized, but the lack of adequate teaching facilities was given as the cause for making them elective to the present time. The officer concurred in thinking that training for citizenship was necessary but, in her opinion, such training should be the responsibility of grade and high schools. If the nurse had not had this training as a prenursing course, it would be necessary to set it up as an extracurricular activity. She did not share the opinion that nurses had been beaten down during their training, but, from her observation of present-day students, she was inclined to the impression that few of them had such an attitude. Commenting on the effectiveness of nurses as supervisors or instructors without additional training for such work, the Army Nurse Corps officers said that it was not to be expected that the three-year basic course would qualify nurses upon graduation for special assignments. Finally, she said:

So long as the number of adequately trained nurses permitted careful selection for assignment to military service, no great problems developed in the Army Nurse Corps. The need for ever-increasing numbers resulted in having to accept nurses who were physically, emotionally, and in other ways unsuited for military service. These posed great problems of administration. Generally, I would say the nurse leaders and educators had prepared sound programs for the selection and education of young women as nurses.

NURSING LOOKS AHEAD

In the February 1945 issue of *The Army Nurse* (Volume 2, No. 2, pp. 8-9) an unsigned article was published under the title "Transitions in Nursing as a Result of the War." This article contains some thoughtful statements on the implications of the wartime experience as they affect the nursing profession, although it is not primarily an article dealing with training. The opening paragraph stated that "the basic, fundamental principles of nursing will never change. It was founded on common sense, cleanliness, simple health care, and training. The procedures of nursing, the demands on nurses themselves, however, are changing, and their changes have been accelerated by the war as a result of necessity." The discourse continued:

Our nursing schools prior to the war emphasized the individual care of the patient. It was, and still is, felt that the more knowledge the nurse has concerning the patient she nurses, the more intelligent will be her care of that patient. The fact has not changed, but nurses, particularly those serving with the Army, are beginning to see that excellent individual care of one patient to the exclusion of a great uncared-for public is a mistake. The war has provided some striking examples.

The author of the article thought the prewar picture presented a public health problem which was not the accepted responsibility of the medical profession. At the beginning of the war nursing had only begun to crawl out of a devastating depression, and professional nurses were in no position to aid the general public in its fight for national health. Nurses were not satisfied either with their social or their professional positions but they did not know how to remedy existing conditions. Civilian hospitals were loathe to increase wage standards, and the nursing schools were raising their standards and producing nurses with better qualifications although their salaries were in many cases less than those of untrained hospital attendants. The "general duty" nurse performed *all* nursing duties including some at a nonprofessional level, simply because her services were cheap. The average citizen understood nothing of the situation and "to put it bluntly, the public was not interested."

In peacetime the Army, prior to the establishment of the Army Nurse Corps, had used hospital stewards to care for its sick and wounded. The corps was composed of graduate nurses who were employed to (1) supervise the duties performed by nonprofessional personnel, and (2) to give nursing care to patients. This system has never changed. Enlisted men, and enlisted women after the war began, trained in the rudiments of certain specialties, work on the wards under the supervision of nurses and doctors. "One nurse with the aid of three enlisted men cares for as many patients—and as well—as four graduate nurses on 'general duty' in the civilian hospital of today."

The article continues with a description of the Army nurse who will return to civilian life after the war. She is a different person in many ways. When she left she was "one of the nurses" and now she is an officer in the United States Army, she has become accustomed to behave as an officer, and she has supervised the work of nonprofessional men and women. The nurse coming back has traveled and has become an experienced person. She has received the pay and prestige of an officer, and the respect and admiration of other veterans.

Nursing in the light of this war has taken on a new meaning. For the first time the public is interested in hospitals and the nursing profession, and "it is amazed at its own ignorance." Here, throughout the years, has been an answer to the problem of public health. One nurse attending fifteen critically wounded men in a tent in Italy or France has had to give nursing care to all with the help of nonprofessional personnel. She has been surprisingly successful. This practice can be, with proper attention to the necessity of supervision, applied to our civilian hospitals.

There has been talk of compulsory military training for women. How much better it would be to make one year of domestic art and home nursing compulsory for American women over the age of 18. In that way, health measures would be brought into every home; mothers would know how to take care of their children; juvenile delinquency would die a natural death; and in the event of another war, the situation of nursing would be less acute. Hospitals, always lacking finances, under new streamlined conditions could increase their care to patients and the health standards of the United States could keep pace with the progress of the rest of the nation.

APPRAISING THE CADET NURSE CORPS

The director of the Division of Nurse Education, United States Public Health Service, Miss Lucile Petry, wrote an excellent evaluation of the work of the Cadet Nurse Corps which formed the conclusion of her article, "A Summing Up," published in *The American Journal of Nursing* (Vol. 45, Number 12, December 1945). Miss Petry was not concerned primarily with evaluating the program in terms of its contribution to postwar civilian education, but in fact her statement does state such implications, both affirmative and negative:

While the wartime contribution of the Cadet Nurse Corps has been tremendous—providing a great reservoir of nursepower for the military and preventing the collapse of civilian nursing service on the home front— certain long-range benefits stand out in bold relief.

In accelerating programs, schools of nursing have eliminated repetition and nonessentials in the basic curriculum. Schools have found also that they were able to purchase a great deal of instruction, especially in the sciences, from junior and senior colleges, and that by planning cooperatively, they could take advantage of the vast instructional facilities available in their own or neighboring communities.

The senior cadet period has proved that our student nurses are qualified to accept higher responsibility earlier than was previously thought possible. Retaining some elements of this "internship" period merits serious consideration.

Through increased affiliations and the senior cadet period, nursing service has been distributed to hospitals without nursing schools, especially the federal services, and the education program has been improved by providing additional experience in a variety of nursing technics.

Preparation of budgets for federal funds by schools has focused attention on financial problems and solutions, and has improved accounting procedures. Educational enrollment records have also improved noticeably, so that a greater amount of vital and needed information is now available.

On the other hand, there are a number of practices resulting from the stress of the national emergency, rather than from the initiation of the Corps program, which should be discontinued. The 80 percent of service now given by student nurses in hospitals with schools, should be decreased in the interest of quality of patient care and of the educational program, as well as to prevent an overproduction of nurses. The vast amount of nonnursing service performed by students should be lessened considerably, if not entirely eliminated. Weaknesses in school administration, brought to light by the demands of war, must be studied and the quality of individual staffs improved.

Probably one of the most lasting beneficial effects of the Corps is that a greater public than ever before is informed on the needs and uses of nursing. National, state, and local organizations (professional and nonprofessional) have cooperated in their common need. Civic groups and community leaders have become "nurse conscious" eager to devote time, effort, and money to the development of first-rate nursepower in their localities. Hospital administrators and members of the medical and nursing professions have learned to work together as natural allies in the cause of better nursing education.

Because of this combined enthusiasm and unity of purpose, a greater number of superior candidates have been attracted to a career in professional nursing, and there has been an increase in the number of college students now going into nursing.

We shall not realize the total impact of the Corps program for several years until Corps graduates have matured professionally and have accepted their rightful place in the profession, but the shadow of coming events is growing longer and longer. From young cadet nurses, educated during the war and in these golden days of peace, I expect to see the finest leadership the nursing profession has ever known.

At a later date, Miss Petry added two further contributions which she believed that the corps program had made: (1) the amount of upgrading of schools which was accomplished because these schools wanted to meet the corps requirements; and (2) the improvement in schools which resulted from the continuous consultation services offered by the Division of Nurse Education.

ON THE TRAINING OF WAVES CORPSMEN

In an earlier chapter, reference was made to an unpublished article by Lt. (jg) Margaret H. Wolff (NC) USNR in which she discussed the training of WAVES corpsmen in the naval hospital in Philadelphia. The concluding paragraphs indicate certain important implications of this program:

All in all, we have contributed nothing new in our teaching program, but we have endeavored to observe the best teaching principles possible, so as to eliminate nonessentials and, quoting Ellen L. Aird, "to present a sure-fire method of teaching a person on the job to do a job correctly, quickly, and conscientiously." In addition, we have stressed observation, comfort, and safety of the patient.

Needless to say, the work has been most stimulating because of the enthusiasm and earnestness shown by these trainees. They have acquitted themselves well, and so far have proved most helpful in their work on the wards at this station. It is true one sometimes pauses to contemplate the future of nursing as a result of the training of all these young women. Will it elicit further interest in professional nursing after the war, so that we will find many of these women applying for admission to an accredited school of nursing? Or, will these women wish to enter the field of practical nursing? One is inclined to feel that the latter field will reap the greater harvest. When I have inquired why they did not enter a school of nursing when they had finished high school, I am informed, either the family needed money at that time, therefore immediate employment was sought, or parents insisted upon a college course, or other advanced education, other than nursing. As one can surmise, the hospital corps presented an opening for these women; an opening, which precluded any delay in beginning active duty. Even the fourteen hours spent on the ward on their "long day" does not seem to act as a deterrent to their enthusiasm. One does not encounter motivation problems with these Waves.

Perhaps we should revamp our nursing education along the lines first advocated by Florence Nightingale, that is, provide instruction for two classes of nurses, namely the bedside nurse and the executive. Miss Nightingale would have had a shorter training period for the bedside nurse, wherein I believe most of these Waves would find a desired place. A longer and more comprehensive program would be arranged for those who show aptitude for leadership in teaching and administrative work. Will there be a place for these trainees who will doubtless retain their interest in nursing after the war? The answer to these questions must be carefully considered by those concerned with the future of nursing and nursing education.

IMPLICATIONS AS SEEN BY TEACHER-NURSES

In correspondence with Army and Navy nurses who held important teaching posts during the war period, several statements concerning civilian educational implications appeared.

One woman who taught courses in nursing to enlisted men in three Naval Hospital Corps schools reported that audio-visual materials were used to great advantage. The courses which she taught varied in length from six to sixteen weeks, and when the course was the latter length thirty-two nursing films were in active use.   In the seven-week course "still on a wartime, rush-rush status" in May 1946, nine films were used.

These films are a boon to our teaching.   They show in ten to twenty minutes what it takes us sixty to a hundred minutes to talk about.   Educational films are a "must" in this department.   We use a greater number of "Silent Teachers," display cabinets which are placed in classrooms, corridors, et cetera.   These cabinets usually deal with one particular phase of a subject.

A "Silent Teacher" on a lumbar or spinal puncture was cited as an example.

The Navy nurse continued with the statement that methods of teaching were similar to those used in civilian life.   She said further:

I would like to stress the importance of proper indoctrination of a new teacher.   New teachers on my staff audit a nursing class from beginning to end and do not do actual classroom teaching until they have seen each lecture taught.   If at that time they wish to see a particular class again they may feel free to enter as an auditor.   This occurs very rarely because by the time they have finished the period of indoctrination they are eager to see what they can do with their own class.   During the period of indoctrination, they assist with demonstration classes as well as auditing classes in theory; therefore when they teach their first class they will feel at home in the demonstration rooms.   I feel that it is very important for all nurses to teach the same way in a demonstration room.   In that way, anyone can take over at a moment's notice.   Due to orders and emergency leaves, my schedule seldom remains unchanged for any length of time.

An Army nurse who had been an instructor in a university school of nursing in civilian life, and who taught surgical nursing courses for male hospital corpsmen during the war, wrote that many methods used in Army training courses had been used to a certain extent in civilian life but that there were a few exceptionally good points which had impressed themselves upon her.   Films and other visual aids were used to great advantage.

This nurse wrote that the Army stressed orienting a new person on the job completely during the first day or so on the job. The teaching of a new lesson by the following method was very effective: (a) a lecture explaining basic principles underlying a procedure; (b) demonstration by the instructor or use of a film with explanation of the procedure; (c) the student himself performs the procedure with the supervisor making necessary corrections or giving added instruction in the classroom; and (d) the student performs the procedure on the patient, under the supervision of the head nurse who might help him with variations according to the particular patients, as well as exercising general supervision of the procedure.

Three additional points were described. The Army instructs all its personnel to teach the individuals immediately under their charge to know their jobs so well that they can replace the superior at any time. In the attempt to give concentrated, inclusive educational programs, some of these programs go into unnecessary detail, and time could be used to better advantage if fewer subjects were treated with very slight mention of less important ones. Some orientation to other departments aids the students as they later come into contact with them on their tour of duty, and they are better able to understand rules and regulations of these departments.

A third nurse who was in charge of the senior cadets in a large Army general hospital mentioned the following features of her program as of value to civilian education: (a) the most important feature was the direct, practical application of the thing learned—first, the demonstration by the teacher followed immediately by application by the student; (b) cadet nurses in Army hospitals had completed basic training and could be assigned to the specialized fields in which they were interested; (c) instructional materials were available and easy to obtain; (d) all material learned was for practical and sometimes immediate use by the student; and (e) incentive to learn was strong because the student nurse felt that she was an active member of the group caring for soldiers who gave their health and limbs for their country.

A fourth reply came from a woman who had been a director of nursing education before she entered the Navy Nurse Corps. While a member of the corps she taught courses in fundamental nursing, psychiatric nursing, and indoctrination for nurses. Her students were nurses and men and women hospital corpsmen.

In discussing morale and leadership she stated that she believed that more instruction was needed in this field and that it appeared to her "that we need more careful training and guidance in the art of leadership and group living, in our civilian education." She went on:

In my indoctrination program for nurses I tried to inject the appreciation of true leadership because so many young nurses had to learn quickly how to supervise men and women in the hospital corps. I had at my disposal several short films, put out by the Navy, on "Discipline" and "Giving Orders," also one by the Army. However, these accelerated programs were not too successful—yet I know that I reached some. As our society becomes more complex, it seems more and more urgent that we include in our required school curriculum classes on morale, group living, and leadership.

PLAN FOR NURSING EDUCATION

The most comprehensive plan for nursing education in the postwar period which has come to the attention of the writer was an unpublished report by Miss Lucile Petry to the National Nursing Council for War Service, Inc., at a meeting in November 1944.

A six-point health program was assumed, as follows: (1) provision of sanitary environment, (2) expansion of health facilities including construction of hospitals and health centers, (3) greater expenditure of public funds for "public health," (4) continued and rapidly expanding research, (5) preparation of needed personnel, and (6) formulation of a medical care plan either through insurance, taxes, or both.

The assumptions as to national economy and trends which would condition the health program were, in Miss Petry's opinion, the following: (1) The United States is headed for dynamic socio-economic conditions in which full employment of all is predicted, (2) all citizens should have equal opportunity and realize optimum health, (3) research and science will yield new principles and their operation will include the prevention and cure of disease, (4) federal-state cooperation will expand, and (5) public and private endeavor will combine for optimum benefit to all.

In recent hearings before a subcommittee of the Senate Committee on Education and Labor, the Surgeon General of the United States Public Health Service had described postwar health needs costing an estimated two billion dollars. These plans included an integrated hospital system with a base hospital serving as a center of research and teaching, and with interchange of personnel and patients within the system. Probably a medical school connection service of a very high level for the most complicated types of cases would be given there. In addition, there would be smaller district hospitals, next smaller rural hospitals, and a health center combining the work of the local health officer, public health nurse, and similar services.

Miss Petry's report next described a combination of professional and vocational nursing care to handle the duties in the previously described integrated systems and in public health agencies and homes. She predicted a much higher ratio of vocational to professional nurses than presently existed and, although she did not make the comparison herself, the situation which she proposed resembled that which existed in Army and Navy, as well as in many civilian hospitals, during the war. During the transitional phase supplemental postgraduate courses would have to be offered to prepare professional nurses from traditional types of schools for supervisory and administrative positions.

"Fewer and better" basic schools for professional nurses would prepare them thoroughly in the preventive, social, and mental hygiene aspects of nursing in addition to the usual four services, and all would be instructed in their responsibilities for the supervision of vocational nurses. A curriculum for schools for vocational nurses would range up to twelve months, approximately three months of which would be concentrated theoretical instruction with practice extended throughout the program. Other details of the curriculum for professional and vocational nurses were included, and postgraduate work of a truly advanced level was planned.

The amount of service given by learners in all curriculums would be only incidental, the experience being chosen only for its educational value, and subsidies were proposed to aid the hospitals if they could not provide nursing service without dependence on students. These subsidies should be "for nursing service" and not "for nursing education." The subject of governmental aid for the various types of nursing education led to the conclusion that federal, state, or local subsidies would be needed in most cases.

XI. EDUCATIONAL IMPLICATIONS OF WARTIME TRAINING IN NURSING AND RELATED PROFESSIONS

To a student of education a most interesting cooperative relationship is apparent in the wartime programs of nurse training described in the preceding chapters. The Army through its Medical Department and the Women's Army Corps, and the Navy through its Bureau of Medicine and Surgery and the Women's Reserves of the Navy and the Coast Guard, were the two agencies responsible for procurement, assignment, training, and utilization of several different types of female personnel needed to care for the sick and wounded of our armed forces. In the process of achieving this goal numerous governmental and civilian agencies were asked to aid, and the result was a complex, large-scale, cooperative venture which produced remarkably successful results.

NATIONAL COOPERATIVE RELATIONSHIPS IN THE TRAINING OF NURSES

The Federal Security Agency, through the United States Public Health Service, was responsible for an important part of the program, the Cadet Nurse Corps. In this case a nonmilitary governmental agency utilized professional nursing organizations, state boards of nurse examiners, civilian and Army and Navy hospitals, and schools of nursing to increase the available supply of nurses for essential military and civilian services. The Red Cross and other volunteer agencies furnished semiprofessional personnel. In short, every military, governmental, professional, educational, and volunteer organization in the field of nursing was utilized to the full in the wartime emergency, and their efforts were cooperative to a high degree.

The outstanding characteristic which dominated the wartime training program for nurses was not arbitrary *centralization* but democratic *cooperation*. In spite of an acute shortage of nurses in Army and Navy hospitals the solutions were cooperative ones. It will be recalled that even the proposal to draft nurses was deemed to be unnecessary. Only one entirely new agency was established—the Cadet Nurse Corps. This corps trained no nurses directly, but as a coordinating agency worked entirely through the customary nurse training schools, administering federal funds to aid the schools and the students in producing more nurses at an accelerated rate. The certification of nurses through the state boards of nurse examiners was unchanged. Wacs and Waves were trained and used as semiprofessional aides in both services, but the only new characteristic of that use was the fact that women were added to the men personnel who had long performed such duties.

There was, however, an urgent national demand which served as the cohesive force. The military need for fairly well-standardized nursing personnel of high quality prevented fragmentation of the training program.

One major question arises. For the acute military and civilian need for more nurses in the shortest possible time which served as such a strong stimulus to cooperation and joint action during the war, less potent springs of action must be substituted now that the war has ended. The two most obvious substitutes in the nursing profession are the responsibility of the profession to the public and the advancement of the individual nurse in her profession. These are less dramatic and less immediately compelling motives than those which operated during the war, and it will not be surprising if a measurably slower rate of progress results in carrying the new five-year plan into effect.

Necessarily, national cooperation and national programs for other professions would not resemble those which have developed in the nursing profession. It is, however, submitted that the wartime experiences of the latter profession and its plans for the future are worth serious consideration by the other professions. All professions have the problems of attracting suitable recruits, furnishing their training, and placing them suitably. In all cases, the public interest is increasing, the attitude that the profession is a self-contained group entitled to handle its affairs chiefly in its own interests is weakening, and the necessity for considering the problems of the profession on a public and a national basis is becoming more apparent. The war accelerated and strengthened and made more evident these important trends, and the results are strikingly exemplified in the programs of nurse training during the war and those planned for the future.

THEORETICAL TRAINING, PRACTICAL TRAINING, AND DUTY

A second characteristic of the training of nurses and other women medical personnel during World War II was the inseparability of training and duty, of didactic and applicatory teaching, of theory and practice. The "learning" and "teaching" phases were very much intermingled, and this characteristic, which had existed before the war, was increased during that period. There was a separation in time between three periods: (1) the first months of training in which didactic, classroom instruction in basic fields predominated and beginnings of applicatory instruction were made; (2) a period including either the last months of training or the first months of duty, in which applicatory, practical instruction predominated, small amounts of didactic training continued, and the student was permitted to assume small duty responsibilities; and (3) a succeeding period in which the graduate nurse had three roles.

Her main business in an Army or Navy hospital was, of course, to render nursing care to patients. However, she was in turn required to assume important tasks as a teacher of newly inducted nurses, enlisted male hospital attendants, Waves and Wacs, senior cadets of the Cadet Nurse Corps, various specialists, as for example, physical and occupational therapists and dietitians, and numerous paid and volunteer civilian personnel. This function of "teaching" was a fundamental part of her duty as a supervisor of the various military and civilian, commissioned and enlisted, volunteer and paid, professional and nonprofessional men and women who were added in such large numbers to Army and Navy hospital staffs during the wartime emergency. Supervision under such circumstances involved far more than the word usually implies, and in practice much teaching was included. In other instances the teaching of new or subordinate personnel was directly provided, and formal teacher training for nurses was instituted in large military hospitals. Finally, the nurse on duty was herself a student in many cases. The number of on-the-job specialist courses during the war cannot even be estimated because in many instances they were instituted and operated within a single hospital as urgent need arose and the supply of specialists was insufficient. Little record of such courses exists.

In fact, it is virtually impossible to separate teaching and practice in the field of nursing in military hospitals during the war. The two phases were so intermingled that the unit—the individual nurse—was simultaneously a student, a practitioner, and a teacher in her profession. As indicated above, her time was not always equally divided between these three occupations, but only in relatively rare cases was she occupied in one to the exclusion of the other two for any considerable period.

Without attempting to make carefully considered comparison with other professions, it can safely be said that in no case is there a situation like the one described above, although similar conditions exist as more or less unusual and isolated examples in every profession to point the way. One of the major implications of the program of nurse training during World War II is that the practitioner should also be the student and the teacher and, consequently, that there should be little institutional separation between the training agencies and the institutions in which the profession is practiced. From the standpoint of time, learning the profession completely does not precede the beginning of its practice, nor does practice mean that the practitioner ceases the study of his profession. Furthermore, he does not have to choose either to practice or to teach, because he will be expected to do both.

ACCELERATED CURRICULUMS DURING THE WARTIME EMERGENCY

Under the scheme of the Cadet Nurse Corps, only those schools which were able and willing to reduce the length of their courses were eligible to receive federal aid, and another significant factor was the fairly specific contents of the regulations of the several states as they related to the certification of nurses. Cooperation between all agencies within the profession facilitated the prompt and satisfactory revision of curriculum, and by a shift in customary timing it was possible to accelerate training without necessitating modification of state regulations. Specifically, a large part of didactic and theoretical training was included in the shortened period spent in the basic course offered by a school, and a formal period of internship in a hospital concluded the training period and served to meet existing state requirements. This had the two immediate results of increasing the teaching capacity of the schools and of getting semitrained nurses into service at an earlier date at a time when they were needed most seriously.

Undoubtedly there were difficulties, and it could not be true that there was perfect agreement and cooperation in carrying out the accelerated programs. Nevertheless, sufficient success was attained to justify examination of the particular type of acceleration which was adopted. The nursing profession itself, acting through the National Nursing Planning Committee of the National Nursing Council for War Service, Inc., has included in its comprehensive program for nation-wide action in the field of nursing a study of present curriculums preliminary to the making of recommendations. Many nurses who have worked with the wartime programs have stated to the writer that the accelerated program plus an internship period, which was in effect during the war emergency, is an improvement over the prewar program, and they gave cogent reasons for this belief.

The particular devices used should be considered and, in particular, the reduction of time for basic training and the addition of a relatively long internship as a means of reducing the overall length of the training period ought to be considered by persons who make it their concern to evaluate the proper timing of instructional programs.

There are probably important implications here for educational programs in law, medicine, teaching, public administration, business administration, and similar professional fields. In some cases the excessive length of time needed to complete general, preprofessional, and professional training and an internship period is a major disadvantage to the young persons wishing to be educated in these professions. There is always the possibility that too much relatively unimportant detail is included and that there is unnecessary duplication. "Overteaching" of certain materials or procedures may be adding unnecessarily to the time of training. These questions were raised by the educators in the field of nursing and wartime emergency answers were made when the necessity of accelerating their programs was forced upon them by developments of the war. That these answers appear to have a considerable degree of validity in connection with the planning of postwar training programs for nurses is a fact of importance to all educators.

SPECIALIZATION WITHIN THE PROFESSION OF NURSING

To the layman there are usually only two kinds of nurses—"trained nurses" and "practical nurses"—and the description of the numerous varieties of nursing and other medical assistants which were used in military hospitals during the wartime emergency presents to him a surprisingly complex situation. The effect of this specialization in function of course produced effects in the training programs.

The causes of this situation are not difficult to understand. There was an increased demand for nurses with special training in anesthesiology and other nursing specialties at exactly the time that acute shortages in such personnel existed. The only solutions were to devise very highly concentrated courses in these specialties so that nurses detailed to enter them would be absent from duty for the least time possible, or to provide on-the-job courses which would take the nurse off duty for a few hours of a working day. Both types of courses were used extensively. In addition to the shortage of nurses trained in specialties, there was an equally serious lack of graduate nurses qualified for membership in the Army Nurse Corps and the Navy Nurse Corps, to be utilized for general duty nursing. The magnitude of the job of nursing in military hospitals at home and abroad made it apparent that, even with the increased supply of nurses produced through the Cadet Nurse Corps program, enough nurses could not be obtained without withdrawing more from essential civilian nursing service than it was safe to do. The solution was the division of the work of nursing into several parts, and the delegation of the simpler duties to semiprofessional or nonprofessional personnel who were specially trained in short, specific courses to perform such duties. Waves and Wacs were trained as technicians and assistants and the Red Cross trained many civilian women who worked both as paid and as volunteer assistants.

The graduate nurse, an officer of a military nurse corps, became a more important element in the nursing service in a military hospital as a result of the situation just described. Her supervisory duties were increased, and her time was used entirely for the professional duties of a nurse and not for the tasks which formerly occupied much of her time.

Among professional nurses there are two points of view. The writer has heard the argument presented most convincingly that the process of breaking down the job of nursing into several professional, semiprofessional, and nonprofessional sets of duties and training perhaps a half-dozen or more different types of nurses and technical aids and assistants, very much as was done during the war, is economical of time in training and efficient in its use of personnel. Consequently, nursing service is improved for the patient which is the proper objective of all plans. In reply, other nurses also considering the patient first, believe that the personal relationship between nurse and patient is of such importance that he should be attended by as few different people as possible, and they favor the training of general duty nurses of professional and semiprofessional grade prepared to take full care of the patient. This plan would reduce the extent of training of specialists very considerably.

As a part of its proposed research program, the National Nursing Planning Committee included "the study and evaluation of the function of professional and practical nurses in relation to the entire community nursing program and to each other" and specific studies of the duty and training of the various types of nurses, aides, technicians, and assistants. The profession has not closed the case, and the publication of its plan will be of importance to other professions.

THE STATUS OF WOMEN AND THE IMPROVED STATUS OF NURSING

One of the implications for civilian education of the wartime training programs for women is that more women can be taught to do more kinds of work than they were doing before the war, and that we have a greater labor pool than was realized before the war.

The implications to be derived from wartime practice in military hospitals are that either men or women can be trained and employed successfully in the numerous semiprofessional and technical jobs closely associated with nursing and laboratory work, and that, if women were entering a man's occupation in this field during the war, there is no apparent reason why men should not now enter the same field in civilian hospitals and doctors' offices, even though this has previously been considered to be "women's work."

The status of the profession of nursing appears to have been appreciably improved as a result of the war, and this, too, is a fact of importance to nursing education. The acute need for many nurses led to several results. There were more positions and several new kinds of positions in the Army and Navy medical departments, and the standards and the pay were high. Recruiting programs of both military services and the Cadet Nurse Corps did much to improve public opinion toward the profession of nursing and that, taken in connection with the strong patriotic desire to further the war effort, led to the enrollment in nurse training of better students with better educational backgrounds than had been the case before the war. The increased prestige of nurses which resulted from their attainment of full commissioned status and the excellent publicity which was given to their service, added to the other causes, resulted in a marked change of attitude toward nursing on the part of the public.

The federal government through the Cadet Nurse Corps program spent considerable sums of money for aid to schools and to teaching institutions, which certainly was one of the major causes of the improved educational program in the nursing profession. Education, like everything else in this world, must be paid for, and subsidy in some form by the benefited public is necessary to supplement payment by students, if an adequate educational program is to be offered. High standards and high pay in the profession are not within the control of the schools which prepare its members, however direct their results may be on the caliber of students who enter training, nor can the schools directly control the attitude of the public toward the profession. Those who are in charge of educational planning need to take these factors into consideration.

APPARENT IMPLICATIONS FOR EDUCATIONAL PRACTICES

Nine salient features of the wartime training experience are worth considering with a view to their continuing adaptability.

1. *The recruitment of the best trainees is a fundamental part of all teaching programs.*

As a consequence of acute wartime labor shortage, there was a limited number of young women to be attracted into business and industry and the professions, government service as civilians, the four women's military services (WAC, WAVES, SPAR, MCWR) which were established early in the war, the military nurse corps, and similar occupations. Never before had there been such a sudden and intensive campaign to recruit women, and there was much to learn about the most effective methods. Excellent publicity materials and techniques were developed by the Army, the Navy, and the Cadet Nurse Corps. In general, emphasis was placed with approximately equal weight on patriotism and on the learning of a profession which could be continued after the war. There was sufficient attention to "glamour" and to excitement and change to make the proposals attractive, and in the case of publicity for nursing there was far more emphasis on the "womanliness" of the work than was the case with recruitment materials for other women's services.

Prospective trainees wanted very detailed information about their work and their living conditions. They were not attracted by publicity limited to the glamorous aspects. If promises, direct or implied, were made at the time of recruitment and it was not possible to carry them into effect, there was considerable resentment.   Great care was exercised to state conditions very clearly and to make specific promises only when there was certainty of being able to fulfill them.   These lessons are important to admissions officers in schools and colleges and, in general, to all persons who are recruiting or counseling young people.   A thorough study by an expert of the recruiting procedures of the women's services during the war would produce a study of value to a considerable number of school officials.

2.   There was a continual effort to adapt courses to the needs and capacities of students with varying amounts of education and experience.

The dietitians and physical therapists and occupational therapists, in particular, were forced by the shortage of civilian women in these occupations, and even by the difficulty in getting enough trainees with the prerequisites which had formerly been required, to devise many plans by which educational requirements for admission were stated with arrangements for the substitution of many varieties of "equivalent experience."   After students were admitted to courses, arrangements for varying the contents of the courses were necessary because of the difference in the backgrounds of the trainees.

Some attempts were made to prepare special courses for enlisted women with low AGCT scores.   There was an "opportunity" school, and later a special training unit at Des Moines. In all, about one thousand women were involved.   Utilization of these women for Army duties was difficult.   As already observed in chapter vii, efforts to train them for service as hospital orderlies were not markedly successful.

Negro women were trained separately for a time in some services, but in general there was no segregation in training, and the only implication which is apparent is that there is no necessity for segregation.

In general, civilian education can learn from the various nursing and medical training courses that it is both possible and advisable to offer students alternative prerequisites for admission, in order to be certain that no competent trainees are barred by inability to meet rigid technical requirements. If such an admissions policy is adopted, it should be accompanied by arrangements for varying the content of courses to meet the variations in the background of the student.

3. *Particular attention was devoted to curriculum revision.*

The accelerated training program for nurses had several important characteristics. The impetus was the acute shortage of trained personnel, and this cause produced a program of liberal federal aid which was available only to those schools which offered courses of a prescribed length. The schools themselves were left with the responsibility of curriculum revision in which task they were aided by their own professional organization, and, as explained in chapter ix, by the nurse education consultants in the Division of Nurse Education of the United States Public Health Service. They had only one academic limitation— namely, that their courses must continue to meet the requirements of the state boards of nurse examiners in their respective states. This latter provision protected the quality of graduates, but it meant that acceleration could not be achieved by the relatively simple process of omitting whole courses. Vacation time had been so short for most schools of nurse training that little leeway existed which could be used to shorten the total course. Real analysis and evaluation of the customary 36-month course was necessary if it was to be reduced to the required length.

The circumstances just outlined united to produce a result which appears to many experienced teachers in schools of nursing to have been good for the war period and also for permanent use. The general principles which guided the reduction in time spent on the course were sound and, in so far as it is possible to evaluate the quality of students trained under the accelerated programs at this time, they would appear to be the equals of the prewar graduates. Admittedly, they were in training under the strong motivation of rendering a war service, and competent observers frequently state that "better" trainees entered the schools during the war. Such intangibles cannot be measured, and in any case the students who took the shortened courses during the war have attained full professional status so recently that it is too early to know exactly how they will compare with graduates of standard courses.

Commendation of the method of curriculum revision is based upon the fact that this method was not arbitrary or mechanical. It is quite simple to tell every teacher to take 5 percent or 10 percent of the material out of his own courses, and let him use his judgment as to the material to be excluded. An accelerated course is undoubtedly produced. But the professional organizations of the nurses chose to examine all materials of all courses in the attempt to insure (1) that sufficient time was given to those subjects which were judged to be of prime importance, (2) that relatively unimportant materials received less emphasis, (3) that unnecessary repetitions were eliminated, and (4) that materials of slight importance were omitted. They also examined the methods of teaching in the attempt to facilitate speedy learning, they evolved many varieties of teaching aids, they used the faculties and laboratories of neighboring schools to expand their own staff and plant facilities, in short, they used marked initiative and ingenuity in solving their problem, and the schools of nursing consequently had competent assistance in the revision of their respective curriculums.

4. *There was considerable training of groups intended to function as permanent units.*

This raises a question: to what extent could or should we train "teams" in civilian schools? We emphasize the values of participation in sports and other extracurricular activities and possibly we underemphasize group action in the more academic studies.

The football and basketball and tennis and debating teams which are trained for action in a unit do not intend, of course, to continue to operate as such after graduation. Yet it is repeatedly stated—and if the statements are not proven, neither are they disproven—that this team training in school or college in extracurricular activities does have carry-over value into civilian life and that the student who has received such training is better able to work with a group in a business, industrial, professional, or social situation. It is a common criticism of college graduates that they are not "able to work with people," and the more advanced work they do, the more this disability increases. The cause is alleged to be that college training is highly individualistic and that, while more importance is attached to increasing opportunities for teacher-student cooperation than was formerly the case, we do little or nothing to train students to work as committees or any other typical work-group. Research workers at the graduate level are trained to carry out individual studies; most of the so-called cooperative research projects are found upon close examination to consist of a number of purely individual projects related only in that they deal with the same subjects. The researchers never deal with each other!

The Army Medical Department knew that certain important functions would have to be carried out in the field, in some cases under combat conditions, just as soon as the assigned personnel arrived at the duty station. There would not be time for a group assigned as individuals to work together until smooth teamwork resulted. Such perfected joint action had to be ready to go into operation immediately. The solution was "team training."

If the present tendency toward business and industry and government and education—and even living—on an increasingly large and complex scale persists, it is evident that one task for educators is to teach students how to work and to live together on a cooperative basis to achieve results which they have jointly determined to be in the common interest. If no help is given in this, one of the most difficult of human social problems, the way is open for the development of patterns of aggressive control far removed from the democratic conception of group action. The Army Medical Department did not trust to sending a dozen individually trained specialists into the field under the denomination of a medical unit, merely hoping that "a boss" would develop and whip a team into shape, or that by some miracle these specialists would develop an effective cooperative technique. There seems to be no better reason for depending on our luck in the civilian world.

5. Intensive programs for instructor-training preceded the initial operation of new training programs.

This aspect of the training programs is related closely to their emergency character, but the methods used in instructing teachers in the uses of all available materials and teaching aids has significance for methodology in civilian teacher-training schools. The Army and Navy did more than merely provide adequate materials and call them to the attention of teachers. Courses of study were prepared in advance to include the use of all such aids and they were demonstrated in the preliminary training period. Whether or not it can be proven, it is commonly believed that every teacher tends to teach in the same manner that he himself was taught. If this is true, the chances of a good grade of teaching can be increased by proceedings like those in the instructor-training programs for nurses and other medical personnel. These were usually short and intensive, and they were conducted during periods which were usually less than two weeks immediately preceding the opening of the new school or course. If the course was to be given in a hospital, as was frequently the case, the hospital staff conducted the courses. The courses for new teachers included indoctrination into the Army or Navy and the particular corps, full explanation of the operation of the hospital, refresher courses in skills which the teachers had not recently used, courses presenting new aspects of a standardized course in order that uniformity of presentation would be insured when numerous teachers taught the course, and courses in which teaching personnel had to learn both new materials and the methods of presentation.

6. Teaching the significance of the job has implications for civilian education.

Especially is this true of training for technical workers, particularly for those who perform routinized, specialized duties. It is easy for such groups of workers to perform their duties without any comprehension of the relationship between their work and a larger, more important, more dramatic whole. Through wise indoctrination the morale and the efficiency of workers, even those who are engaged in relatively uninteresting work, can be greatly improved. The technique of indoctrination of technical workers in Army and Navy hospitals was based upon a plea to patriotism plus full explanation of the work of the medical department, corps, and unit, and the significance of the individual's particular job in the complex whole. This same method was used with good effect in many industries during the war, and there is a wealth of military and civilian experience to serve as basis for planning similar courses in any public or private agency which operates on a large scale, employing many workers whose satisfaction and efficiency would be improved if they understood clearly their importance in the total operation.

7. *The evaluation of student performance was specific and continuous.*

Examinations in courses were usually of various objective types, but rating procedures involving subjective opinions from teachers and supervisors were widely used. The necessity for determining whether a student had suitable personal qualities as well as adequate skills meant that two types of evaluation had to be made.

A highly novel situation would be presented if this twofold method of evaluation were to be used in the teaching of other professional students. Student lawyers and teachers, for example, receive their grades on their work in courses. Their fitness to pursue the profession may be given some more or less formal consideration but a grade, or a series of grades, is not entered in the registrar's office. The usual practice is to ask a few teachers who have known the student through work in their courses to write confidential letters to a placement agency (either a commercial agency or one operated by the professional school) and these letters, which the student has not seen, are used in connection with his academic course grades as the basis for advising prospective employers. There are several disadvantages in this plan. The teacher, particularly in a large university, knows little or nothing of the personal characteristics of students in his classes. Furthermore, he keeps no record on such a basis and probably thinks little about it until he is asked to write letters of recommendation for graduating students. Students do not know whether these letters of recommendation are favorable or unfavorable, fair or unfair, nor does the placement agency have any way of judging them. The prospective employer has adequate information on the academic ability of a new graduate seeking appointment, but he has to depend on inadequate and undependable information about characteristics of the individual which may have just as much importance as his grades in course. The personal interview offers a slight check, to be sure.

Even conceding all the sources of error inherent in the use of subjective rating sheets, it would appear that there are enough possible advantages to warrant further study and experimentation. If such a study were made, it would be important to use the rating data which must be in existence in many Army and Navy hospitals as a result of their use during the war. If the researcher could get one thousand personal records of a group graduated three or four years previously, and compare such records with an evaluation of the same characteristics by the present supervisors, the correlation rate would offer some evidence of the values of this type of evaluation. It would be so important to be able to recognize the presence or absence of character or behavior traits of significance in the practice of a profession that effort spent in that direction would be well worth while.

8. *Nurses in training could undertake professional responsibilities earlier than had been previously realized.*

Perhaps nothing except an emergency in any profession can lead to such a discovery. The conclusion has a relationship to two subjects discussed in this section—acceleration and the evaluation of student ability.

In the course of all discussions as to the advantages and disadvantages of an accelerated curriculum, the question arises as to the "maturity" of students under the two plans. One group argues that we really do not know exactly what "maturity" means, that there is no particular reason to believe that you add a proportionate amount of this desirable quality by adding a year to a high school or college course, and that it might even be produced more effectively if the course were shortened sufficiently to keep students working at a rate somewhat nearer capacity. In reply, opponents of acceleration say that what is learned rapidly, under pressure, and without opportunity for reflection is merely "skill" not "education" and that it is not absorbed into the total personality—in short, no "maturity" results. They would believe that the nurses who were trained in less time during the war emergency would not have a sound appreciation of many fundamentals of their profession even though their superficial skills were not to be distinguished from those of nurses with the "maturity" resulting from a longer training period. Although people who take this position are often accused of arguing that there is a maturing effect in the mere passage of time, this is not a fair charge in more than a few cases. Even the most ardent defender of acceleration concedes that *adequate* time must be spent to permit a student to grow into a subject, but he is not prepared to believe that the conventional time allotments, which in some cases have become almost sacred traditions, are necessarily the best. He would say that nurses, for example, had become accustomed to training courses of a particular length which the war compelled them to shorten. The statement of a competent professional observer that the trainees were able and willing to assume professional responsibility at an earlier stage than had previously been believed possible would indicate that trainees achieved a useful degree of professional maturity more speedily than had been anticipated.

This returns the discussion to the subject of evaluation of student progress which certainly ought to include discovery of this trait of "maturity," as yet undefined and not isolated. The questions of the content of courses, methods of teaching, length of courses, and many others depend in part for solution upon our ability to know what traits we wish to produce, how to do the job, and how to know when we have done it. At present there is more than a suspicion that some first-year students are more "sensible" and more "mature" than some second-year—or even graduating—students, and we must even face the fact that if "maturity" is something which can be achieved in a school or college it is also something which can be weakened or lost.

A study of the relative professional abilities (including the characteristic ability to undertake responsibility) of students from the war emergency accelerated courses, and of students from courses of conventional time duration, could be made and, until it has been done carefully, thoroughly, and objectively we will have no satisfactory answer to one of the most hotly and subjectively contested arguments in the educational field. The necessity of defining and evaluating characteristics less tangible than the ability to learn facts presented in courses, or to acquire skills, must precede evaluation of the results of the shortened courses in comparison with those of conventional length.

9. *It was found that specific provision must be made for a health program for the young women in training.*

The program was developed by a group of health authorities and its contents were based upon sound understanding of the situation. The findings were published as Supplement No. 189 to the *Public Health Reports* of the United States Public Health Service, under the title "A Study of Nursing School Health Practices and a Recommended Health Program for Student Nurses." The recommended health program was described under the following headings: responsibility of the school of nursing, administration, pre-entrance examinations, immunization, medical, dental and nursing service, hospital care, subsequent medical and dental examinations, preventive medical service and general hygiene, environmental sanitation, and recreation and physical education.

There is a strong implication in the action just described, for other educational and business institutions, in connection with their responsibilities for students and trainees. Undoubtedly many institutions have done what the Public Health Service did in setting up a competent committee to investigate actual conditions and to make recommendations, and, just as certainly, many others have been content to evade this responsibility. There is far too much mere assumption that young students are getting along fairly well under health programs which were created piecemeal without too much attempt to examine their efficacy in practice. Just because a school has a physician and a nurse, even such an obvious result as that students are consulting them cannot be assumed to be a fact.

If civilian institutions wish to evaluate their health programs the method used by the United States Public Health Service should be studied because it would appear to be adaptable to other types of schools. The findings and recommendations are, to be sure, peculiar to schools of nursing but they are decidedly worth consideration by civilian educators.

THE AMERICAN COUNCIL ON EDUCATION

George F. Zook, *President*

A. J. Brumbaugh, *Vice President*

The American Council on Education is a *council* of national educational associations; organizations having related interests; approved universities, colleges, and technological schools; state departments of education; city school systems; selected private secondary schools; and selected educational departments of business and industrial companies. It is a center of co-operation and coordination whose influence has been apparent in the shaping of American educational policies as well as in the formulation of American educational practices during the past twenty-eight years. Many leaders in American education and public life serve on the commissions and committees through which the Council operates.

The Commission on Implications of Armed Services Educational Programs began its work in July 1945. It undertakes to identify features of the wartime training and educational programs worthy of adaptation and experimentation in peacetime civilian education of any and all types and levels. It also undertakes to make available to the public well-considered answers to the questions: What should education in America gain from the experience of the vast wartime training efforts? What are the implications for education and the national culture and strength, now and in the future?